David Lewis

Philosophy Now

Series Editor: John Shand

This is a fresh and vital series of new introductions to today's most read, discussed and important philosophers. Combining rigorous analysis with authoritative exposition, each book gives a clear, comprehensive and enthralling access to the ideas of those philosophers who have made a truly fundamental and original contribution to the subject. Together the volumes comprise a remarkable gallery of the thinkers who have been at the forefront of philosophical ideas.

Published

Saul Kripke
G. W. Fitch

David Lewis
Daniel Nolan

John McDowell
Tim Thornton

Forthcoming

David Armstrong
Stephen Mumford

Nelson Goodman
Daniel Cohnitz & Marcus Rossberg

Thomas Nagel
Alan Thomas

Hilary Putnam
Max de Gaynesford

John Rawls
Catherine Audard

Wilfrid Sellars
Willem deVries

P. F. Strawson
Clifford Brown

Bernard Williams
Mark Jenkins

David Lewis

Daniel Nolan

McGill-Queen's University Press
Montreal & Kingston • Ithaca

ISBN 0-7735-2930-6 (hardcover)
ISBN 0-7735-2931-4 (paperback)

Legal deposit first quarter 2005
Bibliothèque nationale du Québec

Published simultaneously outside North America
by Acumen Publishing Limited

McGill-Queen's University Press acknowledges the financial support of
the Government of Canada through the Book Publishing Development
Program (BPIDP) for its activities.

Library and Archives Canada Cataloguing in Publication

Nolan, Daniel Patrick, 1972-
   David Lewis / by Daniel Nolan.

(Philosophy now)
Includes bibliographical references and index.
ISBN 0-7735-2930-6 (bound).—ISBN 0-7735-2931-4 (pbk.)

   1. Lewis, David K., 1941-2001. I. Title. II. Series.

B945.L4554N65 2004   191   C2004-907311-7

Designed and typeset by Kate Williams, Swansea.
Printed and bound by Biddles, King's Lynn.

Contents

Acknowledgements

I owe thanks to many people for assistance and encouragement while writing this book. I won't even try to mention all the people who encouraged me. In addition to encouragement, Steffi Lewis was kind enough to provide me with copies of forthcoming Lewis papers and provided me with a bibliography of his works.

Particular thanks also to those who gave me feedback on one or more chapters: Alan Hájek, Ishani Maitra, L. A. Paul and especially Chris Daly, who gave me much useful feedback on many chapters. Thanks to the School of Anthropological and Philosophical Studies at the University of St Andrews for giving me leave to write this book, and thanks to the several Australian departments that made me feel welcome during the composition: the philosophy department at Monash University, the philosophy program at the Australian National University, and the philosophy discipline at the University of Queensland. Thanks to the series editor, John Shand, and to Steven Gerrard at Acumen, for giving me the opportunity to write this book. Thanks to Robert Williams for the index and Kate Williams for copy-editing. Finally, my greatest gratitude goes to my family, who made me welcome and cheerfully put up with me while I was writing.

Page numbers in citations throughout the text refer to the collected editions of Lewis's works, but the original publication date is also given in square brackets to give the reader a sense of the chronology of publication.

Daniel Nolan
St Andrews

Introduction

David Lewis's work is among the most influential in many areas of contemporary philosophy, but much of his influence has been as a "philosopher's philosopher": his main impact to date has been on the work of other professional philosophers. His work deserves a broader audience, since it is full of thought-provoking ideas, breadth of vision, a clear and incisive treatment of issues and plain good sense. He deals in a straightforward and unpretentious manner with many of the deepest philosophical issues, and his picture of the world and our place in it is one that deserves to be widely known.

Lewis's work covers topics in many of the central areas of philosophy: metaphysics, philosophy of language, philosophy of mind, decision theory, philosophy of mathematics, epistemology, philosophical logic, philosophy of science, value theory and many others. Despite this, his views have a unity to them. A comprehensive philosophical system emerged gradually from Lewis's writings, somewhat of a rarity in Anglo-American philosophy in the second half of the twentieth century. It emerged somewhat unexpectedly, even for Lewis. "I should have liked to be a piecemeal, unsystematic philosopher, offering independent proposals on a variety of topics. It was not to be," he commented in the introduction to his first volume of collected papers. Indeed, many of his readers may only have a vague idea of how his views fit together, since it is possible to engage in one set of issues dealt with by Lewis without engaging very much in the others. His papers on causation, laws of nature, chance and conditionals, for example, form a connected body of work, but a philosopher could be heavily engaged with Lewis's ideas on those topics without knowing much about, say, his views about language and meaning and convention. This book is intended to provide an overview of Lewis's contributions in different areas, both well-known contributions, such as his views in metaphysics, and less well-known ones, such as his contributions to ethics. Those who have come across Lewis's work in one area may find this book useful to get a sense of how his different projects relate to each other.

While I hope this book might be useful to those who already know something of Lewis's work, no familiarity with any of Lewis's writings nor any philosophical background are presupposed, except perhaps inadvertently. Apart from anything else, Lewis's work does have an impact in areas outside philosophy, and those concerned with linguistics, game theory or cognitive science may be just as interested in an overview of his work as those with more narrowly philosophical concerns.

Lewis's written work includes four influential books and approximately 100 articles (including responses, critical notices and so on), and his philosophical interests are very wide-ranging, so on occasion this book may resemble a whistle-stop tour rather than a detailed critique. In particular, I have not tried to discuss all of Lewis's more technical works. Lewis's contributions to formal semantics, the foundations of mathematics, decision theory, game theory and other technical areas are important, and they have significant philosophical implications. I shall certainly address some of the philosophical implications, but those seeking a discussion, for example, on the effect on the semantics of conditionals flowing from Lewis's triviality results (1976b, 1986e), or Lewis's contributions to deontic logic (e.g. 1988b, 1974b), will find little here. In particular, I decided with regret not to attempt to convey Lewis's work in the philosophy of mathematics. This is not because I think his book and articles on the topic are not valuable, but rather for reasons of space and accessibility. Some of Lewis's important contributions to the formal understanding of languages, for example his paper "General Semantics" (1970) or his work on double-indexing, are also topics I shall not attempt to address because of their technical level.

I urge readers who are interested in any of the topics discussed to read Lewis for themselves. He has an entertaining and clear style, and deals with issues in much greater depth than I could allow myself in reporting and discussing his work. Many of his papers are as valuable for their introductory sections as for Lewis's actual positions and arguments. He has a way of introducing the issues in a dispute, or clearing up confusions along the way, so that a paper yields useful understanding of philosophical problems even before the reader realizes the paper is underway. Lewis is often a pleasure to read, and one of my hopes for this book is that it will lead people to discover that pleasure for themselves.

David Lewis was born in 1941, and his philosophical writings span the period from 1966 to the time of his death in 2001 (and more than half a dozen posthumous papers are still appearing or due to appear). Lewis did his graduate work at Harvard, and his supervisor was W. V. Quine, one of the most influential philosophers of *his* generation. Lewis was in many respects a Quinean, although he was always an independent thinker. His PhD thesis, which became his first book, *Convention* (1969), was in part a defence of the analytic–synthetic distinction, a philosophical thesis, it is probably fair to say, that Quine was most famous for attacking.

His philosophical influences and his own subsequent influence were almost entirely in so-called "Anglo-American" philosophy, the dominant philosophical tradition in Britain and North America, which is standardly contrasted with "continental" philosophy, supposedly the philosophy of continental Europe. This distinction is not drawn very satisfactorily with these expressions. Anglo-American philosophy is the dominant tradition in places outside North America and Britain – Australia and New Zealand, parts of Scandinavia, Ireland and elsewhere – and it is not even clear that continental philosophy is currently the dominant tradition in Europe, particularly in France and Germany. Nor have the "Anglo-American" and "continental" labels ever been entirely apt; it is arguable that some of the mainsprings of today's Anglo-American philosophy were found in Austria and Poland before the Second World War. Anglo-American philosophy is also called "analytic" philosophy, although contemporary Anglo-American philosophy is not analytic in the narrow sense, the sense in which all philosophical problems are to be solved by the analysis of language, for example. Labels for broad philosophical movements are agreed on all sides to be unsatisfactory. Nevertheless, to the extent that there is a distinction between "analytic" philosophy in some broad sense and other traditions (not only continental), Lewis was an analytic philosopher. My remarks about how Lewis fits into broader debates and trends should be read in this light.

From early in his career, Lewis entered into a fruitful engagement with the school of "Australian materialism" represented by figures such as J. J. C. Smart and D. M. Armstrong, and this engagement, in the philosophy of mind and also in metaphysical debates, was a constant throughout Lewis's career. He spent a good deal of time in Australia, as the number of Australian examples in his writings shows, and most Australian philosophers would consider him an honorary Australian. Lewis shared many Australian philosophers' preference for a down-to-earth, no-nonsense writing style, and many of Lewis's philosophical proclivities were shared by prominent Australian philosophers. A taste for philosophical materialism, a respect for the natural sciences, and an unabashed sense that metaphysical problems are real questions whose answers we can make real progress towards answering are only three of the philosophical traits Lewis shared with many Australian philosophers. I was a postgraduate student at the Australian National University when I first met him, and I experienced his kindness and patience with students first-hand.

After Harvard, Lewis's first job was at the University of California, Los Angeles, from 1966 to 1970. Lewis was there at the height of a boom in the philosophy of language and philosophical logic, and along with other UCLA faculty, including Richard Montague and David Kaplan, was part of an exciting new wave of theorizing about language, which combined technical virtuosity with philosophical insight. In 1970 he moved to Princeton University, where he worked for the rest of his life, becoming one of the most influential philosophers of his generation, and one of the best. His death at the age of 60 in 2001 came as a shock to the philosophical community, and greatly saddened those of us who knew him. Lewis's contributions remain at the cutting edge of philosophy, and they are part of an ongoing philosophical conversation. It is a tragedy that one of the most important participants in our collective philosophical conversation fell silent so suddenly.

Chapter 1

Metaphysical and scientific realism

Where to begin?

There are a variety of possible starting-points for discussing David Lewis's work. I suspect the most common way in is for people to start with his work on a particular topic they are interested in – causation, the mind, convention, properties and relations, or whatever – and then gradually come to see how his views and arguments in one area connect with his views and arguments in another, until some greater or smaller piece of an entire system emerges. So where should a general introduction start? I have decided to start with Lewis's metaphysics, perhaps the most philosophically influential part of his work, and a part of the system that can be seen as being at the base of an entire worldview. Lewis's views in other areas do stand or fall to an extent independently of his metaphysical views. Whereas Lewis does have a system, it is not a system where every part presupposes the others, but rather a system where views in many different areas are developed and argued for in their own terms, although there are many points of contact between different doctrines. Looking at his metaphysical views first will establish a framework for locating his other doctrines.

So if I am to start with metaphysics, what is metaphysics? Lewis, who did so much to shape the debates in metaphysics in English-speaking professional philosophy, never, to my knowledge, attempts a definition of the subject. Perhaps this is because it is difficult to say anything both concise and informative about what contemporary professional philosophers are doing when they are doing metaphysics. Etymology does not really help, since the word derives from a title of one of Aristotle's works, and Aristotle's *Metaphysics* is so called because in the ancient lists of his works it comes after (*meta-*) his book on physics (called *On Physics*). Attempts at snappy definitions, such as the one that defines metaphysics as "the science of being *qua* being", do not really help. We could say that metaphysics attempts to answer a variety of fundamental questions about our world, but this might not distinguish it from some other areas of philosophy, or some areas outside philosophy such as physics or theology. (There is also the problem of getting a grip on what sorts of questions are fundamental – without that, this characterization of metaphysics may not be very clear.)

Perhaps it would be better to give a sense of what metaphysics is with a list of example topics metaphysicians grapple with, which traditionally include questions about the nature of time, causation, existence, possibility or the laws of nature, or the extent to which questions about the world are independent of our conception of the world; or questions that are about us – about the nature of mental states, or the possibility of survival after bodily death, or the freedom of the will. Of course, other categories of philosophy touch on these questions: philosophers of science also deal with questions about time or causation or laws of nature, philosophers of mind deal with questions about the connection between our concepts and the world or the connection between states of mind and states of body; and philosophers of language have a role to play in most of these areas. To take one example in the philosophy of language, when we are trying to work out whether we have free will, as well as information about whether our actions are predetermined, or how our decisions affect our movements, we want to know exactly what we mean by "free will" and what sort of thing deserves that name.

Lewis has plenty to say about many topics in metaphysics, so the next thing to do is determine what part of his metaphysical views should be dealt with first. Rather than starting with the details of any particular dispute, let me begin with two general metaphysical strands that run through much of his work. Lewis is both a "scientific realist" and a "metaphysical realist". Both of these attitudes are present throughout his work, although both are perhaps more often presupposed than argued for. Together, they provide a metaphysical framework for more specific questions to arise.

Realisms

There are various attitudes we can take to what science tells us. We could think that science reflects nothing more than our cultural preferences and assumptions; or offers nothing more than models that yield useful predictions but should not be taken as attempts to tell us what is really happening in the world; or that science is in the business of telling us how the world really is, although we have no reason to believe that it has had any success in getting it right. Lewis would have rejected all these takes on science. For Lewis, the natural sciences are substantially correct, and substantially correct not only in making correct predictions of the outcomes of experiments, but also about how the world really is. This attitude is often called "scientific realism": the combination of the belief that science aims to describe how the world really is, and that it is to some extent successful in that aim. Indeed, Lewis goes further. He identifies himself as a "materialist", and at various places he describes materialism in ways that make his materialist position an endorsement not only of the *correctness* of much of the scientific picture of the world, but also of its *completeness*: in some sense, all there is in our world is what is revealed to us by the sciences (particularly physics). Here is one statement of Lewis's optimism:

> We have no *a priori* guarantee of it, but we may reasonably think that present-day physics goes a long way toward a complete and correct inventory [of fundamental properties and relations]. Remember that the physical nature of ordinary matter under mild conditions is very well understood. And we may reasonably hope that future physics can finish the job in the same distinctive style. We may think, for instance, that mass and charge are among the fundamental properties; and that whatever fundamental properties remain as yet undiscovered are likewise instantiated by very small things that come in very large classes of exact duplicates. We may further think that the very same fundamental properties and relations, governed by the very same laws, occur in the living and the dead parts of the world, and in the sentient and insentient parts, and in the clever and the stupid parts. In short: if we optimistically extrapolate the triumph of physics hitherto, we may provisionally accept that all fundamental properties and relations that actually occur are physical. This is the thesis of materialism.
> ([1994b] 1999a: 292)

David Lewis

There is a lot that follows from Lewis's conviction that physics, in something like its current form, provides a complete inventory of the fundamental properties and relations of our world. Lewis accepts, of course, that there are living creatures, and creatures such as ourselves, with minds and consciousness, and that there are things such as nations and currencies and economies. But these will all be ultimately explainable in terms of patterns of arrangements of fundamental properties, and those fundamental properties will be the ones in the inventory of physics. For example, Lewis's system will not be one in which there are irreducible features of consciousness that set human beings and human agency apart from the rest of the world. Human beings may be distinctive in various ways, but ultimately they are natural creatures interacting with the rest of the natural world, just like anything else. Likewise, Lewis's system will not find a place for gods or other supernatural creatures in the functioning of our world: no divine creator, no theological story of the progress of humanity. These presuppositions are shared by many contemporary philosophers, and I suspect many professional philosophers would find them barely worth commenting on. But they still form part of a minority view in society at large, and those not familiar with Lewis's work may be interested to notice to what extent he was able to provide materialist theories of such things as meaning, mind and values.

The relation between the fundamental properties and relations in our world, and the familiar objects of experience such as chairs and people is a difficult one to spell out, and not one that Lewis ever attempts to spell out in full detail. (Nor could he, in *complete* detail. The question of how assemblies of chains of molecules make up a living cell, for example, is an extremely difficult one in biology and biochemistry, and not one that we should expect anyone, let alone a philosopher, to be able to answer in complete detail.) But in general, Lewis is confident that "every contingent truth is made true, somehow, by the pattern of coinstantiation of fundamental properties and relations" ([1994b] 1999a: 292), and those fundamental properties and relations are of the sort discovered by physics. (The "instantiation" of a property or relation is a case of it being had by some thing or things, so a "pattern of coinstantiation" of properties and relations is a pattern of properties and relations being had by things.) So, somehow, all the rich variety we come across in the world, and all the truths we discover, are ultimately made the case by the pattern of physical properties and relations, such as charge or mass, or spatial and temporal relations.

Is Lewis, then, a *reductionist*? That is a hard question to answer because "reductionist" means so many things to different people. Lewis is prepared to describe himself as a "reductive materialist" (*ibid*.: 291), although he often avoids putting his views in terms of "reductionism" because of the "contested" nature of that word. There are some things associated with the expression "reduction" that Lewis would not have endorsed. Some philosophers, for example, think that if we "reduce" mental processes to physiological processes, or "reduce" biological systems to physical systems, then we have said that after all there are no mental processes or biological systems. They interpret reduction as a kind of elimination. Lewis is not this sort of reductionist. Although, in some sense he wants to hold that "physical science will, if successful, describe our world completely" (1983a: xi), he does not think this means that there *are no* donkeys, people, beliefs, countries and so on. Indeed, his "reductions" are often achieved by establishing identities. For Lewis, people, chairs, cows, or whatever *are* certain kinds of very complicated arrangements of sub-atomic particles. Others take it that if we have a "reduction" of the entities talked about by one science to the entities of another, then that shows that the science being "reduced" is in some sense redundant or unnecessary – if we could reduce chemistry to physics, that would show that there was no need to do chemistry any more. Lewis would also, I imagine, have had little sympathy for this view. Napoleon may have been an extremely complicated swarm of physical particles (or whatever the basic physical story is, in terms of fundamental particles, fields or something else), but it would be disastrous to try to discover the course of his military exploits using the methods of physics alone. Likewise, providing a mass of information about the fundamental physical goings-on in a region may provide a bad explanation of what happened in that region. If I ask about why I cannot find my keys, there would be several things wrong with giving me information couched in the language of fundamental physics: I would not be able to make much sense of it; it would be terribly hard to process even if I did understand it; and it would tell me too much that was irrelevant to my question, among other vices. (Lewis discusses what makes for a good answer to a question, including an explanatory question in "Causal Explanation" ([1986c] 1986b: 226–8).) Better just to tell me that the keys have fallen behind a cushion. Even if the whole truth about my keys, their location and my ability to find them is made true, somehow, by the fundamental physical goings-on in the world, we do not have to give up all forms of enquiry and explanation besides those of physics.

In those senses of "reductionist", Lewis is not one (and there are probably not many such reductionists, except perhaps in the minds of anti-reductionists). In one other sense Lewis's view does seem reductionist: in addition to all I have said so far, Lewis also believes that the basic laws of nature can be cast in terms of the patterns of fundamental physical properties and relations ([1983c] 1999a: 42, 292). Why Lewis thinks this will be discussed in Chapter 4, but for the time being let me note that this means that the "laws" of less basic sciences, such as biology, astronomy, psychology or economics, will either have to follow from the laws of physics (in the sense of being strictly implied by those laws), or will not be true laws of nature at all. This will strike many as objectionably reductionist. There are many philosophers who might well agree that, for example, biological systems such as rabbits and rainforests are made up of fundamental physical constituents, but would want to hold that there are laws of biology or ecology that do not follow from the laws of physics. In rejecting such "emergent" laws, Lewis would count as more reductionist than the philosophers who accept them.

Why, then, is Lewis a scientific realist and a materialist? He never gives a systematic defence of either, and seems to hold both positions from his very earliest philosophical writings (see, for example, "An Argument for the Identity Theory" (1966)). Nevertheless, there are clues in different parts of his writings, so we can reconstruct at least some of the reasons. While scientific realism and materialism have a certain affinity (it would be particularly unusual to believe the second without believing the first, I imagine), it is worth considering separately Lewis's reasons for being a scientific realist and his reasons for being a materialist.

Lewis's scientific realism seems to be grounded in his philosophical naturalism, which he shares with W. V. Quine, who was an important influence on Lewis. There are several strands to naturalism in philosophy, including respect for the findings of science, and for the progress that has been made by science, in particular by the natural sciences (physics, chemistry, biology, etc.). The methods of science have enabled us to construct technology that would have seemed like magic to people only a few hundred years ago, and have given us a vast amount of information that has stood up to rigorous testing and that we can use for correct predictions and satisfactory explanations. An endeavour this fruitful is one that we should think is succeeding on its own terms, so we should think that science, particularly natural science, is discovering the truth about the topics it covers; we should be scientific realists.

Another general argument from naturalism is that there is no better epistemological position to criticize science from. However fallible science might be, any other area of enquiry is even more fallible, and so we should not reject the claims of science for any reasons other than scientific ones. Something like this argument is found in Hilary Putnam's *Philosophy of Logic* (1971: 73). I do not know whether Lewis would have endorsed either of these arguments, but there is reason to think that he would have had sympathy with the second sort of argument at least. Here is Lewis, in the context of discussing philosophical proposals that the claims of mathematics are systematically false:

> Renouncing classes means rejecting mathematics. That will not do. Mathematics is an established, going concern. Philosophy is as shaky as can be. To reject mathematics for philosophical reasons would be absurd. If we philosophers are sorely puzzled by the classes that constitute mathematical reality, that's our problem. We shouldn't expect mathematics to go away to make our life easier. Even if we reject mathematics gently – explaining how it can be a most useful fiction, "good without being true" – we still reject it, and that's still absurd. Even if we hold onto some mutilated fragments of mathematics that can be reconstructed without classes, if we reject the bulk of mathematics that's still absurd.
>
> That's not an argument, I know. Rather, I'm moved to laughter at the thought of how *presumptuous* it would be to reject mathematics for philosophical reasons. How would *you* like the job of telling the mathematicians that they must change their ways, and abjure countless errors, now that *philosophy* has discovered that there are no classes? Can you tell them, with a straight face, to follow philosophical argument wherever it may lead? If they challenge your credentials, will you boast of philosophy's other great discoveries: that motion is impossible, that a Being than which no greater can be conceived cannot be conceived not to exist, that it is unthinkable that there is anything outside the mind, that time is unreal, that no theory has ever been made at all more probable by the evidence (but on the other hand that an empirically ideal theory cannot possibly be false), that it is a wide-open scientific question whether anyone has ever believed anything, and so on, and on, *ad nauseum*?[1]
>
> Not me! (1990: 58–9)

11

David Lewis

While this is about mathematics, rather than the natural sciences, I think Lewis would have a similar reaction to extra-scientific attempts to cast doubt on the natural sciences. This quote should be taken with a grain of salt, perhaps, since by 1993 Lewis was advocating a view of mathematical language that did look like a revision (1993c), and a revision that did, according to Lewis, "rebuke the mathematicians for a foundational error" ([1993c] 1998: 222). Although he does admit that this rebuke is "presumptuous and suspect", he goes on to do it anyway. So perhaps the quote expresses an attitude to mathematics that he did not quite endorse, although he felt the appeal of it.

On the other hand, Lewis is not content to be a passive receiver of information from the sciences, including physics. On the question of taking metaphysical lessons from quantum physics, in particular lessons in what exists in the world (ontology), he writes:

> I am not ready to take lessons in ontology from quantum physics as it now is. First I must see how it looks when it is purified of instrumentalist frivolity, and dares to say something not just about pointer readings but about the constitution of the world; and when it is purified of doublethinking deviant logic; and – most of all – when it is purified of supernatural tales about the power of the observant mind to make things jump.   (1986b: xi)

Although Lewis admits that after this purge quantum physics would be the "best of authority" about the ontology of physics (*ibid.*), this sort of sentiment does strike some as in tension with naturalism, and with the sentiment that the natural sciences are too successful and secure to be seriously challenged by a discipline such as philosophy. There are ways of trying to reconcile the two. Perhaps Lewis thinks that his objections to quantum mechanics as it is sometimes interpreted are themselves scientific objections: and even the hardest-bitten naturalist does not think we ought to believe a scientific theory if there is a better alternative by scientific lights themselves. Or perhaps Lewis thinks that the "frivolity" and "impurity" are somehow not due to the physical theory itself, but due, for example, to philosophical interpretations of that theory (although many would doubt that a line like that could be successfully drawn). Or perhaps they are not to be reconciled, and Lewis goes too far on one occasion or the other. (Lewis discusses what he *does* think that quantum mechanics might show in "How Many Lives has Schrödinger's Cat?" (2004b), but he does not tell us there whether his objections to alternative views are to be understood as scientific, philosophical or

something else, nor whether he thinks that there is an interesting line
to be drawn here.)

I shall return to a discussion of Quine's methodological influence
on Lewis in Chapter 9, so I shall not go further into Quinean naturalism here, or the support it lends to scientific realism. Lewis's materialism goes further than scientific realism. For him, the picture of the
world we get from the natural sciences, particularly physics, is not
only true as far as it goes, but it is in some sense complete. (This sort
of view is often called "physicalism", although there are many different views that go under that label.) Lewis himself, incidentally,
prefers the more old-fashioned label "materialism". While some people prefer not to use that label because it suggests a metaphysics of
matter alone, rather than one that encompasses charge, spin, field
strengths, and the other materials of twentieth-century physics,
Lewis writes:

> it would be pedantry to change the name on that account, and
> disown our intellectual ancestors. Or worse, it would be a tacky
> marketing ploy, akin to British Rail's decree that second class
> passengers shall now be called "standard class customers".
>
> ([1994b] 1999a: 293)

Lewis comes closest to defending materialism when he discusses
the philosophy of mind, since he is particularly concerned to defend
the view that experiences and other mental occurrences are physical
occurrences (1966, 1994b). In his very early "An Argument for the
Identity Theory" (1966) he offers an argument for materialism about
the mind that he later generalizes in "Psychophysical and Theoretical Identifications" (1972). This argument has as a premise that a
"true and exhaustive" account of *physical* phenomena can be given in
physical terms ([1966] 1983a: 105). Lewis labels this premise "the
explanatory adequacy of physics". Others have called a similar
hypothesis, put in terms of causation rather than explanation, the
"causal closure of the physical". This might seem to have already pre-
judged the question against the opponents of materialism, who may
precisely think that non-physical minds, or non-physical gods, or
non-physical "historical forces" make a difference to the distribution
of physical things. Lewis points out, though, that his premise "is not
an ontological thesis in its own right"; it does not by itself rule out
anti-materialism, since it is compatible with the claim that physical
things have complete physical explanations but that there is also
non-physical stuff doing its own thing. He also cites arguments by

Oppenheim and Putnam (1958) that make it plausible that something like contemporary physics will at least provide a complete physical explanation of all *physical* phenomena. (At least as far as there is an explanation. Perhaps some physical events just happen, or can at best be only partly explained.)

With this principle of explanatory closure – anything that explains a physical occurrence is itself physical – we are in a better position to argue that anything that is supposed to influence the physical world is to be identified with something physical, or its existence is to be rejected. For example, Lewis defends an identity theory about experiences and other mental states. We discover what they must be by seeing what sort of causal work they are supposed to do (they result from perception, and result in action, including specific bodily movements), and when we look at the "role" mental states are supposed to have, we discover that the states that do this sort of causal work are specific states of the brain, and so we identify mental states with relevant states of the brain. (For a discussion of Lewis's view of the mind, see Chapter 5.) Lewis rejects the existence of other supposed influences on the physical, such as psychic powers or the guiding hand of a deity; he thinks that nothing plays the causal role of an overseeing deity, for example. Lewis's strategy here can be generalized: we find out what something is by discovering what role, often what causal role, it has according to our theory of it. (I discuss this in detail in Chapter 9.)

To take a frivolous example, our theories of rabbits tell us that a rabbit interacts with its environment in certain ways, it bears certain relationships to other rabbits and other animals, it digs holes, and so on. We discover that, in fact, certain complex assemblages of complicated molecules do what rabbits are supposed to do (or close enough – our theory may be wrong in some details): they can be found in holes in the ground, they consume vegetation, they look like rabbits and so on. We discover that those complex assemblages are the rabbits. This example is a bit silly since we do not worry about whether rabbits in fact exist, or worry about whether they are physical creatures or some kind of spirit. But something like it might be more sensible when it comes to settling whether there is something extra-physical about being alive (some "vital spirit", as some early biologists thought). Once we can show that cells behave the way they do because of complex physical processes in them, we might come to decide that cell reproduction is a very complicated physical and chemical process, rather than that process *and* a transmission of vital spirit.

The above case is one where we discover that a biological process (reproduction by a certain sort of cell) is actually a physical process, rather than one that requires an extra-physical process as well, such as the transmission of vital spirit. We can also imagine that our theory tells us about something where nothing fits the role. A famous historical example of this is the planet Vulcan (not the *Star Trek* one). Some astronomers, puzzled about wobbles in the orbit of Mercury, postulated that there might be a planet between Mercury and the Sun that had a strong enough gravitational field to make Mercury's orbit behave the way it did. We had a fairly specific causal role for Vulcan: it needed to behave like a planetary body, with a mass in a certain range that would explain Mercury's orbit (but not so large that, for example, it would produce deviations that were too large in Mercury, or have large effects on orbits such as those of Venus or Earth). Astronomers training their telescopes at where Vulcan would have to be could not see anything (no light was being reflected in the way it should be by a planet), so they concluded that there was no such planet after all.

Lewis's story about identifying a physical and/or causal role for something (e.g. a mental state like an experience, or a biological state like reproduction), and then seeing what physical object or process fills that role, gives us a story about how we can justify a claim that, for example, mental states are complicated physical states, rather than something else. But even if we grant that this works where it is supposed to – so that everything that is supposed to have a physical influence is shown to be a physical thing after all, or else is shown to not to exist – is there anything we can add to get an argument for materialism across the board, and not just materialism about things that are supposed to have some physical effects? Part of the story might be in terms of an argument that our minds and the rest of us are physical, for then anything that had any influence on us, or was part of the explanation of anything we thought or did, would also have to be material. That would still leave a gap. Why suppose that there are no immaterial things in our world that fail to interact with the physical realm, including ourselves? Why not be undecided about whether there is such "epiphenomenal rubbish", as Lewis calls it (1986a: 119)?

Lewis suggests (*ibid.*) that we can rule this out using Ockham's razor (a simplicity principle, often summarized as "Don't multiply entities beyond necessity"). Indeed, while Lewis was reluctant to base materialism about the mind on Ockham's razor (Lewis [1966]

1983a: 99–100), I think it is this principle, or some similar principle of simplicity, that is implicit in much of Lewis's metaphysics. In many areas, Lewis seems to be engaged in the project of accounting for as much as possible with as few resources as possible (this will become apparent in the discussion of Lewis's "Humean supervenience" in Chapter 2). Simplicity considerations can also motivate materialism; given that we can come up with an account of the phenomena we encounter in terms of the resources given to us by something like contemporary physics, we can try to explain the movements and sounds that people make in terms of people being very complicated systems of physical particles and forces. Simplicity considerations would then say that to go beyond that, say by postulating some extra-physical aspect of people, we would need some good reason, since it is better to explain the phenomena with fewer theoretical commitments rather than more. Simplicity suggests that materialism should often be our default, provided we agree that the world does indeed contain physical systems of something like the sort the natural sciences tell us about. (We could see simplicity considerations either as a motivation for the "closure of the physical" supposition, or perhaps as an alternative to it; even if we have no general reason to suppose that every physical event is fully explained by physical causes, in any particular case we may find it simpler to account for it in terms of physical causes alone, rather than physical causes and some extra-physical ones as well.)

Realism and metaphysics

Scientific realism and materialism raise important and wide-ranging philosophical questions, and *aficionados* of these questions will have noticed that I have glossed over some subtleties. Some of them will come up again, most notably when we turn to Lewis's views in the philosophy of mind in Chapter 5, since materialism necessarily looms large there. As well as a scientific realist and a materialist, I claim that Lewis is also a realist in some other senses as well. Lewis is certainly happy to identify himself as a proponent of "the realist philosophy we know and love" ([1984b] 1999a: 56). He distinguishes at least two realist positions in metaphysics that he wants to endorse (*ibid.*: 67). One is a rejection of various sorts of claims that how the world is depends on our concepts, our classifications or our abilities to find out about it. Lewis has argued against Putnam's claim, for example, that there cannot be anything more to a sentence being true than that it would turn up in an "ideal theory", where an ideal theory is whatever theory we would get if we applied our current theoretical standards (consistency, simplicity, etc.) repeatedly to the sentences we accept (Putnam 1977, 1980).[2] Realists typically think there is room for us to go wrong even in this ideal limit; the question of whether we have the truth is a different question from whether we have applied our theoretical standards properly. Of course, realists hope that our enquiries will get us to the truth, and often they will, but for a realist, there is a world out there that we are trying to engage with, and there is no a priori guarantee that our engagement will be successful. For some anti-realists, on the other hand, which sentences turn out to be true is some sort of reflection of our theoretical practices or conception of the world, and so for them there is not the same gap between what our theories *say* about how the world is and how the world in fact is.

Opponents of this sort of realism are often called "idealists" or "anti-realists"; according to them, facts about the world are somehow mind-dependent or language-dependent, or otherwise dependent on human capacities. I expect Lewis, following Jack Smart, would have thought that this was rather too anthropocentric: why would *we* be so important to the nature of the world (Smart 1963)? But Lewis did not very often argue for realism against idealism or other anti-realist theories of the world. Realism was more often a presupposition than something explicitly argued for.

There is another position in metaphysics that often goes by the name "realism". This name goes back at least to medieval disputes between so-called "realists" and so-called "nominalists". They were on opposite sides of a metaphysical dispute about the "problem of universals", a dispute that in one form or another existed in ancient times, and in various forms is still raging in contemporary metaphysics. One part of this dispute is over whether properties and relations (such as greenness, or humanity, or being taller than, or the parent–child relationship) have a real existence, or whether such expressions are "mere names", or in some other way a figure of speech not to be taken literally. (Properties and relations, especially the sorts of properties and relations that distinct objects can share, are sometimes called "universals"). A traditional nominalist will reject the real existence of roundness or squareness, or red or green, although she will accept the existence of objects that are round or square, red or green. Where a nominalist sees only a red ball, the realist sees a ball with at least two distinguishable properties, redness and roundness.

David Lewis

Another facet of the dispute between realists and nominalists, in at least some of its guises, is a dispute over the objectivity of our classifications. The realist picture suggests that what kinds objects are sorted into, what species they belong to, or what their natures share, is an objective matter, to be settled by what real properties and relations they share. A traditional nominalist picture suggests that the way we divide up the world does not answer to any real, independent principles of classification, but instead is something that flows entirely from us. This second facet can cross-cut the first. For example, some realists about properties and relations think that there is a property for every grouping of objects, no matter how gerrymandered the grouping may appear, and that all of these properties and relations are on a par. On the other hand, some nominalists may think that, strictly speaking, there are no properties or relations, but nevertheless the similarities and differences between objects are perfectly objective and our classifications have to answer to them. The existence of properties and relations, on the one hand, and the objectivity of classification, on the other, are distinct issues. Nevertheless, from time to time people have felt that the rival positions come as package deals: the existence of properties and relations plus the objectivity of classification, on the one hand, and the rejection of properties and relations plus the rejection of the objectivity of classification, on the other.

Lewis accepts both parts of the "realist" picture, in this sense of "realism".[3] He believes in the existence of properties and relations, and he accepts "the traditional realism that recognises objective sameness and difference, joints in the world, discriminatory classifications not of our own making" ([1984b] 1999a: 67). It is this defence of "objective similarities", of distinguished aspects of reality that he calls "natural properties", that I want to focus on for the remainder of this chapter: this is an interesting and influential doctrine of Lewis's in its own right, but it also played an important role in much of the rest of his metaphysical picture.

Lewis had always believed in properties, although he followed Quine in thinking that properties were best seen as sets or classes of their instances: having a property (such as redness) was a matter of being a member of the set of red things. Since sets are so plentiful, this would give us a property for any old collection of objects; some would be recognizable, but many would be entirely gerrymandered. Lewis did not, however, always think that some of these properties would have to be identified as a special elite: that there were any special "natural" properties. "Formerly I had been persuaded by [Nelson] Goodman and others that all properties were equal: it was hopeless to try to distinguish 'natural' properties from gruesome gerrymandered, disjunctive properties" (1999a: 1–2). Lewis signals his change of view in his "New Work for a Theory of Universals" (1983c),[4] in which he defends the view that we should accept that there are *both* the "abundant" properties, one for every group of objects, and also the "sparse" properties, that privileged elite of "natural" properties that mark out the genuine qualitative similarities and differences in things. (Contrast the set of gold atoms, a fairly natural grouping, with the set of things I thought about last Tuesday. This second set of things is unlikely to have any natural features in common that they do not also share with things I didn't think about last Tuesday; the set of those objects does not correspond to a *sparse* property.)

A similar thing can be said about relations. Relations are different from properties because they have more than one "place", or take more than one "object". The relationship of being a parent holds between two things: the parent and the offspring. Being between is a relation that holds between three things: one thing that is between two others (as when a chair is between a table and a wall). There are four- and five-place relations, and presumably there are relations that hold between any number of objects (although we shall not often have convenient expressions for relations with, say, 53 objects). Those who like to identify relations with sets will often identify them with sets of ordered pairs for two-place relations, sets of ordered triples for three-place relations, and so on. So the relation of "... is a father of ..." will include, for example, the ordered pairs <Vespasian, Titus>, <Henry VIII, Mary I> and <George H. W. Bush, George W. Bush>. (Note that the order is important for this relation. The ordered pair <Mary I, Henry VIII> would not be a member of it because Mary I is not Henry VIII's father.) A distinction between natural relations and gerrymandered, artificial relations can be drawn as well as a distinction between natural properties and gerrymandered ones: nevertheless, rather than constantly talking about "properties and relations", with the suitable qualifications to capture relations as well, let me focus on the case of properties, since the same kinds of points can be carried across to relations.

What reasons does Lewis give us to believe in properties at all? What reasons in particular does he give us to believe that there is a distinction worth making between natural properties, on the one hand, and the unnatural abundant remainder on the other?

David Lewis

One reason to believe in properties that Lewis endorses is that it makes straightforward sense of many of the claims science and common sense make.[5] We have many abstract nouns that we use in everyday language, such as "red", "humanity", and so on. We also have words for properties that we use in general statements: characteristics, features, kinds, qualities and so on. (We could quibble about whether all the expressions in this list are synonyms, but they seem to do the same kind of linguistic job.) Consider a sentence that uses some abstract nouns, such as "Humility is more valuable than cruelty" or "Purple is a more interesting colour than brown". If we believe in properties, we can treat these nouns as straightforward referring expressions: "humility" refers to the property of being humble, "purple" refers to the property of being purple, and so on. If we reject the existence of properties, we need to tell another semantic story about what is going on with these abstract nouns. Similarly with generalizations. In "You have more characteristics in common with your mother than with your father", or "I like seven colours and dislike three", we appear to be talking about a range of things: characteristics, in the first case, and colours in the second. If properties exist, these sentences are about things in just the way they seem to be. If there are no properties, then we must tell another story about what these sentences are doing. Perhaps we could paraphrase the first as "You are more similar to your mother than to your father", and paraphrase the second as "I like red and green and ... and yellow, but dislike blue, orange and brown, *or* I like blue and green and magenta ... and scarlet but dislike ... *or* I like black and brown and grey and ... but dislike ... *or* ..."; it may have to be a very long paraphrase![6]

Furthermore, many people think it would be fair to require of a nominalist not only that she provide us with paraphrases of sentences that use this vocabulary and that we think are true (or which stand or fall with the original sentence), but also that she do this in some fairly systematic way. After all, the meanings of most bits of language (idiom aside) seem to work in a fairly systematic fashion, and we manage to understand new sentences because of our grasp of how the system works. Providing a systematic account of these apparent references to properties and apparent generalizations over properties has proved very difficult, so difficult that the pendulum of philosophical opinion has swung quite sharply away from nominalism. Of course, a nominalist could always decline to offer a paraphrase and claim that ordinary and scientific talk is just false and mistaken when it employs these abstract nouns, but why suppose we have been going that badly wrong all along?

If we need a property whenever we have a "property nominalization" word, and we need a range of them whenever we generalize about characteristics or features, then we shall have a rather large array of them. We may have an even larger array if we think that meaningful *predicates* need to each be associated with properties. Predicates such as "is red" or "is a tiger" or "is seven metres tall" are often given a set of objects as their "semantic value", or what they mean. A simple subject–predicate sentence is *true* if the object referred to by the subject term belongs to the set associated with the predicate. So "Jack runs" is true if the object referred to by the word "Jack" belongs to the set associated with "runs", that is, if Jack is one of the runners. Other proposals say that a simple subject–predicate sentence is true if the object referred to by the subject *has the property* associated with the predicate. These two proposals come to the same thing if the property just is the set, of course. Some people suggest we need properties to be the meanings of predicates (or an important part of the meaning of predicates), and this would be another argument for having an abundance of properties. Lewis does not offer this argument in "New Work for a Theory of Universals" (1999a), but he would be aware of it.

Another very similar argument concerns the meaning of our mental states, our beliefs and desires. When we believe, we represent things as being a certain way, and when we desire we want things to be a certain way. If we had very abundant properties, we could characterize these "ways" as properties, and let those properties be part of the meaning of our beliefs and desires. Lewis does give something like this argument ([1983c] 1999a: 19). See Chapter 6 for more discussion of Lewis's account of the content of our mental states.

None of these arguments support having properties as abundant as Lewis wants them to be; even if we need a "property" for any group of objects our language picks out, or our minds pick out, or even that our languages or our minds could pick out with similar resources to the resources we have, then there are still many sets of objects we have no hope of picking out in particular. Why suppose there is a property for each of those, or, even if we allow that there is a set of any arbitrary group of non-mathematical objects, why suppose that this set deserves to be called a "property"? Lewis does not say, and so his argument that we should have one sense of properties in which they are as abundant as can be is incomplete. Perhaps he could argue that given that we have sets of objects anyway, it is simplest or most convenient to identify sets with properties, and so we get the extra abundance for free.

How about the other side? Why suppose there are some groups of objects that are special in being associated with a special sort of classification, in sharing a "natural" property? Here Lewis gives a variety of reasons. Some have specifically to do with the need for them in accounting for laws of nature and causation, and in accounting for mental content. The roles natural properties play in the contexts of these accounts will be discussed in Chapters 4 and 6, respectively. An appeal to natural properties happens in many places in Lewis's metaphysics. If belief in natural properties cannot be justified, that would be serious trouble for Lewis's system. On the other hand, if the notion of natural properties does useful work in metaphysical problem-solving, that might show that we have good reason to believe in them. (Many metaphysicians use this sort of "inference to the best explanation" argument. For more discussion of this kind of reasoning see Chapter 9.)

As well as playing a role in explanations of such things as laws of nature and mental content, natural properties are also supposed to help us do justice to some of our common-sense views of the world. The first use is to account for similarity between things. We are inclined to say that when two things are similar, they have a lot in common (many properties in common). Abundant properties would allow us to say that two things had a lot in common, but they would make it too easy. Everything has infinitely many abundant properties in common with everything else. If we think that similar objects (say, peas in a pod, or even better two protons or two points of spacetime) have more in common with each other than dissimilar objects (a proton and a tree, or a human being and a dust mote orbiting a star in another galaxy), then we shall want to distinguish some properties from others: some make for real similarity, and others of these abundant properties don't make for much similarity at all. There is a set containing all the badgers and the Taj Mahal, but this "property" does not make the Taj Mahal similar to badgers.

If it is properties out in the world that make for real similarity between objects, then similarity will not be entirely relative to what we are interested in. Sometimes our judgements of similarity depend on what project we have in mind. If we are interested in sexual development in primates we might think that a male chimpanzee and male gorilla are more similar to each other than either is to a female chimpanzee, but for other purposes we might judge that the two chimpanzees are more similar to each other than either is to the male gorilla. Some philosophers, such as Nelson Goodman, have thought that judgements of relative similarity are entirely "non-objective", objectively speaking, no similarities are special, and we do not discover "joints in nature" but we do the carving up ourselves. Lewis takes it to be self-evident (or close to self-evident) that there really are objective similarities and differences in things, or, at any rate, that this is so much a part of common sense that we should be very reluctant to give it up. One reason, incidentally, why we might want objective similarities and not merely the ones we impose, is to explain why we make the classifications we do. Across times and across cultures, human beings make similar similarity judgements in many different ways; ask anyone to pick the odd one out from two badgers and the Taj Mahal, and they'll be able to do it! It is probably vital to our being able to learn anything that we make fairly stable similarity judgements, and learning a language would seem to require that we spontaneously make similarity judgements that are approximate to those of others in our community.

Perhaps we could try to explain this similarity without an appeal to property-sharing. Maybe some things are similar to each other, and others aren't, and that's that. (No mention of properties here!) One problem with doing this is that when we start to talk about similarity we often end up talking about similarity *in respects*, rather than overall similarity. (Is my hand more similar to a fork or a spoon? It is hard to say, but we can cite respects in which it is more similar to one than the other.) What are these respects? They look like properties, or families of properties. It is a tricky business to do justice to similarity without mentioning properties at some point. Even if we could, though, this would give us a "natural" distinction between groups of objects (the groups of objects that are all similar to each other in some particular respect), and this might well be enough to mark out a "natural"/"unnatural" boundary. If we already have abundant properties, we could use this distinction to mark out natural properties. The natural properties would be the properties corresponding to the natural groupings.

Lewis expects the perfectly natural properties of our world to be the ones discovered by fundamental physics (or at least they will be discovered if fundamental physics succeeds). The somewhat-but-not-perfectly natural properties will depend on these; presumably "being a rabbit" is a property that marks out a more genuine difference in arrangement of physical qualities than "being a badger or the Taj

Mahal" does. Lewis never tells us exactly how a property's degree of naturalness depends on the purely natural properties: at one point he suggests that it has something to do with the length of the possible definition of a property in terms of the perfectly natural ones ([1984b] 1999a: 66), and at another he suggests that there is some cut-off of sufficiently natural properties that will correspond to "not-too-complicated chains of definability from the perfectly natural properties" (1986a: 61), but we are not provided with a recipe for the definitions. Perhaps Lewis means any definition couched in terms of names of the perfectly natural properties, plus any sort of logical machinery (or any standard logical machinery). If this is the proposal, though, it's far from clear that the length of the chain of definability has much to do with naturalness: a book-length gerrymandered definition with terms from fundamental physics ("neutrino or electron or proton one metre from an electron or ...", or whatever the ultimate physical kinds would be) would seem extremely unnatural, but it would still probably be much shorter than many perfectly reasonable properties, such as being a rabbit or having a certain timbre, if we tried to define these in the language of physics (if that could even be done). Perhaps an alternative proposal for specifying degrees of naturalness could be devised: it may even turn out that the proposal best suited for specifying meaning and mental content might be different from the proposal best able to account for the contribution to degrees of objective resemblance.

A final question to address is what makes a property a perfectly natural property: what is the difference between electron charge, say (supposing for the moment that this is a fundamental physical property), and some other property such as being a rabbit, or some gerrymandered property, such as the property of "having a name in English starting with C *or* a name in German ending in P"? Lewis explores three alternatives, without definitively settling for any. One option is to just take the distinction between the perfectly natural properties and all the others to be a primitive distinction: a distinction that is basic and unanalysable. This might seem unsatisfying, but most metaphysical systems will end up postulating something primitive at some stage; explanation comes to an end somewhere, in metaphysics just as in everything else. (You could think that everything is infinitely complicated, with every feature of the world, or some features of the world, susceptible to unending explanation and analysis. Everyone else will probably have to rest content with taking some things as primitive). If we take the distinction to be a primitive one, then there will just be a difference between some sets and others; some will be perfectly natural, and others will not.

Alternatively, we could offer theories to explain the difference between the perfectly natural properties and the rest. Two theories that Lewis discusses are a theory of "universals" such as the one defended by Armstrong (1978a), and a theory of "tropes", such as that of D. C. Williams (1953) and others. Armstrong's "universals" are properties that are conceived of not as sets but as entities located in space and time; a certain "negative charge" universal is located where each electron is, for example. What is distinctive about Armstrong's universals is that they are supposed to be *multiply located*: the same negative charge universal is found in many different places, and each electron literally shares its universals with other electrons. (Sometimes a universal might only appear once, but even if it does, it is still *potentially* multiply located.) Armstrong only believes in universals corresponding to "sparse" properties; there may well be a universal of electron charge, but there will not be a universal for "being a cabbage" or "being owned by Bill Gates". These universals, distributed across space and time, and literally shared by the objects that possess them, could be what marks out the natural sets from all the others. (The "natural" set would then be a set corresponding to the objects that shared a certain universal.)

"Tropes", on the other hand, are meant to be property instances: *this* electron's negative charge rather than *that* electron's negative charge. If there are tropes, then they are particular "natures" or "aspects" of objects, exactly the same as tropes of the same kind in nearly all respects, differing only by when and where they are found, and which objects they belong to. If we had a set of tropes for each sparse property, then we could say the "natural" sets were those that gathered together all the objects that shared a specific kind of trope (e.g. all the objects with the "negative-electron-charge" trope, or the "point-of-spacetime" trope, or whatever the fundamental tropes turn out to be). There would only need to be sparse tropes for this to work (no tropes of "being-a-hit-single" or "being-bigger-than-average" would be necessary). Sparse tropes, like spare universals, will give us "markers" to tag the things in the world that get bundled into the natural properties, and fix which natural properties they appear in.

Whether we should believe in either universals or tropes is a difficult question in metaphysics, and what answer we should give will in part depend on what other things we take ourselves to have good reason to believe. (If you already believe in one, you have less reason to believe in the other.) However, for most of Lewis's uses of natural properties, the metaphysical details of naturalness do not matter. As long as some properties (and relations) are marked out as the elite of "perfectly natural" properties, and for some of his purposes there is a sliding scale of "natural but not perfectly natural" properties, he will have what he needs from naturalness. For most of his purposes it will probably even be enough if he has a category of "natural enough" properties, whether or not any are *perfectly* natural, or, in other words, whether or not the scale of naturalness has a top ranking.

The end of the beginning

In this chapter I have examined some of the "big picture" metaphysical positions in Lewis's work. Lewis is a scientific realist who thinks that the picture of the world provided to us by the natural sciences is substantially close to the truth as far as it goes (while it may be wrong in some areas and in detail). He is also a materialist, and in his sense of "materialist" this is a commitment to the claim that, in some sense, the physical story about our world is a complete one: all the truths about our world are made true, ultimately, by the distribution of physical properties and relations. Lewis is also a metaphysical realist: the world has its existence and nature in a way that is largely independent of us, and of what we might think or how we might categorize things. The objects in our world also have "natures" independently of us; some properties and relations are in an important sense fundamental and natural. The distinction between natural properties, features that make for objective resemblance, and unnatural properties, corresponding to arbitrary collections of objects, is needed, according to Lewis, both to do justice to aspects of our ordinary view of the world, and also to do important theoretical work elsewhere in metaphysics and philosophy.

Let us now turn to some of Lewis's particular metaphysical doctrines. He is a defender of a view of the world he calls "Humean supervenience", at least against philosophical objections. He defends a "four-dimensional" view of time and the existence of objects in time. He also, famously, defends a view of possibility and necessity where other possibilities – other "possible worlds" – exist, and are as real as this one. In the next two chapters I shall outline and discuss these distinctive doctrines.

Chapter 2

The Humean mosaic

As we saw in Chapter 1, Lewis is prepared to try to locate everything we come across in a single, physical, realm. Lewis goes even further. Not only is everything in our world to be accounted for in physical terms, but he is also spartan when it comes to accounting for the physical world. For Lewis, many physical objects are not themselves fundamental, but are composed of smaller and less long-lived objects. At the fundamental level, Lewis is prepared to describe the world as an arrangement of instantaneous, point-sized instantiations of perfectly natural qualities: a "mosaic" of "local, particular matters of fact" (Lewis 1986b: ix). The only fundamental relations between different pieces of this mosaic are spatiotemporal[1] ones ("being-one-metre-away-from" is an example of a spatiotemporal relation, although not necessarily one of the most basic ones), and from this arrangement of point–instant-sized qualities, Lewis proposes to provide us with a metaphysics that will be adequate to include everything we find in the world: bicycles, galaxies, orchestras, debates, fashion shows, colours, wars, values, and so on. A rich outcome from a limited basis!

This world and the Humean mosaic

Lewis gives the name "Humean supervenience" to the view that "all there is to the world is a vast mosaic of local matters of particular fact, just one little thing and another" (1986b: ix). The "Humean" comes from David Hume, who is associated with the view that all there is in the world are regularities of occurrence, without any necessary

David Lewis

connections between them. (The world may be regular, but there aren't any hidden connections forcing the world to behave in a certain way.) "Supervenience" is a technical philosophical term. When X "supervenes" on Y, that means there can be no difference in X without a difference in Y. ("Supervenience" can be glossed, at its most general, as "lack of independent variation".) A common example is the way a photograph in a newspaper *supervenes* on the arrangement of ink dots that make it up. Newspaper photographs can have all sorts of appearances, but any difference in the look of the photograph can be traced back to a difference in the arrangement of the small ink dots. In this context, Lewis's claim is a supervenience claim because Humean supervenience is the doctrine that *everything* about our world, every matter of fact that our world settles, supervenes on the distribution of local qualities. The only way for something to be different – whether that something is mental, economic, biological, or whatever – is for there to be a difference in the ultimate arrangement of ultimate qualities.

According to Humean supervenience, we have spatial and temporal relations (which might be different, or might be ultimately the same sort of spatiotemporal relations). These relations will be between point-sized things: points of spacetime, positions in a field (e.g. field strengths at a point in an electromagnetic field or gravitational field), or perhaps pieces of matter (point-sized particles, or point-sized parts of bigger particles). And these point-sized things will have properties. They will be the only things to have the *perfectly natural* properties. (Exactly what these properties would be is presumably something that physics can tell us. Maybe they are field-strength properties, or maybe they are properties of point-sized pieces of matter. The classical electron was often thought of as a point-sized object with mass, charge and spin and so on. Or perhaps the points will have properties not yet dreamed of. Fundamental physics isn't finished yet!) And, in a certain sense, that's all there is. Everything else depends entirely on how the point-sized instances of properties are arranged. So while there are other things in the world – for example, bigger things made up of these point-sized things – what they are, and how they are, depends entirely on this "mosaic" of point-sized qualities.

Humean supervenience comes with some qualifications, some to make it more explicit and some to make it less uncompromising than it might at first seem. One is that Lewis intends it to be contingent (1986b: x; [1994a] 1999a: 226–7). He is not saying it is a necessary truth that everything is ultimately a matter of point-instantiations of properties linked by spatiotemporal relations, but only that this is so in possible worlds like our own. A hypothesis, for example, that there are some fundamental properties that operate only on macroscopic levels – for example, that there is some "vital force" that indivisibly occupies the area a rabbit fills, which keeps the rabbit together and functioning as a single unit – is not incoherent or totally impossible, but Humean supervenience rules out finding such a force in worlds like ours.[2] What a "world like ours" is requires some clarification, unless this restriction turns into "Humean supervenience holds, except if it doesn't", or something equally uninformative. Roughly, a possible world like ours is one where the only perfectly natural properties and relations that are instantiated are ones found in our world.[3] If there are only things like the ones around here, then necessarily the only way to get differences in anything is to get differences, somewhere, in the "local, particular matters of fact" (Lewis 1986b: ix) and their arrangement. Another way of putting this that is intended to be equivalent is to say that it is a claim about the worlds that do not contain any "alien" properties and relations, where "alien" properties and relations are natural properties and relations that are not found in our world, and are not "built up" out of natural properties and relations found here (1986a: 91).

The other qualification is an important one, and one that is sometimes overlooked by Lewis's critics. Lewis discusses and defends Humean supervenience, but it is only a partial defence. He does not endorse Humean supervenience as the *truth*.

Instead, Lewis is only concerned to set out the theory and defend it from certain sorts of philosophical objections. Humean supervenience could turn out to be incorrect because physics could discover that we need fundamental relations other than spatiotemporal ones, or we need fundamental properties that are indivisibly instantiated in regions, rather than just at points. "Really, what I uphold is not so much the truth of Humean supervenience as the *tenability* of it. If physics itself were to teach me that it is false, I wouldn't grieve" (Lewis 1986b: xi). As we saw in Chapter 1, Lewis is not quick to jump to the conclusion that physics *has* shown that it is false, but he does seem to refrain from endorsing Humean supervenience rather than "whatever better supervenience thesis may emerge from better physics" ([1994a] 1999a: 226). So we could reconstrue Lewis as claiming that a world where Humean supervenience is true could seem to its inhabitants much as this one does; a world with a Humean supervenience base could contain the rich diversity of phenomena that our everyday experience of the world indicates.

If Lewis isn't defending Humean supervenience as correct, then what is the point of his defending it at all? Don't we want to work out what the world is really like, and not just the details of a story of what the world is probably *not* like? One justification Lewis gives for his interest in Humean supervenience is that, while the world might not quite be a Humean supervenience world, he thinks it will be like a Humean supervenience world in important respects. Humean supervenience fits the world as described by classical physics. Specify the values of the electromagnetic field and the mass function at every point in space and time, in accord with the constraints given by the equations of physics, and you would have specified the entire fundamental physical description. (This might be a little simplistic for classical physics – we might want to add in nuclear forces, some geometric facts, and perhaps some other values – but it is enough to get the flavour.) The ultimate physical story will be different from the story told by classical physics. But Lewis suspects that the relationship between fundamental physics and everything else will be like the relationship classical physics would have to everything else in a Humean supervenience world. Many of the philosophical objections to this – that the world of physics does not have a place for consciousness, or value, or people, or causation, or dispositions, or whatever – do not depend very much on whether physics is classical or turns out to be something slightly more complicated. So we can see discussions of Humean supervenience as a "worked example", if we like; we are not sure exactly what modifications would be made to it in the light of physics, but whatever they are, Lewis hopes they will not make a difference (or much of a difference) to the interesting philosophical questions.

An analogy might be when an engineer uses Newtonian mechanics to explain something. Newton's laws of motion and gravitation are not exactly right, but when we are trying to explain why a bridge fell down, the respects in which Newtonian mechanics are not quite right don't really matter. If we treat the bridge as a collection of Newtonian systems, and calculate the various stresses and strains caused by mechanical actions and the force of gravity, we might be able to come up with an explanation of the bridge's collapse that we can be confident is pretty much right, even if the true story would have to be tweaked slightly. We could even do this before we know all the details of the full story. (Which is lucky, since nobody knows all the details of how the world works at a fundamental physical level!) In the same way, when we are trying to work out what we need to explain people's minds, or how cars are likely to behave, or the functioning of an ecology, seeing whether we can sketch an explanation with the resources allowed by Humean supervenience might be philosophically interesting. Although physics might require some modifications to the picture provided by Humean supervenience, those modifications will probably not matter to the philosophical question.

There is another reason why we might be interested in seeing how far we can push a theory of the world that respects Humean supervenience. Humean supervenience is in some respects a very parsimonious theory. Not only does it not have any fundamental relations besides spatiotemporal ones, or any fundamental properties of more than point-sized things, it also has no facts or truths that are true even though they depend on nothing in particular. (At least, it has no "contingent" truths made true by nothing in particular. A contingent truth is one that could have been otherwise. Necessary truths, such as "all siblings have parents", are things Humean supervenience says little about). Truths about the laws of nature, or truths about what is morally right and wrong, or truths about what *would* happen if there were a ball of gold as big as the sun, are all truths that on the face of it do not depend on any particular pattern of occurrences. But if Humean supervenience is right, then the laws of nature being one way rather than another, or morality being one way rather than another, or conditional truths being one way rather than another, are all a matter, somehow, of the distribution of fundamental point-sized properties. (That is, assuming these truths could have turned out otherwise, i.e. that they are contingent.)

Perhaps we shall need to postulate things not covered by Humean supervenience to achieve a proper explanation of all the phenomena in the world. But it would be good to get a clearer idea of what requires something extra, and when we are obliged to go further. Many of us will be tempted to accept that there are things in the world like those supposed by the doctrine of Humean supervenience: spatiotemporal relationships and fundamental properties instantiated at a very small scale (whether or not they are exactly point-sized). If there are extra fundamental aspects of the world, we should like to discover a good reason to believe in them, and perhaps the best way to look for these extra reasons is to test the adequacy of explanations of different phenomena that do respect Humean supervenience.

David Lewis

If Humean supervenience is false, then there are possible differences in worlds like ours that do not correspond to differences in the distribution of fundamental local qualities. Some of the differences people think there could be have to do with differences in laws, or in what causes what, or in what dispositions things have, or what chances things have of occurring. (These sorts of matters are together sometimes called "nomological" or "nomic" matters, from *nomos*, the Greek for "law".) Perhaps there could be a world with a distribution of properties just like ours, but where everything that happens is entirely random and a massive "cosmic accident". (This is incredibly unlikely, presumably, but may be possible.) Or maybe things could turn out the same, despite being governed by different laws of nature. These sorts of challenges will be discussed in Chapter 3.

Another style of objection to Humean supervenience comes from those who think that the mental aspects of our world are an extra fundamental component left out by the physical picture. Some think that it is possible to have a world just like it actually is physically, but where nothing is conscious, or maybe where nothing has any mental life at all. (These people, usually called "dualists" in the literature, think that the mental aspects of our world are a genuine add-on.) "Theological dualists" might also think that there could be two worlds that are the same in terms of their arrangement of fundamental properties, except that one is looked over by a deity and another is not. If they think our world is one looked over by a deity, they will probably reject Humean supervenience. The challenge from dualism will be discussed in Chapters 5 and 6, especially Chapter 5.

There are other objections in terms of our ability to account for rules and norms in a world of Humean supervenience (issues about how to get a truth about what *ought* to be the case from what *is* the case, or from what a word *means* from facts about people's dispositions to *use* it), and those will be mentioned in Chapters 7 and 8. Finally, there are some objections about whether Humean supervenience can do justice to some basic physical facts. For example, quantum physics tells us that states of particles at some distance from each other can be "entangled", and it is hard to see how this relationship can be captured except by accepting that there is some fundamental relation that holds between such particles, besides a spatiotemporal one. Spatiotemporal relations might even turn out to be less fundamental than some deeper level of relations, in which case the only fundamental relations would be non-spatiotemporal. (See Oppy (2000) for some other worries.) Even traditional classical physics might include things that require more

32

than Humean supervenience offers: as Denis Robinson (1989) points out, it is hard to see how to construe vector quantities with the resources Lewis offers. A vector quantity has both magnitude and direction, and many of the quantities of classical physics are vector quantities. Force, momentum and velocity, for example, all have directions associated with them, as do the strengths of many fields (e.g. electrical fields). Suppose we have a point-sized particle with a vector quantity associated with it. One natural way of construing this quantity is as a relation to a region of space very near the quantity: the space the quantity is "towards", for example (as if you thought a force was a relation between a particle and where it was headed next, or with the place immediately behind it, which would give a direction just as well). Such relations would require fundamental facts about the non-spatiotemporal relations between objects at different points, and so would be an addition to the Humean mosaic. Lewis may be able to argue in response that vector magnitudes are intrinsic to points, rather than relations (which is an option he suggests ([1994a] 1999a: 226)). Remember that none of these *physical* challenges affect Lewis's own position. Humean supervenience may turn out to be wrong for physical reasons, and Lewis's interest is only to see whether it can resist being shown to be false for the sorts of philosophical reasons people may advance.

From this discussion the reader can see how ambitious the scope of Lewis's philosophy is: one of the tasks he sets himself (a "campaign" he engages in) is to show how *every* aspect of the world can be accounted for in terms of a limited explanatory base, not to provide all the detail, of course (the world might even be too complicated for anyone to provide all the details), but to provide the *kind* of story that would connect the fundamental physical story to the story about minds, meanings, morals or whatever. It is an ambitious project, aiming to connect every aspect of the world we experience. Of course, what Lewis has to say on particular topics might well remain useful even if the overall campaign fails at some point.

Once we have the basic mosaic, we then face the challenge of accounting for everything else. Everything else is supposed to supervene on this basis, but how can we explain how everything else is built up from these beginnings? In the next section I shall describe how we can start to answer this question.

David Lewis

Getting ordinary objects from the mosaic

Parts

To build up the objects of everyday experience from point-sized microstates, Lewis needs another relation in addition to spatio-temporal ones. This is the part–whole relation. The relation that a table leg has to its table is not just one of being in close proximity, it is a *part* of the table. Lewis has a very generous theory of the part–whole relation. Whenever there are any things, together they form a whole. Lewis believes in many scattered wholes, then – such as the Crab Nebula and my left foot – as well as objects we are more familiar with, such as tables and lumps of gold and puddles of water.

Furthermore, Lewis thinks this "unrestricted composition" – that any objects whatsoever go together to make up a whole – is a necessary truth, true no matter how the world turns out (1986a: 211). This has the advantage that he does not need to include the part–whole relation in his inventory of the fundamental objects in the supervenience base. If how parts relate to wholes in this way is a necessary truth, then the only way to have a difference in what wholes there are is to have a difference in what ultimate parts there are. The Humean mosaic fixes how the point-sized parts are, so it in effect fixes what wholes made up from those parts there are as well. (What wholes there are "supervene" on which parts there are.)[4] It does seem curious though. Why should the part–whole relation behave in this way at all and, even if it does, why should it behave this way necessarily?

Our common-sense view of parts and wholes does not seem to be this generous. While we do recognize many objects as having parts (I have hands and feet as parts, for example, and the solar system has Mars and Jupiter as parts), we do not tend to think that there is an object made up of two iron molecules near the middle of Mercury and my left hand. I make up a whole, but tiny parcels of matter scattered in different parts of the galaxy do not. A couple of pieces of terminology would be convenient here from mereology (the study of parts and wholes).[5] Two objects *overlap* if they have at least one part in common. The *fusion* of some objects *O* is an object such that *all* and only its parts overlap at least one of the *O* objects. A fusion can be thought of somewhat like a "least whole". My hands and feet might belong to many wholes (me, the biosphere, the solar system, the universe, etc.), but a *fusion* of my hands and feet would be an object that in a sense would be made up of just my hands and feet and nothing else. (Only in a sense, since the fusion of my hands and feet would contain all sorts of other objects, including the fingernail on my thumb, or perhaps smaller fusions such as my-left-hand-and-my-right-foot). "Unrestricted composition" says that any group of objects whatsoever has a fusion.

Lewis points out that we seem to employ criteria from the following list when deciding whether objects make up a whole: "things that contrast with their surroundings more than they do with one another; and that are adjacent; stick together; and act jointly" (1986a: 211). An object such as a rabbit or a table seems to fit these criteria well. We are more iffy when it comes to less unified objects. Lewis asks us to consider a fleet: "the ships contrast with their surroundings more than with one another, they act jointly but they are not adjacent nor do they stick together" (*ibid.*). Fleets might even come in degrees, I suppose; the US Pacific Fleet, for example, has a unified command and tends to clump together somewhat, but the "fleet" of a petrol company like ExxonMobil will have different ships on different missions all over the world, and we might be less inclined to think that there is a single thing here.

For Lewis, however, these principles should be seen as determining which fusions we *pay attention to* or *have words for* or *bother to talk about*, rather than which fusions exist. One reason some people offer for this is the idea that which objects exist should not be an anthropocentric matter. We could have been interested in quite different groupings of objects, and that would have been equally good, so we should conclude that all of those wholes are out there, and our concerns merely focus on a sub-set that interest us. This is preferable to thinking that our concerns create specially demarcated objects, or somehow happen to line up with which wholes are really out there. Lewis does not exactly offer this argument, but he offers a more sophisticated argument that I think gets some of its force from the same sort of idea. Lewis points out that the sorts of criteria we tend to use are *vague*. How attached is "stuck together"? How close is close enough? A piece of granite seems to form a whole, but what about a clump of sand? A pile of loose sand? A scattering of sand across a floor? A quantity of sand after it has been scattered from an aircraft? Drawing a cut-off line here would seem to be arbitrary. However, Lewis claims, vagueness is a matter of language, not of the world. But how many objects exist is not a matter of language. So how widespread composition is (how often it is that objects have a fusion) is not a matter of language.[6] We would be better off saying that these vague criteria tell us not when there are fusions and when there are not, but rather something else: the boundaries of our interests, or what we bother to keep track of in ordinary language. (These sorts of things are vague.)

So if Lewis is right, we need a non-vague criterion for when objects form a whole. Two extremes present themselves: that parts *never* go together to make up a whole, or that they *always* do. The first goes against common sense and what most of our theory of the world tells us (although for a limited defence of it see Rosen and Dorr (2002)). The other extreme, that an arbitrary bunch of objects always makes up a fusion, is the thesis of unrestricted composition.

Of course, for Lewis's argument to be watertight, we would want some assurance that there are not any other appealing non-vague options. We would want an option that included the objects of common sense, and maybe even the objects that are borderline according to common sense. Presumably we would want something that ruled out objects that were made up of parts that were very scattered and dissimilar and independent. And we would want an option that was not vague. It might be hard to make a case for an option in the middle without any vagueness in its cut-off. It is hard to think of very appealing options like this, but that is hardly a proof of unrestricted composition.

Suppose we grant to Lewis that unrestricted composition is true for the material objects of this world, on simplicity grounds, for example, or because any other cut-off point looks arbitrary. Why suppose that unrestricted composition is a necessary truth? Why suppose it is impossible for the world to have different principles governing the part–whole relation? If we believe in unrestricted composition on the grounds of simplicity, for example, we might be hesitant to generalize it to a necessary truth. When we believe the simplest or most parsimonious option elsewhere in our theorizing, it is not usually because we think that it is *impossible* for things to be more complicated or arbitrary than they seem.

There is another line of thought in Lewis that suggests why we might think that the principles of composition are necessary, not contingent, and so not the sorts of thing that need to be added in as extra facts about a world, over and above the "Humean mosaic" facts. Consider another relation: numerical identity. Identity is a pretty straightforward relation: everything is identical to itself, nothing is identical to anything else. (This is identity in the sense of "is the same thing as", rather than identity in the sense of "exactly similar to", which is sometimes called *qualitative identity*. Two peas in a pod might be qualitatively identical, but if they were numerically identical, they would be one pea, not two.) Furthermore, we are happy to think facts about numerical identity supervenes on what objects there are. It is not as though you have to say what all the objects are, and *then* which objects are identical to which. Every object is identical to itself automatically. Standardly, people are happy to think this is a necessary truth as well. It is hard to describe a coherent situation where something is not identical to itself, or is identical to something else (something other than itself). Identity seems to be a relation that is both supervenient and has its behaviour fixed necessarily. Indeed, philosophers normally take the behaviour of identity to just be a matter of logic, and as necessary as anything else in logic.

Lewis suggests that the part–whole relation is like identity, indeed, that identity is just the limiting case of overlap. Two objects that do not overlap at all are entirely distinct, and two objects that share a part (Lewis uses the example of conjoined twins) are somewhere between entire distinctness and identity. This connection is a matter of degree; almost entirely overlapping things are almost identical, and almost entirely non-overlapping things are almost entirely distinct (see, for example, Lewis (1993b; 1990: 82–5)). He also suggests that the relation that many parts stand in to a single whole is a relation analogous to identity (1990: 83–4). If this is right, then Lewis could argue that overlap and the part–whole relation should be treated like identity. Just as we do not think that which things are identical to which is any extra fact about the world, we should not think that which things overlap with which, or which things make up wholes is an extra contingent matter. Just as the behaviour of identity is necessary and should be treated as part of logic, so the behaviour of the part–whole relation and the axioms of mereology should be treated like logic. If unrestricted composition is a correct principle of mereology, we have a reason to insist that it should be treated as a necessary truth.

I should point out that while Lewis draws on these analogies, he never explicitly offers this as an argument for the necessity of principles of composition and the supervenience of wholes on parts. I suspect this is part of what motivates his view, and, at the very least, it is a consideration that can be drawn from what he is committed to in order to support his belief about the necessity of mereological principles. Obviously such an argument would be controversial. Is the analogy strong enough? Is overlap really like a degree of identity? Does it even make sense to say that a number of things (parts) collectively stand in a relation like identity to a single thing (a whole)? It makes sense if we interpret it as saying the fusion of the parts stand to the whole in a relation like identity. Indeed they do, since the fusion is the whole. But whether there is any other way of making sense of this is controversial (see Baxter 1988, van Inwagen 1994).

Be that as it may, if some sufficiently strong mereological principles are necessary truths, then Lewis will be able to build up large aggregates from tiny, point-sized particles, and so will have objects large enough, and complex enough, to be the atoms and puddles and galaxies of the world we find ourselves in, and these can all supervene on the Humean mosaic. The next challenge concerns time. Lewis's building blocks are instantiations of properties at spatiotemporal points, but the world we are familiar with is full of things with duration; people live for dozens of years, countries can last for hundreds of years, and planets and stars measure their lifetimes in millions and billions of years. Lewis needs objects that are not only large spatially, but are long lived temporally, if he is to get something like the world we encounter to supervene on his foundations.

Time

Lewis treats time as analogous to space in many ways. Just as objects in other places exist, so do objects at different times. There are no triceratops around *today*, just as there are no neutron stars around *here*; but triceratops and neutron stars both exist, they are both part of reality. In thinking this, Lewis rejects several alternative theories of time; theories according to which only the present is real (*presentism*) and also theories that allow for there to be a past and future, full of objects and events like the present, but a past and future very different from the present (for example, a past somehow fixed and unchangeable, or a future still unset and indeterminate).

Lewis tends to dismiss these alternative conceptions of time quickly, although no doubt this is in part because he thinks the case for his preferred conception of time has been made by others (e.g. Quine 1960b: 170–76; Smart 1963; Williams 1951). Against the view that all that exists is the present, Lewis writes:

> In saying that there are no other times, as opposed to false representations thereof, it goes against what we all believe. No man, unless it be at the moment of his execution, believes that he has no future; still less does anyone believe that he has no past.
>
> (1986a: 204)

Presentists are likely to object that they can find a way for talk about the past and the future in the mouths of ordinary people to come out as equivalent to something that is true by presentist lights. But as Lewis's remark points out, presentists who want to say that our ordinary thought and talk is largely correct have a difficult balancing act to maintain. If it really is correct to say and think that there is a past, and a future, and that there are objects and events to be found in the past and the future that are not to be found in the present, then how could presentism be true? And if presentism is true, how could it be correct to say the things we do about the past and the future? (Presentists often say that *strictly speaking*, there are not past or future things, or past or future events, but what sort of strictness is this, if it doesn't apply to the truth of the claims we ordinarily make?)

Something like this appeal to common sense is made against people who think there is no determinate future, or that there fail to be truths about many matters of contingent facts in the future. To use an example from Aristotle, it might be settled that either there is a sea battle tomorrow or there is not (since that is just a matter of logic): but which of the two options obtains (sea battle or no sea battle) is something you might think there is no fact of the matter about, and there will not be, until tomorrow comes and settles the question. Lewis considers two options for someone who holds this view: that there are no future events at all yet, and that there are equally real "branching futures". On the branching model, one future contains a sea battle, and the other does not, which is why there's no fact of the matter about what happens in *"the* future". Against the option that there is no future at all yet, Lewis runs the same sort of argument as against presentism:

> If ever anyone is right that there is no future, then that very moment is his last, and what's more is the end of everything. Yet when these philosophers teach that there's no more time to come, they show no trace of terror and despair! When we see them planning and anticipating, we might suspect that they believe in the future as much as anyone else does. (1986a: 207)

Against the "branching future" option,[7] though, Lewis claims that this does not jibe with common sense either. We think it makes sense to wonder what the future will be like, and to agree or disagree about predictions people make. If all the branching futures are equally real, though, this is not reasonable. Wondering whether the future contains a sea battle is pointless if one future has one, another doesn't, and that's all there is to say. If one person predicts a sea battle and another predicts no sea battle, it's hard to see what they could currently be disagreeing about. Of course, one could be wrong if one or the other option was not found anywhere in the future branches (e.g. if it turned out to be physically impossible, or physically impossible given present conditions), but that's not what is supposed to be going on in a case like the sea battle. Lewis thinks our wondering about how the future turns out does make sense (and so do related things we do when we plan and anticipate), so he thinks we should reject the "branching future" view. Again, this seems to be primarily an appeal to common sense.

Lewis also treats the past like the present; times do not gain some sort of special character of fixedness when they become "past". Some of Lewis's attitudes to the status of the past can be illustrated by his views on the possibility of time travel (1976c). Lewis believes that time travel is possible, in principle at least. Someone could get into a time machine and appear hundreds or thousands of years earlier. Whether this is permitted by the laws of nature is not Lewis's concern. He is more concerned with whether time travel is coherent, or possible in the broadest sense. So Lewis thinks that, in principle, there could be causal influences from the present to the past; the past need not be "fixed" in the sense of being unable to be influenced.

Lewis does agree that the "past" is fixed in another way: things cannot be one way in 1800 "before" the time traveller travels and then another way "after" the time traveller visits. It is inconsistent, for example, for a warehouse to be entirely empty all through 1 January 1800 and "then" be occupied with a time machine on 1 January 1800. Such a warehouse would be empty and non-empty at the same time. But Lewis points out that in this sense, the present and future are fixed too. The present cannot be one way and simultaneously another way, and neither can the future. If I discover a cave on the moon that was going to be undisturbed, and instead store a machine in it, I might bring it about that the cave is occupied on 1 January 2100. But that does not mean that I somehow make an empty future cave also be full. All I do is make a cave that *would* have been empty, but for my actions, come to be full. Lewis argues that it is the same for the time traveller. A time traveller who changes the past by piloting a time machine to an empty warehouse in 1800 does not make the warehouse both entirely empty and also occupied on 1 January 1800. What he does is occupy a warehouse that *would have been empty* on 1 January 1800 *if* he had not time travelled. Changing the past is no more problematic in principle than changing the present or the future. This is because changing what happens is a matter of making a difference in how it *would* have been, and it is consistent, Lewis claims, to say that time travellers can make their past different from how it would have been without the change.[8]

It would be too quick to say that for Lewis the past is not fixed in *any* special sense. As we shall see in the discussion of conditionals, particularly in Chapter 4, Lewis thinks that the past rather than the future is often taken into account when we consider what would happen if things were different. We try to keep much of the past fixed when making our judgements, but allow the future to vary. Lewis also thinks that there is a difference in past and future when it comes to *chances*: the chance, at time t, of propositions about t's past will typically be either 0 or 1 (the chance that a coin tossed yesterday came up heads will normally be 1 if it in fact came up heads, and 0 otherwise), but chances for things in t's future can often have other values (the chances that a particular coin will come up heads when tossed tomorrow might be 0.5, for example). But even in these cases, this will not be because of a fundamental metaphysical difference in the times behind us and the times ahead of us. The differences in what would happen, or what the chances are of things happening, are to be explained in other ways.

What, then, is the difference between the present, on the one hand, and the past and future, on the other? For Lewis, there is no fundamental difference in reality. Words like "now" and "present" function as *indexicals*. Consider the word "here", for example. "Here" is not the name of a special place that I happen to be visiting. "Here" is a word that refers to wherever the speaker happens to be. Two people on the telephone who say to each other "It's raining here" and "It's not raining here" are probably not disagreeing about whether it is raining in a certain special location; they are each referring to their own location, and they may well both be correct. Likewise, if someone in Elizabethan England said "Shakespeare is now writing a tragedy" and I say "Nobody writes Shakespearian tragedies now", we are not disagreeing. It is not that "now" refers to some special time, one that the Elizabethans thought contained Shakespeare and that we think does not contain Shakespeare; rather, "now" gets used to refer to *when* the speaker is, just as "here" refers to *where* the speaker is. Many other words to do with time also have the function of picking out a time relative to some time fixed upon by context: "past", "present", "yesterday", "future", "next week", and so on. The "present" at any given time is just when the people at that time happen to be. Notice that there is a spatial use of "present" and "absent" that seems to be indexical like this. If I am not "present" at a roll call, it is not because I have some other state of being; I just happen to not be where the roll call is taking place.

There is another important question in the philosophy of space and time about the *nature* of spacetime. Some people conceive of spacetime as an entity independent of the objects with spatiotemporal locations, as a "container" where objects can be found. Others think that there is no such thing as spacetime; rather, there is just a system of spatio-temporal relations between objects. When two apples are one metre from each other, this view says that there is a relation between the apples, but there is not, strictly speaking, a metre of space between them. A third view accepts that regions of spacetime are entities in their own right, but that physical objects are just modifications of spacetime. On this view, an apple is not a distinct object located in a spatiotemporal region; rather, a spatiotemporal region instantiates a range of properties (including the property of being an apple). Lewis has little to say about this issue, but I think this is mostly because he wants to stay neutral about the three options. For many of the questions he is interested in, it does not much matter which option is correct (1986a: 76). In so far as he has an opinion, he prefers the third option over the first on the grounds that the first seems "uneconomical". Why have *both* objects and regions when the theory works as well with just one? He prefers theories with spacetime over ones that have only objects, however, largely for physical reasons. As Graham Nerlich and others have pointed out (e.g. Nerlich 1976), someone who tries to capture the truths about space and time with only spatiotemporal relations faces many difficulties. Whether we build the Humean mosaic up from properties instantiated by objects that are located at points, or with properties instantiated at the points themselves, or by objects that stand in spatiotemporal relations, the challenges for Humean supervenience will be rather similar.

There is one topic in the philosophy of time that Lewis does devote a considerable amount of effort to, and it is his theory here that will be important for understanding the next step in getting everyday objects out of his Humean mosaic. Everyday objects continue to exist through time, and continue to exist through many changes. I was once a tiny infant but am one no longer, the earth was once a seething hot sphere, but now has a surface covered with oceans, solid ground and even ice. How can an object survive change? How can one and the same thing come to be different?

Lewis answers this in the same way that we would answer the analogous spatial question. A river can be narrow in one place and wide at another by having a narrow part and a wide part. Rivers (and people and planets and most other things) are spread out through space, having different parts at different places. Lewis thinks that things are spread out in time in the same way. I was a short infant and am now a tall adult, because I have a short "infant part" several decades ago and a tall "adult part" now. In other words, Lewis believes in *temporal parts*: at each time when an object exists, the object has a temporal part at that time. Everyday objects, such as tables or people or planets, are actually four-dimensional "worms" spread out through time as well as space. Existing at different times is a matter of having parts at those different times, and changing from being one way to another way is a matter of having one sort of part at one time, and another at another time. My time slices several decades ago are shorter, height-wise, than my time slices now, and that explains why I am able to be short in the past and taller now, while not possessing any contradictory properties.

The most common alternative to this account is one where an object is "wholly present" at every stage where it exists. Objects might still gain and lose parts, of course, but an object can continue to exist for a period of time without having to have distinct parts at distinct times. Lewis introduces some terminology for the difference. Objects that exist through time in the way Lewis thinks they do are called "perduring" objects, and he labels objects that exist through time in the "wholly present" way "enduring" objects (1986a: 202). Another set of labels that is sometimes used (especially in American philosophical circles) is the distinction between "four-dimensionalism" about objects and "three-dimensionalism" about objects. This terminology is slightly misleading, since it suggests that "three-dimensionalists" think that objects are not extended in time. That would be misleading. People who believe in enduring objects believe that objects exist at different times, it is just that they do not think those objects have to have different "temporal parts" at different times. (Another option besides these two would be the presentist option, where objects do not exist at different times because there is only the present. Presentists usually get classified as three-dimensionalists, although, strictly speaking, they do not seem to fall into either the perdurantist or the endurantist camps.)

There is a question about how to tell when stages form parts of the same object. Which person stages 25 years ago, for example, are stages of me? To the general question "Under what conditions do

43

stages at different times form an object?" Lewis's answer is going to be that they always do. Temporal stages are just parts, for Lewis, and his principle of unrestricted composition means that whenever you have a bunch of objects they form a mereological whole. However, most of these aggregates of parts (e.g. five minutes from an eighteenth-century elephant and the next two hours of my table) are ones that we ignore. For objects we are familiar with, Lewis is going to say that chains of similarity and causal connection are often important. If you want to know which infant stages are stages of me, trace my trajectory back into the past. When you find the infant stages that caused other stages that caused other stages, when this whole series is a series where there is only gradual change in many respects, then you've found the stages that go to make me up. Likewise if you want to tell whether the chair you sit on today is the one you sat on last week, there is a path through spacetime of successive chair stages, and if two stages are part of the right sort of continuous connection, they are parts of the same perduring chair. (Lewis thinks that temporal parts often cause further temporal slices in their immediate future to come into existence. A chair slice will cause another chair slice unless something gets in the way. This sort of causation, sometimes called *immanent* causation, often gets overlooked.)

This doctrine of perdurance, plus the part–whole relation, is what enables Lewis's theory to get objects such as rocks and planets and rabbits from instantiations of properties the size of spatiotemporal points. Various point-particle properties (or field strengths or whatever) that are near each other might go together to make up a time slice of an atom, and a series of these time slices, interrelated by similarity and causation, can go together to give us a chemical atom throughout its history. Bundle together many of these perduring atoms and you get large aggregates. It is these aggregates that are the apples, chairs, rabbits and stars of the everyday world.

Lewis has some arguments for preferring a theory of perdurance as opposed to endurance. The most well known is the so-called "problem of temporary intrinsics" (see Lewis 1986a: 202–5; 2002). Objects change; they sometimes have one property, and sometimes another. Consider, for example, an iron bar that is red hot at one time and quite cool an hour later (suppose we heat it in a furnace and then throw it outside in the middle of winter). Being hot and being cold are *contrary* properties: one drives out the other. So how can one and the same thing be both hot and cold, as the iron bar is supposed to be? This problem generalizes whenever we have a pair of contrary properties that are both apparently intrinsic (the object has them just in virtue of how it is, and not how it is connected to other things). Being 10 kg at one time and 60 kg at another would be another example, or being pale at one time and dark at another, or having an arm at one time but no arm at another. Any of these cases would do.

Perdurantists have a straightforward answer to the problem of temporary intrinsics: the iron bar has a hot part (the time slice at the start of the process), and a cold part (the time slice at the end of a process). Maybe hotness and coldness cannot be found together, but there is nothing wrong with something having a hot part and a distinct cold part. The same sort of answer could be used to explain how an iron bar could be hot and cold at the *same* time; the mystery would disappear if we discover that it is hot at one end and cold at the other, say because one end is in a furnace and the other is being dipped in liquid nitrogen.

Endurantists will not want to give this response to the problem of temporary intrinsics. They may well think that all the parts the bar has when it is hot are also parts it has when it is cold (the bar is "wholly located at different times"). Lewis suggests that the endurantist has several options, but none of them are very appealing. Endurantists could take things such as being hot and cold to really be relations to times. One and the same thing could stand in the relation of "hot at" to one time and "cold at" to another. This would be like other relational claims. Abel can be both shorter and taller, for example, if it turns out that he is shorter than Bill and taller than Bob. "Shorter" and "taller" are contraries, but that only means that they cannot both hold at the same time between the same pair of things; someone can stand in contrary relations to different objects. So if hot and cold turn out to be relational[9] (they turn out to really be "hot-at" and "cold-at"), their being contraries does not rule out one and the same object entirely having both, provided it has them to different things (different times, in this case).

Relational accounts of hot and cold, and other supposedly "intrinsic" properties, are not good enough for Lewis. Hot and cold (bent and straight, being 10 kg and not being 10 kg and so on) are supposed to be *intrinsic*; for them to turn out to be relations to something else goes against what we normally think. In effect, Lewis suggests that an endurantist with this relational strategy has given up on intrinsic properties in favour of relational properties.

Some endurantists have endorsed the relational conception of intrinsic properties, and attempted to argue that this does not run

45

counter too much to what we ordinarily think (e.g. Teller 2001). When we think properties are intrinsic, we ignore relations to the times those objects are and just think about whether having the property depends on a relation to anything else (besides the time of having it). Others have wanted to say that only present objects have intrinsic properties of the usual sort, and that non-present objects have very different sorts of features (I am sitting, but my great grandfather in 1900 only has the property of sitting-at-1900, or something similar). This makes for a big difference between the present and all other times, and the less other times seem like ours, the more the view starts to look like presentism. Still other endurantists have wanted to keep non-relational intrinsic properties (*heat*, rather than heat-at or whatever), and complicate the story of what it is for an object to have them: maybe it is only having-at-a-time, or maybe the "is" in "Godfrey is bald" really has some sort of hidden parameter in it, so there are actually many claims such as "Godfrey is$_{\text{at 11.00pm on 1/1/04}}$ bald", "Godfrey is$_{\text{at 6.00pm on 5/3/84}}$ hairy" and so on. With these variables hidden in our sentences, there is no longer supposed to be any conflict between Godfrey being bald on 1/1/04 and hairy on 5/3/84.[10] Lewis doubts that these attempts help very much (Lewis 2002).

Debate still continues about the "problem of temporary intrinsics": what the problem is, whether it is a problem, and what a theory needs to do to solve it. Lewis at least thinks that perdurance is a better solution than its rivals. Another kind of problem that perdurance helps with is the problem of counting objects when there are cases of "fission" or "fusion", where, we are inclined to say, one object becomes two objects, or two objects become one. One class of cases of fission and fusion occurs when objects of the same kind split or come together, for instance when an amoeba "mother" cell divides into two "daughter" cells. The kinds of cases like this that philosophers often worry about are cases involving people. If I can survive the loss of one of my brain hemispheres (and people have survived injuries this dramatic), and I can in principle also survive losing most of my body (provided life-support machines are good enough, as one day they surely will be), then what happens if I am divided so that each of my brain hemispheres is on life support with half of my original body? Those hemispheres will still be able to think, and with the right prosthetics they may well be able to talk, walk and interact with others. After the operation, it seems as though there will be two people, "Leftie" and "Rightie", but both of them, it seems, are me. How can I become two people? If Leftie and Rightie are both identical to me, then doesn't that mean that Leftie and Rightie are identical to each other? Depending on your theory of what it takes to be the same person over time, other fission cases seem possible. If what is required is continuity of memory and psychology, then a duplicating machine may produce several people with the same memory and psychology.

The reason why so much attention has been paid to these unusual cases is that they seem to rule out tempting views of personal identity: what makes a person at one time the same person as one at another time? If it is impossible for something to be distinct from itself, or have a different history from itself, then any theory that says these things *are* possible must be mistaken. This might mean that we have to rethink our idea of what it is to be a person. Lewis offers his story about perdurance as a way of making sense of what is going on in these cases ([1976d] 1983a: 73–7). Consider my original fission example. Leftie and Rightie, in their superior life-support machines, are both able to talk, think, remember life before the operation that produced the separation, and so on. Let us suppose Leftie is remembering how, as a child, he used to run around on two good legs, go to school, and so on. Four-dimensionally, what do we have here? We have a series of person stages covering childhood and right up to the operation. Then we have two diverging series of person stages: one is a series of Leftie's post-operation stages, and one is Rightie's. Suppose we agree that Leftie was indeed the child who went to school, as was Rightie (after all, it looks as though each has as good a claim to be the child as the other). We can think of Leftie and Rightie having a long series of stages in common: the child stages belong to Leftie's spacetime worm and to Rightie's. Strictly speaking, Leftie and Rightie are distinct people and they each have stages the other lacks. But they have a lot of temporal *overlap*. In this respect they are somewhat analogous to conjoined twins, who may share a part at the same time, a liver, or a shoulder, for example. But Leftie and Rightie share temporal parts. Just as conjoined twins are different people who share parts, so are Leftie and Rightie. This explains how they can have the same childhood but be different people.

To finish the explanation, we need to see how Leftie and Rightie can avoid the paradox. If the child is both Leftie and Rightie, doesn't it follow that Leftie and Rightie are the same individual? And if they are one and the same person, how can they have different stages? Lewis's response is that there were two people all along: the child is part of two different person worms, and so are both Leftie and

Rightie. This might seem strange at first, but when it is explained as a matter of part-sharing it becomes possible to see how there could be two people there even though it seems like only one. It is like hearing a single set of footsteps and seeing a single pair of feet go by, and being told that two people just walked past; there is no mystery if it happens to be a pair of feet belonging to conjoined twins who share a single pair of legs.

Lewis also suggests that when we count, we often count things that share their temporal parts at a time as one thing. So even if we knew the future history of Leftie and Rightie, we would be within our rights to count the child as one person. This is because, even though strictly speaking the child is two people, we can talk of identity-at-a-time as being a matter of sharing temporal parts at that time, and then if we count people by identity-at-a-time we will say the child is only one person. This still strikes some people as odd, but much of this oddness might just be due to the fact that fission of people would be very strange.

One thing that makes the perdurance story of fission and fusion not just of interest in far-out cases is that it can help solve much more ordinary cases of identity between things of different kinds. Suppose someone takes a sword and hammers it to make a ploughshare. According to one way of talking, we are tempted to say that the sword has been destroyed, and a ploughshare created. According to another way of talking, one and the same piece of steel exists through the entire process: first it is a sword and then it is a ploughshare. Do we have an object (a piece of steel) that used to be identical to a sword but now is identical to something else? How could one thing become different from itself, or the same object be something else? Some people respond to this puzzle by saying that the sword and the piece of steel are never identical, that before there was both a sword and a sword-shaped piece of steel, and afterwards there was a ploughshare and the same piece of steel, now ploughshare-shaped. The worry with this is that it is double-counting. Did someone carry around a sword *and* a sword-shaped piece of steel? If each weighed 20 kg, then why together do they only weigh 20 kg and not 40 kg? Don't we want to say that the sword was the same thing as the piece of steel?

If Lewis's story works, then we have an explanation of what is going on here as well. The piece of steel is made up of sword stages and ploughshare stages (and maybe some oddly shaped hammered stages in between). It has parts that neither the sword nor the ploughshare have, so it is a different object from both of them. However, while the sword exists, the stages of the sword and the stages of the steel are the same, and while the ploughshare exists, its stages are the same as the piece of steel's. So the piece of steel is identical-at-a-time with the sword when the sword exists, and identical-at-a-time with the plough-share when the ploughshare exists. That's why we count them as the same thing. There is only one thing-at-a-time that fills the sword's scabbard, and only one thing-at-a-time that gets fastened to a plough. It also explains why we do not have to add the weights of the sword and the steel to get the total weight. What an object at-a-time weighs is a matter of what its temporal part weighs, and when you add up the parts of both at-a-time, you only get 20 kg, since there's only one temporal part.

This satisfies our thought that the steel and the sword are in some sense the same, and in some sense different, and it seems less myste-rious than, for example, the view that says that there are distinct sword parts in the scabbard, as well as all the parts of the piece of steel. It is also a picture that fits with Humean supervenience. Once all the microphysical parts are distributed through time, then the parts of the atoms, pieces of metal, sword and so on are all there. We do not have to find extra parts at a given time to be "sword" parts or "piece of metal" parts, even though we want to respect the thought that the sword is in some sense not identical to the piece of steel, since the piece of steel will do things the sword will not. If they really were identical (and not just identical-at-a-time), this would be like saying *that thing* will do things which *that thing* will not, which sounds impossible to most ears.

Conclusion

If Lewis has been successful so far, then we have built up the arrangement of ordinary objects from a basis of point-sized qualities and their arrangements through space and time. But there are also other sorts of truths about our world that need to be accounted for. Things could have been different. How do we account for the fact that some alternatives are possible, and others are not? The world around us is full of objects with dispositions, and one thing causing another. How do we account for this? The world seems to be governed by laws of nature (we may not be sure what they are, but we often take it that part of the job of physics and the other sciences is to work out what these laws are). How do we explain that? It is these sorts of questions

David Lewis

that will concern us in the next two chapters, since it is Lewis's contribution to the theory of necessity and possibility, causation, laws of
nature, chances, and related topics that is in many ways the most
influential part of his metaphysical views, and one of the central
pieces of his philosophy as a whole.

Chapter 3

The plenitude of possibilities

Possible words

In Chapter 2 I outlined a theory of our world, and what the fundamental facts in it are. As well as what in fact happens, though, we
also want an account of what can and cannot happen. We also want to
understand how it can be true that certain things *would* happen if
conditions were somewhat different. Questions about what could
happen and what must happen, about what is necessary and contingent, about what is possible or impossible, are all called *modal* questions. (The terminology dates back to the medievals, who thought
necessity and possibility were *modes* of sentences or propositions.)
Philosophers increasingly came to recognize the importance of questions about necessity or possibility, or modality (as the subject is
sometimes called) in the second half of the twentieth century. One
reason for this is the role that modal questions seem to play in a host
of other philosophical puzzles. One set of puzzles involves a family of
concepts, including causation, laws of nature, objective chances,
dispositions and powers and conditional statements. Questions
about what causes what are intimately linked to questions of what
must happen if something else does, and also to questions of what
outcomes can be brought about by certain causes. Questions about
the laws of nature seem to concern what must be true, as opposed to
what happens to be true as an accidental matter. Chances or
probabilities sometimes seem to be weighted possibilities: the more
probable something is, the greater the possibility that it will occur.
Statements about an object's dispositions (that a glass is disposed to
break when struck, for example) are statements not just about what

does happen to the glass (it might never be struck, or it might be melted before anything else happens to it), but also what could or would happen if the glass were struck. In each case we have to go beyond the events that actually occur.

How to make sense of causation, laws of nature, dispositions and chances will be discussed in Chapter 4. This chapter will focus on questions of necessity and possibility, on what can and cannot happen. These questions are quite difficult enough in their own right. There are many occasions in ordinary language and when we are engaged in non-philosophical theorizing where we seem to talk of situations other than the ones that actually obtain. When making a decision, for example, we are often comparing different courses of action, even though we think that at most one of them will end up being real. (When I am deciding whether to eat a carrot raw or cook it, I do not expect that both things will happen to that particular carrot.) We talk about possible outcomes when we talk about causes and effects. If I prevent a forest fire, the whole point is that the forest fire isn't real. Or if a ship hits an iceberg because a steering correction is not made, then the unmade steering correction does not actually exist, yet it might be crucial to our investigation. When assessing probabilities, we typically distribute probabilities over an "event space" that includes events that will not happen. The event of the roulette ball landing on red 17 may not occur on a given occasion, but we would still want to give it some probability before the spin of the wheel. (In more technical use of probabilities, the appeal to possible but non-actual outcomes is sometimes even more explicit.) Quantum physics assigns quantitative measures over outcome states, even though on most theories not all of those outcomes become actual.

We talk as if there are possible situations other than the situations that occur. Philosophers often distinguish the "merely possible" from the "actual"; what actually happens is possible too, hence the expression "merely possible" for events that could have happened but didn't, or objects that could have come into existence but failed to. A "possible world" is a maximal possibility: a complete way things could have turned out, or a possible specification for the entire cosmos. There is an "actual world", the way things really do happen, but most people will agree there are other possible states for the world to have. Our world could have been the way some other possible world is. Normally we seem to talk of situations that are less all-encompassing than a complete situation. When we wonder what would have happened if a fire had got out of control, we typically do not consider the entire evolution of the cosmos. On reflection, though, most of us would admit that there are complete ways the world could have been besides the way it in fact turned out. Once we have possible worlds, we can represent these more limited possibilities as being sets of possible worlds. The possibility that squid evolved to have only four tentacles, for example, can be represented by the set of all the possible worlds where squid have evolved to have four tentacles. There are other stories about how we can relate complete possibilities to partial ones, but in general once we have one, we can reconstruct the other.

We seem to talk directly about merely possible situations, and also merely possible objects and events. It was also noticed (partly due to formal work done by Stig Kanger (1957), Saul Kripke (1959, 1963) and others) that possible worlds give us a way to understand the behaviour of the expressions "it is possible that ..." and "it is necessary that ...", and the related adverbs "possibly" and "necessarily". When we attach these expressions to sentences, "possibly p" behaves like the claim "at some possible world(s), p", and "necessarily p" seems to behave like the claim "at all possible worlds, p". So "necessarily, rain is followed by sunshine" seems to mean something like "in all possible worlds, rain is followed by sunshine". "Possibly, dogs outrun tigers" means "in some possible world(s), dogs outrun tigers". Claims about what is necessary or possible seem to function like generalizations about possible situations, and exploiting this analogy has led to significant advances in "modal logic", the logic of necessity and possibility. This has led many to think that our ordinary talk about necessity and possibility amounted to generalizing about possibilities: "quantifying over" possible situations or possible worlds, in the jargon of logic.

We may talk about possible situations, and the objects and events in them, but it is all very puzzling. After all, we are inclined to think that if an object could have come into existence but didn't, then it *doesn't exist*! Mere possibilities, unlike what is actual, are not real. Merely possible situations don't obtain; that seems to be the whole point. So how can we be talking about all of these things, when there *are* no such things?

Lewis proposes a radical solution. He takes the same approach to other possibilities as he does to other times. For Lewis, other possible worlds are just as real as this one, and are much the same as this one. For him, there really is such a thing as a species of land-dwelling squid, not in our cosmos, perhaps, but in some other possible world.

David Lewis

Every possible description of a world matches up to a real, concrete universe out there. Talk of possible worlds is to be taken entirely at face value. This was the doctrine Lewis called "modal realism", although maybe this was not the best name, since it was realism about possible worlds rather than just realism about possibility and necessity, and it included a specific story about what these possible worlds or possible situations were like. Nevertheless, the name stuck, and this doctrine of modal realism is one of the most famous of Lewis's views.

If there really are singing cows, swooping stars, or palaces of solid gold a mile high, then we have a straightforward story of what people are talking about when they talk about the possibility of such things existing. Modal expressions that appear to be generalizations about possible worlds can be treated just as that; necessary truths are true in every possible world, just as eternal truths are true at any time. It is a theory of possibility that is straightforward, and Lewis shows how it answers many of the puzzles people had about modality. However, it gained very few adherents. Most philosophers could not believe that there was an endless variety of universes, or at any rate they did not believe that accounting for modality was a good enough reason to accept the theory that all of these possible worlds exist.

If all possibilities equally exist, we need a story about why one possible world seems special. What actually happens, and what we actually experience, has a significance that mere possibility does not. (Having the possibility of winning a million dollars is not the same as winning a million dollars.) Many people have thought that this means actuality should have some special metaphysical status that mere possibility does not. Lewis, on the other hand, thinks that what is "actual" is an indexical matter, just like the question of which time is "now". There are no Roman legions any more, but that does not mean that there is any fundamental metaphysical difference between Roman legions and nuclear missiles. It is just that the Roman legions are located in a time long ago, while the nuclear missiles can be found at the same time as we are. Likewise, Lewis thinks, there is a difference between dragons and orang-utans, but the difference is not that orang-utans have some special metaphysical status that dragons lack. It is just that there are orang-utans in our world, but dragons are only found in other possible worlds. Actual things can be found in our world (although some of them only in the past or the future), but merely possible things cannot. Actuality makes such a difference to us because actual things are the only things that are here in our world. (Just like presentness makes such a difference because only present things are around now; a million dollars now is more use to us than a million dollars in 500 years time.)

According to Lewis, each possible world is a separate spatio-temporal system; there are no ways of getting from one world to another. Likewise, possible worlds are causally isolated from each other. The only things that could have causal influence on us, or that we could causally influence, are things in our own possible world. Why couldn't there be interaction between possible worlds? Well, for Lewis, there certainly could be largely disconnected regions of space and time with only a few connections – the odd dimension hopper or wormhole or whatever – but he would want to count those only slightly connected regions as part of a single possible world. After all, if we do think it is possible for someone to leave one "universe"[1] and travel to another, we seem to be taking the whole trip to be a possibility, and the complete possibility in which that trip occurs contains both the starting-point and the destination. Lewis also takes his possible worlds to include their contents, so just as you and I and everything else are part of the actual world, so other worlds' contents are parts of them.

We understandably often restrict our attention to the actual, and Lewis claims that much of what we say was said with implicitly "restricted quantifiers". "Quantifiers" are words such as "all", "some", "most", "few" and "none" and expressions such as "at least five", "infinitely many" and so on. In everyday life, we often restrict the application of our quantifier expressions to talk about less than everything. If at a party someone complains "There's no beer left", they are probably not suggesting that beer has disappeared from the universe; they are probably restricting their quantifier to talk only about things at the party. If someone complains "Everyone was mean to me today", then unless they are having a *very* bad day they are probably not thinking that everyone in the world was mean to them; they are probably restricting their quantifier to a much more limited group (their workmates, the people they talked to, or some other group). Context often makes clear how comprehensive a quantifier expression is supposed to be.

There are also quantifier restrictions to do with time. Sometimes we seem to be talking about only present things, and other times we seem to include things from the past and the future. "There are eight English kings called Henry, but only two called Charles, and none called Bugalugs" seems to be true enough. On the other hand, it seems to be true to say that "England does not have a king, it has a queen". We can explain how the second sentence can be true, even though there are several English kings called Henry, through quantifier domain restriction. The first sentence seems to be quantifying over past English monarchs, while the second one has its quantifier restricted to present monarchs. If we only count present monarchs, then England does not have any kings; if we include its history, there are many English kings. It seems more common to include the past than to include the future, but some things we say seem to include the future too. We might be inclined to reject the claim "Elizabeth II is the last queen of England" (given what we expect about the continuation of the English monarchy), but if she is not the last, then there must be queens after her, so if the sentence is false, then it must be because of future queens that we are taking into account.

Lewis claims that we often (tacitly) restrict our quantifiers to only include actual things. When we say there are no giant gorillas who climb skyscrapers, or we say there is no species of bird that spends its entire life underground, or we say that cows never tap-dance, we are restricting our quantifier to the actual world. (We may not realize that we are doing this, but quantifier restriction does not have to be deliberate. Many of us do not realize until it is pointed out that in our talk about objects in time we seem to be restricting quantifiers.) That is why we can coherently say that if something is merely possible it does not exist, or if something is a merely possible outcome it doesn't occur – these are particularly tricky sentences because they require a shift in what is quantified over halfway through – but the sense in which Lewis thinks they are right is that he agrees that if something is merely possible it is not one of the things that *actually* exist, and if something only possibly occurs it is not among the *actual* occurrences. Of course, talking with restricted quantifiers when we are explicitly talking about possible worlds may be very misleading, but if we ordinarily talk as if the only things are actual things, this need not cause any misunderstanding.

Of course, Lewis agrees that his opponents are quantifying without restriction (they really do intend to not leave anything out) when they say that there are no talking donkeys or singing planets. They genuinely disagree with Lewis (just as a presentist, who thinks the only things that exist exist now, can be talking unrestrictedly when they say England has no kings, but only a queen – presentists really don't believe in Henry I–VIII and all the rest). Lewis's opponents do owe us an explanation, then, of what is going on when we seem to quantify over merely possible objects – "several dreadful outcomes were avoided", "anything I could cook with these ingredients would taste funny, so I won't use them", "some races are never run" all seem to be quantifying over merely possible things – and merely possible outcomes (since they were not actual if they were avoided), meals cooked with those ingredients (which will not be actual, if the cook gets his way), merely possible races, and so on.

We can see at least how Lewis's story about restricted quantification might cover much of what people ordinarily say. Whether there is implicit quantifier restriction, or whether Lewis is asserting something that we in effect deny every day (for example, when I claim there are no psychic healing crystals), seems a theoretical question that might be hard to resolve. At any rate, even if Lewis contradicts what we believe when we believe there are no flying pigs or castles of bronze, he has at least pointed out that there is something very close to what we believe (that, speaking with a very natural restriction, there are no flying pigs, and no castles of bronze) that his theory does say is true.

Lewis does concede that his theory is not common sense, and he even admits that it contradicts common sense. Common sense probably does hold that everything is actual (Lewis 1986a: 99, 134). He thinks that despite this it is worth accepting modal realism as an improvement in "unity and economy" over our common-sense opinions (*ibid.*: 134). He does think it is a constraint on his theory (and any other theory, especially a philosophical theory) that it ought not stray too far from common sense, since at a certain point a theory that goes too far from our opinions becomes unbelievable, and nobody can believe a theory that is literally unbelievable. Lewis hopes that the advantages of modal realism outweigh the cost of disagreeing with common sense. The story about restricted quantification goes some way to reduce the apparent disagreement, and so Lewis would hope it goes some way to mitigating what we have to put on the cost side of the ledger.

Lewis believes that every possibility, in the broadest sense of possibility, is represented by a possible world. Possibilities that are less than maximally specific will be represented by a set of his worlds. There are many possible worlds where there are green cows – worlds much like this one where there is a quirk of evolution or some eccentric genetic manipulation, worlds like ours in our galaxy but with very different goings-on in other galaxies, and so on – one for every coherent way we can extend the story of green cows. The set of all the green-cow worlds represents "the" possibility that there are green cows. Philosophers sometimes talk about the "logically possible". In one sense, this includes any claim that does not contradict a law of logic. It rules out "all roses are red and all roses are not red", for example. Lewis's worlds are not quite this generous, since there are claims that do not conflict with logic but nevertheless seem to be necessarily false in the strongest sense. (Standard formal logic will not tell you that everything that is red is coloured: but nevertheless a colourless red ball is impossible.) There are some other principles that Lewis thinks are true in all possible worlds: unrestricted composition is one example, the truths of mathematics are another. But comparatively few things are necessary; the possible worlds include those that do not obey our laws of nature, have a different number of spatial and temporal dimensions, and have all sorts of other strange goings-on. Not all possible worlds are made up of Humean mosaics, either. Lewis wants to defend the view that *our* world was nothing but "local particular matters of fact", but there are other worlds with all sorts of spread-out natural properties, perhaps lots of fundamental relations besides spatiotemporal ones, objects that endure rather than perdure through time, and so on.

Often we are not as generous with possibility as this. Consider talk of people's abilities, what they can and cannot do. In almost any normal context, if I told you I could run 100 metres in ten seconds I would be lying; only the best sprinters can do that. Or if we said it was possible that Hitler was a perfectly lovely person, we would be sorely deluded. Or if a physicist told us it was possible to accelerate through the speed of light, we would take this to be a controversial view that was almost certainly false, rather than an innocuous truth. People often distinguish between different "grades" of necessity. There is "broadly logical" or "metaphysical" necessity, which is the most generous. Then there is "physical" or "nomic" necessity, where the laws of nature are held fixed (it is not physically possible to accelerate through the speed of light, for example). There may be more restricted versions too, such as "temporal" necessity, where we hold the past fixed (it is too late to do anything about the massacres committed by Ghengis Khan, but the massacres of the twenty-second century can still be averted). Claims about people's abilities are even more restricted. When we want to know how fast it is possible for me to run, we not only take as fixed the laws of physics and the physiology of human beings, but also my level of fitness, my level of training, maybe even my will to run fast, and other things.

Lewis handled these "restricted necessities" as another case of implicitly restricted quantification. Considering all the possible worlds, it is possible for a particle to accelerate through the speed of light; considering only the possible worlds compatible with our laws of nature, it is not (or so we believe) – it does not happen in any of those worlds. Considering all the physically possible worlds, I can run 100 metres in ten seconds (human beings can have the right sort of physique to do that, after all); considering the ones that resemble this one in terms of my fitness, musculature and training, I cannot. If this is the explanation (and we need some explanation of the variability of our talk about what is possible and what is not), then this is further evidence that our expressions "necessary" and "possible", "can" and "must" are closely connected with quantification over worlds. It may also provide some support for Lewis's claim that our tendency to talk as if only actual things exist can be understood as implicitly restricted quantification, if only because it suggests there is implicitly restricted quantification going on in language that we are not immediately aware of.

There is another use of possibility and necessity talk that is related to this. Sometimes when we talk about things being possible, or that they must be true, we seem to be talking about what we know, or what we are certain of. It is possible that a war just broke out somewhere in the world. It is not possible that three people are hiding in this room. What we sometimes mean by these expressions seems to be something such as "it is compatible with all I know that a war broke out", or "it is ruled out by what I am sure about that three people are hiding in this room". The same sort of phenomenon can be observed with "must" or "have to be". When we hear many people making noise and say that there have to be at least twenty people at the party next door, we are not guessing that it is metaphysically necessary for the party to be that big, or somehow the laws of physics ensure that the party is large. We are presumably just indicating that there are at least twenty people in every situation compatible with our information. Again, this usage of modal vocabulary ("must", "can", "has to be", "necessary", "possible", etc.) might be treated as a form of restricted quantification over worlds; we consider only possible worlds that are not ruled out by our knowledge, or not ruled out by what we are sure about, or something similar. There are some tricky puzzles here. For one thing, it seems that we could be unsure about something that is metaphysically necessary (e.g. we think something could be the correct solution to a logic puzzle or a mathematics question, but we are not sure). Does this

David Lewis

mean that there are some worlds that are compatible with what we know that are not even possible? Lewis thinks not, but I shall not go into that issue here.

Lewis thinks that we have good reason to believe in other possible worlds – they help make sense of some of our ordinary opinions about modality – and there are considerable theoretical benefits of employing theories that make use of possible worlds. For Lewis's modal realism to be successful, however, he should also show that alternative conceptions of worlds are not as attractive. Lewis's discussion of the range of options available to people who believe in possible worlds have become standard, and his objections to rival theories are still seen as the objections to beat.

The most common alternative to thinking that other possible worlds are like our cosmos is to say that they are some sort of abstract object. Maybe possible worlds are complete sets of sentences (complete in the sense that together they settle every question). Or maybe they represent by being similar to what concrete worlds would be like, in the way a painting or a road map represents by being similar to the thing it is supposed to represent. Or maybe the abstract objects stand in some other sort of relation to concrete things (or at least the one corresponding to our cosmos does, and the others would if they were the one that was actualized). Lewis calls these sorts of theories "ersatz" theories of possible worlds; others looking for a more neutral name often call them "abstractionist" theories of possible worlds (see van Inwagen 1986). Lewis groups the options into three families: "linguistic ersatzism", "pictorial ersatzism" and "magical ersatzism" (1986a: Ch. 3).

Linguistic ersatzism takes possible worlds to be representations: structured descriptions of other complete ways a world could turn out. They might be sets of sentences, or sets of some abstract objects that represent in the same sort of way that sentences do, or some other complicated structures that can be interpreted as complete descriptions. They are "linguistic" because they are supposed to represent the way languages do. Sometimes this thought is expressed by saying that possible worlds are "world books": complete stories about how a universe could turn out. These language-like objects would almost certainly need to be abstract. Most complete possibilities are too complicated to be captured by anything anyone has in fact written down, or ever will. Still, many philosophers do believe in a good many abstract objects. For example, someone who believes in mathematical objects will have many complicated models composed of sets and functions available as the structures that are to be interpreted as representing total states of affairs.

Lewis has several objections to linguistic ersatzism.[2] One is that it does not give an analysis of possibility and necessity. It must simply presuppose that the distinction between the possible and the necessary has already been drawn. Lewis thinks that modality enters into the account in separating from the others the representations that can be possibly complete and correct (for if we have the representational resources to represent all the maximal possibilities, we will presumably have many representations that are inconsistent or are otherwise not possibly correct). The representations, given the relevant interpretation must be *consistent*, and they must be *complete*. Consistency is sometimes understood as being co-possible: a set of claims is consistent if the claims could all be true together. A set of claims is complete if, for any proposition, the claims imply either it or its negation. (A complete set can imply both, if it is also inconsistent). An "ersatzer" (like anyone else) probably does not know exactly what claims are necessarily implied by others. What specifications, couched in the language of microphysics, are such that, if they are true, a donkey exists? Lewis shows how tricky it is to try to give a specification of consistency and the right sort of implication, without implicitly relying on modality.

Another two objections concern the descriptive resources these sorts of world-making languages could have, even if they are abstract and idealized. One is about indiscernible individuals. Consider a possible world where there is an infinite regular array of nondescript particles, or, as Lewis does, a world of infinite recurrence, where there are infinitely many individuals called "Napoleon" who have indistinguishable Napoleonic careers (in indiscernible environments, so we cannot distinguish them by their relationships to differentiated surroundings). We often want to talk about possible individuals, and while Lewis literally has infinitely many Napoleon clones running around in other worlds, the ersatzer had better make do with something else. The obvious thing to use is descriptions of individuals, presumably descriptions extracted from the full-sized world descriptions. The problem is that when a world represents that there are indiscernible objects, there is no difference in the way it describes each of them, and without different descriptions, we cannot have different (ersatz) objects. But it does seem possible to have objects that are not distinguished from any of the others, or at least not distinguished by means of any "external" description. One of the

Napoleon clones might be able to say "all the others are not *me*", but that does not help us. If all of the clones utter that sentence, we cannot pick out a single one of them in the way the Napoleon clones themselves can.

Lewis's other objection involving representation concerns "alien" properties. We might think that there are possible properties that are very different from the ones we find in this world, so different that they cannot be built up as combinations of our properties, or in any other ways we might define complex properties from families of simpler ones. If such properties are possible, though, it looks as though we cannot describe them uniquely. Any description we can give of how one operates in a world will be applicable to some other one of these alien properties in another world. Perhaps we could try to distinguish them by their relationships to other alien properties but, again, when one stands in a certain relationship (say, being a species of some alien genus), there will be another possible family of alien properties that stand in equivalent relations (some quite different species of some quite different alien genus). As far as a language in our world goes, even an abstract idealized one, there will be nothing to single out one of the alien properties from others that have the same profile in some other world. But if they cannot be represented, they cannot appear in the world books: so the linguistic ersatzer seems driven to say that such alien properties are not possible after all.

Defenders of linguistic ersatzism can reply to these objections, but at some cost. In response to the first objection, they can accept that they leave modality unanalyzed. Although it would be nice to have a further account of possibility and necessity, talking about possible worlds and possible objects is useful even if they get explained in terms of modality rather than vice versa. Or they can claim that which descriptions serve as the possible worlds is marked out by some independent feature (rather than marking them out explicitly using modal notions). We could suppose that the relevant descriptions come with some sort of tag. Let's call this tag, whatever it is, W. This would not require the ersatzer explicitly to mention modality in her account of what a possible world is; instead, possible worlds would be a certain sort of abstract representation tagged with W. In another sense, though, this would still have an extra theoretical resource employed just to account for modality: the distinction between things with W and things without. In that sense, Lewis would probably claim, the ersatzer still has a modal primitive (a "primitive" is something posited by a theory that is not further analysed, and the W tag is a "modal primitive", arguably, if it is a primitive introduced just to account for modality). Whether this seems like a problem will depend on your theoretical perspective. Although it is nice to have unified explanations to explain as much as possible with a common set of theoretical resources, adding one distinction to a theory to account for modality might seem like a fair trade. (And critics of Lewis might fairly charge that all of his worlds and their contents are postulated to account for modality, so in that light a single W distinction does not seem so bad).

In response to the indiscriminability charges, again a linguistic ersatzer could bite the bullet and revise our conception of what is possible. Lewis thinks that this is particularly unwelcome in the case of alien properties. He asks us to imagine the point of view of some-one in a simpler possible world than ours, one where protons are simple fundamental particles and not made up of quarks, as in ours. That person cannot distinguish a world such as ours from a world where the properties are swapped around; for example, where quark flavours behave as quark colours do here, and vice versa. (Quark "flavours" and "colours" are distinctive properties postulated by sub-atomic physics. Let us suppose for the time being (perhaps implausi-bly) that in our world these properties behave the way current science says they do.) From the point of view of that simpler world, this possibility cannot be distinguished from another. Does that mean that we should say our world is not possible relative to that one, that a person in such a simpler world would be right to claim that our world could not possibly exist? Or should we claim that somehow our world is special, and while simpler worlds can have the problem of not being able to distinguish possibilities, our world is so rich in prop-erties that it does not face the problem that slightly simpler worlds do? Neither of these claims seem particularly well motivated.

We could try saying that properties have some of their roles neces-sarily, so that quark colour could not behave the way quark flavour does, and vice versa, and that would block this particular example. But more complicated examples might still do the trick. Two families of alien properties might feature in possibilities indistinguishable by us, even if we say that how a property relates to other properties is not a contingent matter. Another approach would be to try to say that this-worldly linguistic resources can go some way further towards permitting the possibility of alien properties than Lewis does. Heller (1998), Nolan (2002: Ch. 5) and Sider (2002) follow this route.

The second sort of ersatzism Lewis discusses is a version he calls "pictorial ersatzism". In many respects, it is similar to linguistic ersatzism. Instead of other cosmoi, we have this-worldly representations to do the job of possible worlds. Where pictorial ersatzism differs is in the kind of representation; linguistic ersatzism represents by means of sentence-like structures, while pictorial ersatzism represents with picture-like structures (or models, if you think "picture" only covers representations in two dimensions). According to pictorial ersatzism, there are picture-like representations that have components that genuinely resemble what possible objects would be like were they to have really existed. (So a world that represents blue swans has something that somehow resembles the way blue swans would be.) Pictorial ersatzism is a puzzling view, and may have no actual adherents. I suspect Lewis includes it in his discussion because many people want to say that worlds work by representation, and pictorial representation is an alternative to sentence-like representation. Lewis thinks pictorial ersatzism requires primitive modality as well. The content of a picture is given by what it *would* resemble, if there were such things, but for most possible objects there are no such things, so we have to use this modal characterization to say what the picture represents.[3]

Lewis's main worry, though, is that it comes so close to his own modal realism that it has the same costs, plus some of its own. If the pictures are adequately to represent through similarity or other isomorphisms, then they must have similar features, or the same features, as the things they are representing. So a pictorial world that represents a talking donkey must have a property (or have a part with a property) almost exactly like the property of being a talking donkey, or perhaps the property of being a talking donkey itself. We are used to pictures having only a few properties in common with the thing represented – a painting may have similarities in apparent colour, a bronze statue has similarities in shape but not in colour and so on – but the more information we want to encode pictorially, the more similar the picture needs to be to the object depicted. A scale model can represent more than a photograph, a life-sized model even more than a scale model (if only because a life-sized model can represent size more straightforwardly). The limit, where all of the information is conveyed by a picture (and all of it is done by isomorphism, rather than by convention, or language, or whatever), seems to be the point where the picture-like object has most or all of the properties in common with the thing it is supposed to be representing. But an object that has a part that is a talking donkey, another part which is a donkey's ear and so on, and has the properties a complete world would have, is for all intents and purposes just one of Lewis's worlds. Lewis thinks that if this is where pictorial ersatzism leads, it is better to drop the attempt to find things that are abstract but that are otherwise just like his worlds.

The final version of ersatzism Lewis considers he calls "magical ersatzism". This form of ersatzism has abstract objects that have various claims true according to them, but not in the way that every-day representations do. "Magical" ersatz worlds might be supposed to work by representation in the strict sense (although not in the way sentences or pictures do), or they might work in some other way, provided various claims are "true according to" them in some other way. The magical theory, as Lewis presents it, is fairly sparse. Worlds are abstract, and they are simple. (They do not have any internal structure, according to Lewis's characterization, although I suppose if they had irrelevant internal structure, that would not make a difference either.) One of them has a special relation to the concrete universe. Lewis calls this relation "selection"; the one that is "selected" is the one that represents the actual truths as true. There are many other objects like this one but that are not selected, and it is a necessary truth that only one of these simple abstract objects is selected. The selected one is the one that gets things right, and since the worlds represent differently, and they are complete representa-tions, there cannot be two that get it right. These objects are such that necessarily, if one is selected, it is the one that is correct; that's the whole story. That's the whole story about worlds, at any rate. If there are ersatz possible objects as well, then there are other simple abstract objects that can stand in selection relations, and there are necessary relationships between one of the "world" objects getting selected, and the "possible objects" objects getting selected. There might, for example, be an object that gets "selected" if I exist. That would be the ersatz representative of me, and it would be selected whenever a world where I exist was selected.

Magical ersatzism, as presented, looks very weird and unattrac-tive, and, of course, this is deliberate. Part of Lewis's point is that the devices it uses are unfamiliar to common sense and not exactly appealing. Again, the account of worlds is partly in terms of neces-sary connections; necessarily exactly one of the worlds is selected, and the condition for a world to make something true is that *neces-sarily*, if the world is selected, then that claim is true. And again, whether this unanalysed modality is much of a problem can be disputed. Lewis's main objection to magical ersatzism is that it is mysterious. What is this relation of selection? Does it hold, when it does, because each world is somehow different, and would therefore relate to concrete worlds differently? If so, then all of these worlds have different simple natures, and Lewis doubts that anyone could understand enough about these simple, abstract natures. (He probably also thought that this is just as extravagant as his own commitment to possible worlds.) If the worlds are all the same intrinsically, but only differ in how the relation of selection would apply to them, then it is the behaviour of selection that is doing all the work, and Lewis thinks this relation of selection is too mysterious. This is why he calls this version of ersatzism "magical"; the behaviour of these things just seems like magic.

Lewis envisages that the magical ersatzers may respond by explaining that the entities with these features have more familiar names – "states of affairs" or "propositions" or something else – and the relation of selection has some more familiar name: for a "state of affairs" to be selected is for it to "obtain", or for a proposition to be selected is for it to be "true". Worlds could then be seen as maximal states of affairs, or maximal propositions.[4] Lewis replies that just applying different names for these objects and this relation by itself doesn't make things any less mysterious. That seems right, as far as it goes. What we label these things seems more of a matter of marketing than something that should make a genuine theoretical difference. However, the magical ersatzer can say that these names are not just relabellings, they are reminders that we talk about states of affairs and propositions elsewhere in philosophy. If we have more illuminating accounts of objects like these in those areas, then this might in turn shed light on what a "state of affairs" is, for example, or what it is for one to "obtain" when we come to accounting for possible worlds. (Or shed more light on what a "proposition" is, and what it is for one to be "true".) Lewis has his own theories of what is going on in the other areas of theory that talk about states of affairs and propositions, and his own candidates to be these things. His theory of propositions will be discussed at length in Chapter 6. But if the magical ersatzer can show that her theoretical resources are explained and justified in some other area of philosophy, then the fact that they look mysterious in isolation will not seem such a problem.

None of these "ersatz" options look very tempting on the face of it. On the other hand, we do want to be able to have the benefits of talking about possible situations and possible objects and events in those situations. There is still no consensus about where to go from here. Lewis's belief in concrete possible worlds is still a contending view, as are both "linguistic" and "magical" ersatz theories of worlds, and there are also theorists who try to show that we can have the benefits of using possible worlds without literally having to accept that they exist. But no matter what the views that different philosophers endorse, it is Lewis's conception of the problems and the alternatives that frames the contemporary debate about possible worlds and their nature.

Essences, identity across worlds and *de re* modality

Some possibilities can be specified without referring to any particular individual: for example, the possibility that all cows are green, or that there is a palace more than a mile high, or that there are 23 spatial dimensions. Other possibilities seem to be possibilities *for* specific objects and people: this lump of timber could be turned into a table, but not into a swan; Bill could become an astronaut, but not a garage. Many people have thought that objects have *essence*, meaning that some facts about what each object is limit the possibilities for that object, that is, limit the metaphysical possibilities for that object. Some people think, for example, that birds are *essentially* animals. This is different from the claim that if something were not a bird, it would not be an animal. It is, rather, the claim about any specific birds that those very creatures could not fail to be animals. Consider Amanda the duck. The claim is not just that if it had turned out that Amanda was not an animal she would not have been a bird. It is also that there is no way that Amanda could have turned out to be something other than an animal. A story where Amanda becomes a very complicated plant is an impossible story, according to these people, as is the story that she could be turned into a sophisticated swimming robot. (At least, she could not be turned into a plant or a robot and survive. The sense in which she can be turned into a pile of ashes by a fire, or turned into dinner by a chef, may be a sense in which she could be turned into a plant or robot.)

This can be contrasted with non-essential properties, or "accidental" properties as they are often called. Amanda is a swimmer, but she could have existed without being a swimmer if she had been largely paralysed, or been so terrified of liquid she always panicked, or in other ways. The terms "essence" and "accident" have other uses in philosophy, but this characterization of an essence in terms of features an object must have is one of the common ones.

So we want to be able to discuss possibilities for objects, and whether objects have distinctive essences. Lewis develops a novel way to account for these possibilities for objects: by employing *counterparts*. Lewis is of the view that each object is found in only one possible world.[5] I am in this cosmos, but I am not found in any worlds with talking donkeys or bottomless oceans or anything like that. However, there are objects that are quite similar to me found in other worlds that are very similar to mine. (Some will be virtually indistinguishable. Consider a world just like this one except that one of the electrons in the Andromeda galaxy is in a different location. The person writing a book just like this one in that world will be just like me!) It is these similar possible objects that represent the other possibilities for me. If there is one that is similar enough to me, it is one of my *counterparts*, and for something to be possible for me is for it to happen to one of my counterparts. So I am possibly red-haired, for example, because in some other world there is someone rather like me who has red hair. Facts about essences turn into facts about similarity. If Amanda the duck is essentially a duck, that means that all of her counterparts are ducks, or, in other words, every possible object that is similar enough to Amanda is also a duck. *Accidental* properties, the properties that an object could lack while still existing, are those properties not shared by all its counterparts. If Amanda has some counterparts that do not quack (because of habit or because of a problem with their voice boxes) then being a quacker is only an accidental property of Amanda's. Facts about an object's essence are thus not mysterious new facts over and above the features the object in fact has. The ordinary properties an object has explain what properties are essential to it, because the ordinary properties an object has determine what possible objects are similar to it.

The more traditional alternative to counterparts in dealing with possibilities for objects is "transworld identity" – which means saying that one and the same object can be found in different possible worlds – so Amanda the duck is found in some worlds not quacking, even though she quacks here. One reason to reject the view that an object like me or my chair is found in many different possible worlds is the problem that I would be different from the way I actually am. Suppose there is a world where I spend most of my time mountain-climbing and none of it doing philosophy. In that world I am a mountain-climber and not a philosopher, and in this world I am a philosopher and not a mountain-climber. But how can I, being only one person after all, be a mountain-climber and not a mountain-climber? This problem (restricted to intrinsic properties) is the problem of *accidental intrinsics*, and Lewis thinks (1986a: 199–202) that if I was entirely in more than one world, this would lead to the same sort of difficulties as endurantism (the view that I am entirely at more than one time, discussed in Chapter 2). Being 5 kg in mass, for example, does not seem to be a matter of standing in a relation to a world; an object just is either 5 kg in mass or it is not. But if an object just plain *is* 5 kg in mass, without qualification, then what sense could we make of it being 5 kg in mass in one world, and 7 kg in mass in another?

Notice that for this objection to objects being in more than one world to work, we need to think of being "in" a possible world as like being in this galaxy: literally found inside or part of it. If worlds are not concrete universes, the problem of accidental intrinsics looks very different. If worlds are only representations of concrete universes (e.g. if they are "world books" providing complete descriptions), then an object having an intrinsic property "in" a world is just a matter of how that world describes that object, and then I can be bald in one world and have a full head of hair in another, just as I can be bald according to one story and have a full head of hair in another. We have less firm a conviction about what it is to be "in" a world than we do about what it is to exist at a time, so the problem of accidental intrinsics does not need to have a very similar solution to the problem of temporary intrinsics, if we are not Lewisian modal realists.

One general reason to adopt counterpart theory, independent of the details of Lewis's theory of possible worlds, is that it permits flexibility in our judgements about essences. In some contexts we are inclined to think different sorts of things are essential to a given object. Some people are strongly inclined to think that, for example, ducks such as Amanda are essentially ducks; others think that it is possible, in the broadest sense, for Amanda to have been some other sort of bird, or a robot, or something else very different. Perhaps there is a deep disagreement here, or maybe what is going on is that different sorts of similarity are relevant in different contexts. Set up a context where much similarity is needed and some strong statement of essence seems appropriate; be more lax, and a duck-shaped robot that acts and thinks like Amanda seems good enough to be a possibility for her. This would at least explain why people have such different intuitions about what is essential, and why the arguments between different sides so often get nowhere.

Variability also solves some problems about essence when an object belongs to several different kinds at once (Lewis 1986a: 252–3). Philosophers often use statues as examples when discussing this sort of problem. Consider a bronze statue, a statue of a horse, for example. Many people are inclined to think that some kind of shape property is essential to such a statue. If you flatten the bronze, you destroy the statue, since the statue cannot survive being flattened. (And if the bronze had always been a flattened square sheet, then the statue would have never existed.) On the other hand, consider the piece of bronze that is in the shape of the horse. We are inclined to think that a piece of bronze has much less of a shape constraint. A piece of bronze can survive being flattened, and could have existed even if it had never been moulded into the shape of a horse. But the bronze horse-shaped statue and the bronze horse-shaped piece of bronze seem to be exactly the same thing; the statue just *is* the piece of bronze, and the piece of bronze just *is* the statue. Consider a case where the piece of bronze and the statue come into existence and go out of existence at the same time; say the bronze is sprayed from 50 different directions into one mould at the beginning, and the statue/piece of bronze is hit with an atomic bomb at the end of its existence (or their existences). Since the piece and the statue exist at exactly the same times, the solutions discussed in Chapter 2, which rely on one object existing at a time when the other does not, are not available. How can we explain that the piece of bronze and the statue seem to have different essences although they seem to be the same thing?

One story is to say that there are multiple objects here, that the statue and the bronze are different things even though they seem to be made up of the same molecules, are found in the same place, and are both horse-shaped bronze objects. Maybe there are even more than two things there, if we can think of other ways of describing what is there that suggest different essences. Lewis thinks that would be "double counting". We should say that there is only one object there: one that is both a statue and a piece of bronze. What is happening is that different ways of describing it bring up different standards of similarity, and how we judge the thing's essence depends on what aspect of similarity is salient. When we describe it as a statue, and think of what possible objects are similar enough to it, we pay attention to the properties relevant to being a statue: shape properties, who the artist was, what its function is, and so on. When we describe it as a piece of bronze, that brings into focus other properties: the material that makes it up, perhaps how the bits are connected together (if it is scattered, arguably it is not the same piece of bronze any more, or maybe not a single piece of bronze at all). One and the same object has a set of statue-counterparts and a different set of bronze-piece-counterparts. Perhaps it could have been the same statue if the artist had used slightly different materials and perhaps it could have been the same piece of bronze even if it had been assembled by a natural process rather than an artist, or if it had a very different shape. If we adopt counterpart theory we can explain why we make different judgements about "the statue" and "the piece of bronze". It is not that there are different objects there with different essences, but rather that what it is correct to say about the essence of the object depends on what sort of similarity is relevant to the context.

Yet another reason to adopt counterpart theory is that it resolves some paradoxes of "transworld identity". One is a problem of transitivity (see Lewis 1986a: 243–8). With many objects we think they could be a little different, but not too extremely different. Suppose I have just assembled a bicycle (let's call it Spinner). Spinner could have had slightly different parts. If I had decided to use a different screw somewhere we would not think that would have prevented Spinner from coming into existence. If, however, I had taken a completely different set of parts and put them together I would have built some other bicycle. Someone else could come along and put Spinner together the next day if I had not touched any of the actual parts. At least, this is what many people find plausible.[6] Lewis himself allows that this is a plausible way to talk about bicycles and talking this way sets up a context where it is correct that a bicycle could not be made of entirely different parts, but in a different context the parts a bicycle is made of may not be essential.

However, if a bicycle can be made of slightly different parts, then we have a potential problem. Consider the bicycle as it would have been made if I had made it with the occasional different screw. *That* bicycle could in turn be made differently from the way it was, so if I had made the bicycle with a few screws different, it could have been made with a few more parts different from the actual construction. And that bicycle could in turn have been slightly different, and so on. Eventually we have a bicycle built of so many different parts that it could not be Spinner. But if we have literal transworld identity, we have trouble. At each step, when we say that the bicycle built could have been a little different, at each stage we are talking about *Spinner* itself, so we seem to be pressed to say that Spinner could have had a certain construction (because a bicycle identical to Spinner could have been a little different), but also that Spinner could not have had that construction, because the construction is too different from Spinner's actual construction. We seem to have an inconsistency.

We can even plausibly simplify the series down to two steps (Lewis 1986a: 245). Consider building a bicycle with quite a few parts different from the ones I actually used, almost enough to stop the bicycle being built from being Spinner at all, but not quite. Call the world in which it is built with the somewhat different parts W_1. According to the person who believes in literal transworld identity, the bicycle built in W_1 is Spinner itself. Now, the bicycle in W_1 itself can be built with some parts different while still being the same bicycle. Consider a world, W_2, that has a bicycle constructed with parts not too different from the bicycle in W_1, but even more different from the way Spinner was actually constructed. That is, the bicycle built in W_2 has significantly fewer of Spinner's actual parts than the bicycle in W_1. We have the paradox again. A bicycle built like the one in W_2 can be the same bicycle as the one built in W_1, since it is not too different. It cannot be the same as Spinner in the actual world because it has too many parts different from Spinner's actual parts. But Spinner and W_1 are supposed to be the same bicycle, so a bicycle like the one in W_2 both is and is not transworld identical with Spinner. Something has gone wrong.

Counterpart theory gives us a way of diagnosing what has gone wrong. The identity relation has to be transitive: if $a = b$, and $b = c$, then $a = c$. But the counterpart relation does not need to be. Just because the bicycle in W_1 is a counterpart of the actual bicycle, and the bicycle in W_2 is a counterpart of the bicycle in W_1, it does not follow that the bicycle in W_2 is a counterpart of the actual bicycle. So the bicycle in W_1 can be a possibility for Spinner, the bicycle in W_2 can be a possibility for the bicycle in W_1, but we do not get the contradiction that the bicycle in W_2 both does and does not represent a possibility for Spinner. Counterpart theory seems to tell us what we want about this case. Alternatives with literal transworld identity seem to have to compromise: maybe bicycles cannot have slightly different parts, or maybe they can have completely different parts, or maybe W_2 is not possible, but is possible according to W_1 (whatever that means). Not having to say any of these odd things is an advantage of the theory of counterparts.[7]

Applications

Properties and events

Once possible worlds and possible individuals are available, some of Lewis's other philosophical positions can be fine-tuned. You may remember from Chapter 1 that Lewis's theory of properties is that properties are sets of individuals: the property of being red is the set of red things; the property of being 1 kg in mass is the set of everything that is 1 kg in mass; and so on. One traditional problem with this is that sometimes apparently different properties are had by exactly the same individuals. Suppose the property of being *one of the hundred best cricket players of all time* and the property of being *one of the hundred best professional cricket players of all time* belong to exactly the same people. Many people think that still would not mean those were one and the same property: one involves being a professional, and the other does not.[8] But sets that have exactly the same members are just the same set; sets are "extensional" (which is a way of saying that you can't have two different sets with the same members).

Once we have possible objects as well, we can take the properties to be sets of *actual and possible* individuals and not just sets of actual individuals. Even if all of the best cricket players are in fact professional cricket players that does not seem to be a necessary truth. There is some possible amateur cricket player who is one of the hundred best (in her world).[9] So the sets have different members after all and we do not have to say that we have just one property here.

These extra resources also allow room for Lewis's theory of events (1986d). Lewis thinks of events as properties of spatiotemporal regions. So, for example, the Second World War was a property of a long stretch of spacetime that included much of the globe and lasted for about six years, or longer if we include the Japanese invasion of China. Lewis wants to say that events (as opposed to event types) only happen once in a world (so they are unlike most properties, which can have many instances), but one and the same event can happen in many different worlds. Stretches of space and time in other worlds can have the property corresponding to the Second World War.

This theory of events has the advantage that we can have more than one event associated with exactly the same region of spacetime. Lewis uses as an example the event of an electron's being in a certain electromagnetic field, and the electron's accelerating. These are supposed to happen at the same place at the same time, but seem to be different events. Another example, due originally to Donald Davidson, is the example of a metal sphere that is simultaneously spinning and heating up. The event of the sphere spinning is a different event from the event of the sphere heating (they may have different causes and effects, for instance), but they are happening in the same place at the same time. Identifying events with regions of spacetime, or with the contents of a region of spacetime, would not allow us to say these events were distinct (unless we could find some part of the region or some object in it to include in one event, but not in the other, but it is hard to do this in these cases). One odd result of Lewis's theory is that he has very different stories about transworld identity for objects and for events. Objects have possibilities for them in virtue of counterparts, as we saw above, but events have the possibility of occurring differently by literally being located in different worlds.

Counterfactual conditionals

As well as what in fact happens there are hypothetical and conditional truths: what happens *if* something else happens, or what *would have happened if* certain circumstances held. "If" is one of the simplest words in the English language, but explaining how it works is far from simple. Part of the reason for this is that whether a conditional claim is true seems to depend not just on what does happen, but rather on how different possible situations are connected. Lewis argues that employing possible worlds could help make the behaviour of conditional sentences more understandable.

One simple theory of conditional sentences, still often taught in introductory logic courses, is that saying something of the form "if p, then q" means something like "either not-p, or p-and-q". So, for example, "if the dog had got out, it would have chased traffic" means something like "either the dog didn't get out, or it got out and chased traffic". (For those who have encountered logical notation, "not-p or p-and-q" is equivalent to $\sim p \vee q$, which is in turn the definition of $p \supset q$, which is often offered as the symbolization of conditional sentences.) This has some advantages as an account of conditional sentences. After all, the case where it is most obvious that a conditional sentence is *false* is one where the *antecedent* (the p in "if p then q") is true but the *consequent* (the q) is false. If you want to disprove the sentence "If you flip the switch, the light will go on", the best way is to flip the switch and for the light not to go on. And if the light does go on when the switch is flipped, that is good evidence that the conditional sentence is true. So if the antecedent and the consequent are both true, that speaks in the conditional's favour. The analysis of "if p then q" as $p \supset q$, or the "material conditional", gives both of these results: it rules out the combination ($\sim p$ and q), and it is true if (p and q) is true. Also $p \supset q$ validates two of the central forms of inference involving conditionals: *modus ponens* and *modus tollens*.

modus ponens	*modus tollens*
If p then q,	If p then q,
p	Not-q
Therefore q	Therefore not-q

So $p \supset q$ ("not-p or (p and q)") has many of the features we want a conditional to have. The most obvious place where this account falls short is when the antecedent is false. Indeed, often we utter conditionals when it is obvious that the antecedent is false, and we do not settle the question of whether the conditional is true or not just by working out whether the antecedent is false. Consider the conditional sentence "If everyone with cancer last year injected themselves with mercury, they would have been cured within two days". It obviously has a false antecedent: not everyone with cancer injects themselves with mercury. Just as clearly the conditional statement is not true; it is a disastrous piece of medical theory. The "material conditional" account says that conditionals with false antecedents are automatically true. It says that provided the claim "everyone with cancer injected themselves with mercury last year" is false, that is all we need to know to establish that the conditional is correct.

One traditional way that people tried to improve on the material conditional account first proposed by C. I. Lewis (Lewis & Langford 1932) was to say that our "if . . . then . . ." statements should be understood as involving some kind of necessity. In particular, "if p then q" means "necessarily, either not-p or (p and q)", or equivalently "necessarily, $p \supset q$". This necessitated material conditional is called a "strict conditional" in the literature. If we adopt this view the antecedent's being false would no longer settle the truth-value of the conditional. In the mercury case the strict conditional would come out false if there is some possibility where cancer patients are all injected with mercury and are not cured after two days. Since there surely is such a possibility the strict conditional account would classify the conditional as false, which seems right.

David Lewis

Unfortunately, the strict conditional account seems to be too restrictive. Often it is *possible* for a conditional to have its antecedent be true while its consequent is false, and yet we think the conditional is true. Consider the conditional "if I hit the Z key, the word-processor will register a Z". Normally, if you said that while you were using a word-processor, that would express a truth. (If I could not rely on conditionals like that I could not be confident of getting very much typed!) But when I believe that conditional it does not seem that I think that it is *impossible* for my hitting the Z key to fail to produce a Z. There could be a blackout, or there is the possibility of a computer malfunction, or there is the possibility that practical jokers have switched the keys on my keyboard. In some possible world I suddenly become so weak that my hitting the Z key fails to register. None of these possibilities are very likely, of course, but it doesn't seem that I am saying any of them are *impossible* when I utter the conditional. (The degree of "necessity" associated with the strict conditional is presumably one of the "restricted" necessities like physical necessity, but even so, it does not seem that anything makes it necessary that hitting the Z key is followed by a Z on the screen.)

Lewis's account can be seen as an improvement on the "strict conditional" account. Lewis in fact offers two different accounts for different sorts of conditional claims. There seems to be a difference between two sorts of conditionals, which becomes clear when we consider past-tense conditionals. Consider the following two conditionals:

> If America had tried to invade Sweden last year, the attempt would have received much media attention.

This seems correct. The media pay attention when America attempts to invade another country, and would pay especial attention if it was a European country (especially a peaceful and stable one such as Sweden).

> If America did try to invade Sweden last year, the attempt did not receive much media attention.

This seems right as well. Nobody (or at least nobody I saw) in the media mentioned America trying to invade Sweden, and so if America did try it, they must have covered it up well, or the attempt stalled extremely early, or something else like that happened.

This is a puzzling phenomenon. The two conditionals seem to concern the same sort of antecedent and consequent ("America tried to invade Sweden" and "The attempt received much media attention."), and the difference seems to be related to things such as the fact that the first talks about what *would* have happened in the second part and the second talks about what *did* happen. Sometimes these conditionals are classed as "subjunctive" and "indicative" conditionals, respectively, on the basis of grammatical mood. Lewis's term for conditionals of the first sort (the "subjunctive" ones) is "counterfactual", because they are often used when the antecedent is explicitly taken to be false. The other sort, the "indicative" is more likely to be uttered when there is a live possibility that the antecedent is true (but not always).

Counterfactual conditionals can seem true when their consequents diverge radically from reality. We know there wasn't much media attention devoted to a US attempt to invade Sweden, but the first conditional still seems correct. With indicative conditionals that we accept we often seem to tolerate less divergence in their consequents, as in this case. Lewis considers indicative conditionals only briefly and is prepared to endorse the "material conditional" account for indicative conditionals, and explain the apparent counter-examples away in terms of what is and is not worth saying (the *pragmatics* of language, rather than facts about how the truth of the sentences is determined). Lewis's main attention was devoted to the first sort of conditional, the "counterfactual".

Lewis says, in effect, that a counterfactual conditional is true if, in the possible worlds most similar to the actual world where the antecedent is true, the consequent is true as well. So when we want to know whether it is true that "if America had tried to invade Sweden last year, the attempt would have received much media attention", what we want to know is whether the possible worlds where America tries to invade Sweden and that are the most like ours, are worlds where the media pays much attention to the American attempt.[10] This is like the "strict conditional" account in a way. Where the strict conditional account says that we consider *all* possible worlds where America tries to invade Sweden to see what happens, Lewis's account says we only focus on the ones most like the actual world. That gets a better result in the Z-key case. Although worlds with blackouts, practical jokers, sudden attacks of weakness and so on are possible, they are less like the actual set-up, since in fact I am not plagued by these interferences at the moment. So a world most like this one, except that I hit the key for a certain uncommon letter on my keyboard, is a world where that key does what we would all expect.

This provides for much more flexibility in the counterfactual conditional. It needs more than the "material conditional" account, but it does not need the necessary connection between an antecedent and a consequent that the "strict conditional" account requires. If we allow that there are different sorts of similarity, this gives the counterfactual conditional an extra degree of flexibility. Depending on context, "If Bill jumps in front of the train, he'll be killed" and "If Bill jumps in front of the train, he will have first made sure it was going to stop in time" can both seem right on one and the same occasion. If we weight similarity highly in terms of the mass and speed of the train, the first statement seems most reasonable, but if we count similarity in Bill's mental state as being the most relevant sort of similarity, the second seems the right thing to say. It would be very odd to say both at once, since once the standard of similarity gets set one way by context, it may take some shifting. (Out of the blue, either on its own would be fine.) When we are communicating information with counterfactuals, much of what we communicate may be sensitive to the context, and Lewis can reflect some of this contextual contribution in a principled way. How context determines the relevant similarity will be discussed further in Chapter 4, in the section on causation.

Lewis also argues that his account respects several features of the logical behaviour of conditionals that both the material conditional account and the strict conditional account do not. Consider just one of these: "strengthening the antecedent".

If p then q.
Therefore,
If (p and r) then q.

This inference is valid for both the material conditional and the strict conditional. But it does not seem to work for the English-language "if ... then ..." construction. Consider:

If I have a cup of tea now, I shall enjoy drinking the tea.
Therefore,
If I have a cup of tea now and someone puts pieces of broken glass in it, I shall enjoy drinking the tea.

Is it possible for the premise to be true and the conclusion false? Apparently so. Often when I'm looking forward to a cup of tea, I wouldn't be equally happy with one containing broken glass. You could say that this just shows that the first sentence is almost never true as it stands, that "If I have a cup of tea now, I shall enjoy drinking the tea" is best understood as "If I have a cup of tea now *and* it doesn't have glass in it, I shall enjoy drinking the tea". But if that's right, then the usual utterance of "If I have a cup of tea now, I shall enjoy drinking the tea" will have to be shorthand for a lot more than that, because there are all sorts of other possible factors that could intervene to make my tea-drinking unenjoyable: other contaminants, being punched in the head, going insane, spilling the tea all over my computer and so on. Do we really build all of these exception clauses into a simple claim about what would happen if I have a cup of tea?

It seems preferable to say that strengthening the antecedent *is* invalid. Just because *q* would happen if *p* did, it does not follow that *q* would happen if *p* and anything-else-you-like were to happen. Lewis's story about counterfactuals explains why strengthening the antecedent fails. For a counterfactual to be true, the closest worlds where the antecedent is true (that is, the worlds most similar to actuality where the antecedent is true) are worlds where the consequent are true. The closest (most similar) world to the actual one in which I have a cup of tea now may well be a peaceful one where I enjoy my cup. But the closest world where I have a cup of tea now and someone puts broken glass in it is a quite different one. The most similar of the tea-and-glass worlds is considerably less like the actual world than the most similar tea-worlds. The two conditionals take us to different possibilities so it is no wonder that in one I enjoy the tea and in another I do not.

Lewis's book *Counterfactuals* (1973a) had a significant impact when it was published partly because it showcased how the tool of possible worlds could be applied to specific puzzles in philosophical logic and philosophy of language, such as the behaviour of the conditional. Of course, Lewis was not the only person who was taking possible worlds seriously in order to provide new insights into the functioning of language. Richard Montague and Robert Stalnaker are particularly notable among many others.[11] Lewis also employed possible worlds in understanding other features of language and the world. See in particular Chapters 4 and 6 for other examples. It is the fruitfulness of applications such as this that is the strongest argument for taking possible worlds seriously.

Chapter 4

Laws, causes, dispositions and chance

Questions about causation, laws of nature, probability and chance are part of the domain of both metaphysics and philosophy of science. Saying what causation is, or what it is to be a law of nature, will presumably shed light on some of the most basic aspects of our world. Sorting out what causes, laws and chances are would also shed light on the foundations of both the natural and social sciences, since both of these make use of notions of causation and laws of nature, and reliance on probabilistic reasoning and estimating chances of events is ubiquitous. That is not to say that these are entirely technical notions to be dealt with only in the sciences. Thinking and talking about causes is to be found throughout human endeavour, and to the extent we are interested in making predictions or finding explanations in everyday life, some dim sense of what is physically impossible and what the laws of nature permit also seems to play a role. Even at the high point of suspicion about metaphysics in Anglo-American philosophy in the twentieth century, few could rid themselves of the view that some things cause other things, or that there is something special about the regularities scientists uncover, as opposed to regularities that are entirely coincidental. The notion of causation is also caught up in the notion of explanation, and Lewis is a champion of a distinctive theory about explanation that related explanation to causation. A principled theory about laws, causes, explanations and probability would be well on the way to dealing with a good number of the traditional concerns of metaphysicians and philosophers of science alike.

It will be no surprise to hear that Lewis wants to not only provide plausible accounts of these phenomena, but also to do so in the framework of Humean supervenience. Given arrangements of local particular matters of fact, he wants to explain the emergence of the "nomic family"[1] of causes, laws and chances. Lewis also has a story about dispositions and powers, two other concepts with very widespread application, since abilities, tendencies, dispositions or whatever are everywhere. They are also, of course, of interest to the philosopher of science, since one thing science is particularly interested to discover is what things (including animals and people) do, and what they are liable to do in a range of circumstances.

If all of these things could be accounted for in Lewis's Humean framework this would have several advantages. One would be a unified story; many different sorts of facts about the world could be explained in terms of a common core. Another may be parsimony; Humean supervenience seems to offer the prospect of doing a lot with less, and the debates between Lewis and his opponents often have the form of his opponents granting the facts Lewis believes in, but trying to argue that something else is needed as well. Of course, we should not shrink from believing in more kinds of things or more things if we have a good reason to, but if Lewis can show that we have no reason to believe in more, his parsimonious basis will have the advantage in this respect. Lewis also complains that the sorts of phenomena postulated by his opponents are mysterious. If he is right about this then that may be another reason to prefer his account since it is relatively easy to see what is going on.

The devil is, of course, in the details, and whether Lewis's interrelated projects succeed depends on what arguments are available for his views and how much they can do for us in providing a systematic and adequate understanding of what we take to be going on around us.

Laws of nature and physical necessity

As well as what does happen, the world seems to obey laws of nature about what has to happen. Certainly, our opinions about what those laws of nature are change frequently. Two hundred years ago, many people would have thought that "bending space" either did not make any sense or at any rate was impossible, whereas now we are inclined to think that any object with mass warps the space around it automatically. But there are some things that contemporary physics tells us cannot happen: you cannot accelerate through the speed of light; you cannot build a perpetual-motion machine – one that continually does work without using up internal energy or getting it from out-

David Lewis

side; there cannot be a reaction in a closed system where the mass-energy of the output is greater than the mass-energy of the input plus the mass-energy of the system itself; and so on. Any particular example runs the risk of seeming dated a few hundred years from now, but it is reasonable to conjecture that future understandings of how physics works will themselves rule some things out as impossible.

It does not seem, though, that these "impossible" things are inconsistent or incoherent. It is no kind of logical contradiction to say that the speed of light in a vacuum is 10 metres per second, although it is false, and is something that may well not be possible. This seems to be necessity that is supplied by the world, rather than by our way of describing things (although how to unpack this metaphor of "supply" is a difficult question). Are these sorts of constraints new facts, over and above facts about the distribution of "local particular matters of fact"? This sort of necessity is often thought of as being given by the "laws of nature": basic principles about how the world works that permit some set-ups and forbid others. It is frequently called "nomic" necessity, or "physical" necessity (although some people might use these two labels slightly differently). Any theory about what laws of nature are must answer at least two questions: how do laws of nature make certain things possible and others impossible; and what are laws of nature?

In Chapter 3 we saw that Lewis would regard the sort of necessity and impossibility associated with laws of nature as a variety of "restricted modality": talk about what does or does not happen in some restricted range of possible worlds. So the necessity associated with laws of nature, whatever they are, has a relatively simple explanation. When we make judgements about what is possible or not, keeping in mind the laws of nature, what we are doing is ignoring all of the possible worlds that do not obey our laws of nature. So when I say that it is impossible for anything to accelerate through the speed of light, this can be interpreted as saying that nothing accelerates through the speed of light *in any possible world that obeys our laws of nature*. We may even make this explicit sometimes by saying something like "it cannot happen, given the laws of nature ...", (or "... the laws of physics ...", or "... the laws of chemistry ...", or whatever particular laws we have in mind). This should be seen as one of many kinds of necessity or possibility we can talk about. When we say that Bill cannot afford his dream car, we are not saying that it is against the laws of nature for Bill to buy his dream car, let alone logically impossible; we are probably only considering those possibilities where Bill has the same amount of money as he actually has and his dream car costs the same as it actually does. If a historian says that it was impossible for the ancient Romans to defeat the Chinese empire, presumably the historian is not saying that there was some law of nature ruling it out (let alone that it is inconsistent or incoherent). It was impossible, if we only consider possibilities that are not too different from the way things were. In ordinary talk, we probably only rarely consider all of the possibilities (in the most generous sense of possibility). It makes sense for us to consider more restricted sets of possibilities when we are talking about what "can" happen or "must" happen, what is "necessary" and what is "possible". Laws of nature are one more kind of thing that are contingent, according to Lewis, but they have some kind of special status for us, which is why we often only consider possibilities where they obtain.

So, if Lewis is right, we have explained the "nomic" variety of necessity once we can say what it is for something to be a law of nature. Let us consider this problem then:what is a law of nature? It can be hard to even know where to start the investigation (and the same might be said for many metaphysical questions). Considering some examples of supposed laws of nature throws up some features that provide a start. Consider Newton's laws of motion, not as examples of genuine laws of nature, but at least as examples of the sorts of things that, had Newton been right about how the world behaved, *would* have been laws of nature. One thing to notice is that they are general statements ("every action has an equal and opposite reaction", for example). So they have something to do with *regularities* in the world. Some might identify them with certain regularities but, at the very least, when a law obtains it must somehow ensure that there is a regularity in what happens in the world that corresponds to that law. "Laws of nature" do not just lay down guidelines about how things *should* behave in the way that laws of a legal system do; when there is a genuine law of nature that things behave in such-and-such a way, then things *do* behave that way.[2] Another thing to notice is that there are two ways of talking about "laws of nature": as a certain kind of *statement* or *proposition* (such as the ones found written down in textbooks), or a certain kind of *state of the world* (e.g. whatever it is that ensures that every action has an equal and opposite reaction). A discussion of laws of nature could be conducted in either way, about what was special about a certain class of general statements, or what has a special connection to certain general regularities in the world. Lewis talks about laws as being a certain kind of general proposition

([1994a] 1999a: 232), and we shall be discussing them in that sense. So the question is: what about the world makes one proposition rather than another a law of nature?

Laws must correspond somehow to regularities in how things behave, and discovering a law of nature is useful for predicting the future, and presumably explaining what occurs. On the other hand, not every regularity is of the right sort to correspond to a law of nature. "All of the pens Mary owns are black", for example, would not be a law of nature. One style of accounting for laws of nature that was perhaps the orthodoxy in the 1950s and 1960s was to take laws of nature to be regularities of some distinguished sort. By *identifying* laws of nature with regularities, the mystery of why a law of nature must go along with the corresponding regularity is explained. If Newton's third law just *is* the regularity of every action being followed by an equal and opposite reaction, then of course when the law obtains the relevant regularity will obtain, since the law and the regularity are the same.

The problem in stating a regularity theory of laws is specifying which regularities count. A variety of attempts were made, often in terms of constraints on law statements: for example, must not make any reference to individual objects; must be unrestricted in space and time; must be formulated in some specific formal language. Lewis defends a proposal first suggested by Frank Ramsey (Ramsey 1990) that the laws are those regularities that would be ones implied by a description of the world that was ideally *simple* and *strong* (Lewis 1973a: 72; [1994a] 1999a: 232–3). Imagine that we (or some omniscient beings more suited to the task) set out to capture as much information as possible about the world in as compact a statement as possible. Including things about the laws of motion and gravity would presumably be part of that project, but that all of Mary's pens are black would presumably not be worth explicitly mentioning. Simple, powerful generalizations about the world is also presumably one of the things scientists (particularly of the sort that look for laws) look for when they are seeking to describe the world. Furthermore, coming up with simple, powerful (and true) generalizations about the world would be a way to gain the ability to predict as yet unobserved processes, and understand what apparently disparate phenomena have in common.

Simplicity and *strength* are desirable features that must be somehow traded off against each other. The body of information that is strongest, in the sense of saying as much as possible, could just be a list of every truth. Such a list might be great to have, but it would not make any distinctions between laws and anything else. On the other hand if we went for maximum simplicity or compactness without worrying about informativeness we could come up with a system that said virtually nothing. (Pure mathematics forms a fairly simple system, probably a more simple system than we would get by adding a bunch of claims about how physical objects behave, but that does not mean that we should think physicists would rest content with mathematics alone.) The right sort of trade-off should preferably entail a great deal about the behaviour of the world, but not by just being a list of curiosities and particular facts.

Many philosophers of science, information theorists and others have come up with measures of simplicity and strength of sets of information, but there is little agreement about the best ways to compare theories in these respects. Furthermore, how simple a system of information is usually seems to be language-relative; the number of characters it takes to communicate a certain amount of data varies a lot from language to language (whether we are talking about natural languages such as English or artificial languages). For Lewis's proposal to work, it must make sense to be able to compare quite different sets of information in terms of their relative simplicity and strength, and if we do not want to make the question of what the laws of nature are a question whose answer somehow depends on language or representation, there must be some objective, language-independent standard for simplicity and informativeness. (Many people would think that which propositions are laws of nature should be an objective matter; people mostly do not think that Newton's laws of motion are the sorts of things that could be genuine laws in English but accidental coincidences in Russian.) Lewis does not tell us what these objective standards are, but he claims that there are such standards to be discovered.

For Lewis, the laws are the theorems of the simplest, strongest axiomatization of a correct theory of the goings-on of our world. This means that the laws are not just the statements in the ideal theory itself; they are also any statements that follow from that ideal theory. This allows for "derived laws": statements about how the world works that are useful, non-obvious consequences of the basic laws. The risk that comes with including in the category of laws all of the consequences of the basic laws is that too many claims about the world will turn into laws of nature. In the limiting case, if there is a sufficiently simple way of describing all the truths of the world, then

David Lewis

every true claim would be a law of nature. Again, it is hard to tell whether Lewis's characterization of laws of nature is too generous, since we are not given much guidance about what simplicity is, or how it is to be traded off against strength. Lewis's theory of laws should not be seen as a final answer to the questions about laws of nature. It is better to see it as a reasoned partial conjecture about what the final theory will look like.

There is a third constraint on laws of nature besides forming a simple and strong encapsulation of facts about the world. For Lewis ([1983c] 1999a: 42), the basic laws of nature must also be statements about the *perfectly natural* properties and relations in the world (see Chapter 1 for a discussion of natural properties). Otherwise, we could get bogus simplicity just by employing abbreviation. Imagine if we had the entire list of truths about our world available and decided to introduce an abbreviation, *P*, that abbreviated the entire list. *P* seems to be a very simple sentence, and it certainly does not have any syntactical complexity. (If you want to encapsulate a total insight into the world on a T-shirt, just print "*P*"!) Or for a slight variant of this strategy (which Lewis discusses in "New Work for a Theory of Universals" (*ibid*.: 8–55)), introduce a predicate, *F*, such that it is true of an object just in case *P* holds (so it applies to all the objects in worlds just like ours, and no others). Then "Everything is *F*" is a very simple general statement, apparently, and is as strong as can be, since it captures all the truths! Obviously, if either of these shortcuts worked, Lewis's theory of laws of nature would be ridiculous. It is not that easy to discover the sorts of truths that, for example, fundamental physics is looking for. Whatever the "objective simplicity" is that Lewis needs, it has to be able to distinguish some more genuine simplicity from the abbreviations I mentioned. Framing the generalizations in terms of the perfectly natural properties would be one non-artificial way to rule out these abbreviations, and it has the additional advantage that it explains why, in fundamental science, discovering laws and discovering objective natural classifications seem to go together.

This insistence that the basic laws of nature concern perfectly natural properties, together with Lewis's conviction that the perfectly natural properties in our world are the fundamental properties of physics, together imply that there are no basic laws of nature discovered by biology, chemistry, psychology, or any of the other sciences outside some branches of physics (unless those other sciences come across some laws of physics, of course). Whether these other sciences (sometimes called the "special sciences" in the literature) have laws of their own is controversial. Perhaps the generalizations discovered by biology, linguistics, archaeology and so on are not "laws", but instead interesting but nomically contingent facts about the world around us. Or perhaps the "laws" of these disciplines are derived laws, that somehow necessarily follow from the laws of physics. (Some principles of chemistry might be like this.) If, on the other hand, these other disciplines *do* have genuine laws that are not derived from the laws of physics, then, if Lewis is right about what laws of nature are, his materialism would have to be modified. For it would mean that there were perfectly natural biological or psychological properties and relations (or they would be economic or archaeological or whatever), and these additional "joints in nature" would have to be part of our account of the world.

Regularity theories of laws of nature, including Lewis's, face several objections. One is the intuition that what the regularities are depends on what the laws are, rather than vice versa. (The laws *make* things conform to certain patterns – such as every action having an equal and opposite reaction – rather than there being a law because, in part, every reaction has an equal and opposite reaction.) It means that what has to happen here and now depends on what does happen in places and times very distant from here. Whether there is a law that like charges repel, for example, depends on a regularity of like charges moving away from each other across all of space and time. To some people, this seems backwards. Lewis's laws depend on patterns of particular occurrences, and those patterns extend throughout space and time. To the extent that we think that the truth about what has to happen here and now does not depend on what happened a long time ago in a galaxy far, far away, Lewis's theory will seem implausible.

Lewis admits that some things like this about his view will come as a surprise, and even an "unpleasant surprise" ([1994a] 1999a: 232). He is prepared, however, to "bite the bullet", and accept that his theory has some counter-intuitive consequences. One of the reasons he is prepared to accept these consequences is that he finds many of the alternatives mysterious or even "unintelligible".[3] Lewis's theory is in a family called "regularity theories", that say that what makes something a law is a matter of what general patterns of particular events obtain. The main alternative would be to say that there is some extra fact about the world that makes something a law, some fact that somehow necessarily ensures that when it holds, the corresponding regularity holds. (These law facts themselves may or may not be contingent, but the crucial thing that is necessary is that *if* the law fact obtains, so

David Lewis

does the corresponding regularity.) Fred Dretske (1977), D. M. Armstrong (1978b, 1983), and Michael Tooley (1977, 1987), for example, suggest that the extra fact is the holding of a special sort of relation between properties. Armstrong calls it a "necessitation" relation and, in the simplest case, for example, it is postulated that when necessitation holds between two properties, F and G, then anything with F must have property G as well. Others, such as Robert Pargetter (1984), suggest that there are just further modal facts about what is and is not physically necessary: facts without a further explanation. Lewis objects that the connection between these extra facts and the regular patterns is mysterious, unexplained and "unintelligible" ([1983c] 1999a: 40). I am not sure why Lewis claims these views are unintelligible, but it is clear why he might find them unappealing. They must insist on some extra piece of metaphysics, one that has a connection with regularities, that is not to be further explained.

Another source of worry about Lewis's theory (and other regularity theories) is that some find it hard to see how we could discover what laws are, or use them in prediction, if they were merely regularities (albeit a particular privileged set of regularities). We only come across a tiny fraction of the goings-on in the universe, and from that we have to come up with our best conjectures about what the laws are. If the laws depend so much on patterns of occurrences beyond anything we can observe directly, how can a regularity theory explain our being able to find out what is physically necessary or possible (Armstrong 1983: 52–9)?

It certainly is a striking fact that human beings are able to predict the future and the happenings in places that we have never visited or studied. (We had a fair idea of what we would find on the far side of the moon, for example, even though we had never seen it until the space programme.) A regularity theory of laws by itself does not explain this fact, but it is not obvious we should ask it to. Somehow, our methods manage to be reliable; that is common ground (except for sceptics, who may well doubt that we can reliably make correct predictions). And it is not as if rival theories of laws, by themselves, explain this striking fact either. This is particularly true when we notice that many people think our evidence for the laws of nature come from observed regularities: our evidence that it is a law that like charges repel largely comes from us observing, in a range of circumstances, that like charges repel (and other regular patterns of interaction). Whatever the laws are, we can somehow reliably generalize from observed samples to the general behaviour of objects. This

88

may seem mysterious, but it seems to be no more of a mystery for a regularity theorist than anyone else.

Lewis offers us a theory of laws where laws are ultimately a matter of "local particular matters of fact". It is a theory consistent with Humean supervenience, and while there are still things to be explained (what objective language-independent simplicity is, what informational strength is, how they are supposed to be traded off), the metaphysics of laws is relatively sparse. What makes something a law is ultimately a matter of regular patterns of properties and relations. Let us examine what Lewis has to say about some related topics: causation, dispositions and chances.

Causation

Talk about one thing causing another is very common in everyday life as well as in areas of science and philosophy. We spend plenty of our time planning to bring certain things about, we seek to find out who made things happen that we like or do not like, and when we are trying to understand how something behaves, finding the causes of events is a big part of what we do. As well as explicit phrases like "causes", "makes", "brings about" and so on, many (perhaps most) of our verbs are *causal* verbs. If you kick a ball across a field, more happens than the leg moving to the ball and the ball moving away; the foot *causes* the ball to move. If an oven heats a potato, it causes the potato to become hotter. If you question someone, you cause them to be asked questions. Most transitive verbs are associated with causal processes of one sort or another (tearing, stroking, cutting, amusing, flattening, detonating, etc.). Despite our familiarity with causation, understanding what causation is, in general, is something that philosophers are still grappling with.

We also seem to use our understanding of causation when we provide explanations of things. ("Cause" and "because" are related words for a good reason.) Indeed, Lewis argues that what an explanation *is* is the providing of causal information,[4] although the information might be indirect, or it might be about structural factors that underlie more than just the event to be explained, and it might even be negative (some explanations might be about how certain factors were irrelevant to what occurred, especially if they seemed to play a role on first sight). And bad or mistaken explanations may be bodies of information, or acts of communicating that information, that are

David Lewis

supposed to provide causal information but instead provide mis-information. Whether Lewis is right that all explanation is somehow tied up with giving causal information, certainly some of it seems to be, so if we are to understand what explanation is, it may help to have a good understanding of our concept of causation.

Lewis famously defends a "counterfactual theory of causation": a general analysis of what it is for one thing to cause another is a matter of the right sort of counterfactual statements being true. The simplest form of a counterfactual theory of causation is to say that, when we have two events C and E,

> "C causes E" is to be analysed as "C and E occur, and if C had not occurred E would not have occurred".

This basic case expresses a connection between particular events. It is designed to handle claims such as "the electrical fault caused the fire" or "John's smoking caused John's tumour", and not general causal claims such as "electrical faults cause fires" or "smoking causes cancer". It is also primarily aimed at elucidating the notion of what it is for one thing to be *a* cause of another, not *the* cause of another. (One event usually has many causes, and which one we call "the" cause might be a matter of which cause we take to be particularly important in the context.) Lewis does not, in fact, endorse a theory quite this simple. The account needs to be complicated in a few different ways.

First, the right sort of relationship has to hold between *distinct* events. Otherwise we get odd results when we, for example, let C and E be the same event. For instance, take my standing up. It is true that my standing up occurs, and that if it had not occurred, it would not have occurred. It should not follow from that that my standing up caused *itself*. It would not have happened without itself, but that is not enough for causation. A similar point can be made about events that overlap each other. My writing "sation" in this section heading would not have happened without my writing "causation". I would not have any reason to write the sequence "sation" in the heading unless I was trying to write "causation" (and let us suppose that I am careful enough that I would not have left off the initial letters by accident, as indeed I didn't). But it seems strange to say that my writing "causation" caused my writing "sation", or vice versa. The point also seems to hold for more specific events and more general events (if we want to distinguish these as distinct particular events, as Lewis at least would want to). Bob's talking loudly, and Bob's talking, are

90

events with counterfactual dependence between them; Bob would not have talked loudly unless he was talking. But again it would seem strange to say that Bob's talking *caused* him to talk loudly (or in a case where Bob was either going to shout or be silent, it would be equally odd to say that Bob's talking loudly caused him to talk). It might be tricky to specify exactly what this distinctness that is required between events should be. But it seems plausible to have some such restriction.

Secondly, Lewis would not call the above relationship "causation", but rather "causal dependence". Lewis's basic account ([1973b] 1986b: 167) is that one event causes another if they stand at either end of a *chain* of causal dependence (where that chain may have only one link). Causal dependence implies causation, but in principle there can also be causation without causal dependence. When B causally depends on A, and C causally depends on B, then A causes C even if C would have happened without A. Examples will be given in a moment.

Lewis, and many other people, thinks causation is *transitive*: if A is a cause of B, and B is a cause of C, then A is a cause of C. (A is not necessarily a very interesting cause of C, but nevertheless one of the causes of C.) Lewis's "cause" is transitive, but "causal dependence" in general is not. Recently, several people have begun to question the transitivity of causation, even in the counterfactual analysis tradition. (For some recent critiques of transitivity, see McDermott (1995) and Hitchcock (2001).) Sometimes there is a chain of causal dependence from something not-very-much-like what we would usually call a cause to some effect. Hartry Field has a nice example (cited in "Causation as Influences" (Lewis 2004a)). One person (let me call him "Bomber") sets a bomb on "Victim's" doorstep. Victim goes outside early, notices the bomb and defuses it. The defusing causes Victim to survive, and placing the bomb caused the defusion (since Victim would not have defused the bomb if it wasn't there). Surely this does not mean that setting the bomb caused Victim's survival? We certainly would not expect Victim to thank Bomber for saving his life! Michael McDermott (1995) has another example, also involving a bomber. In this example, a right-handed bomber going to detonate some explosive is attacked by a dog, which manages to injure severely his right hand. The bomber nevertheless perseveres, and manages to detonate the bomb with his left hand. In this story, the attack causes the bomber to use his left hand when detonating, and the bomber's detonating the bomb with his left hand causes the explosion. But it does not seem that the dog attack causes the explosion.

Lewis suggests (2000b: 194–5) that these sorts of counter-examples seem most pressing when the supposed "cause" is the sort of thing that would tend to interfere with the effect happening, and may in fact interfere to some degree (the dog attack makes it harder for the bomber to set off the explosion, not easier). And they are cases of causation without causal dependence. Lewis is prepared to say that these are cases of causation after all, albeit unusual cases. One reason for doing this is that he thinks that when we are considering causes over many intervening steps we neglect to worry too much about whether the initial cause made the final outcome more or less likely, or whether the final outcome would have happened anyway. These sorts of things are very difficult to tell when we are doing historical investigation, and, as Lewis writes, "every historian knows that actions often have unintended and unwanted consequences. It would be perfectly ordinary for a move ... to backfire disastrously" (*ibid*.: 195). Events can be the cause of outcomes that they were intended to prevent, and even trigger outcomes that they would normally prevent.

Another thing that defining causation as a chain of causal dependence does is that it helps deal with the most immediate problem facing counterfactual theories of causation: the problem of *redundant causation*.[5] Sometimes when an event *C* causes an event *E*, event *E* would have happened even if event *C* did not. Suppose Saboteur 1 has been ordered to make sure a certain bridge blows up (to keep with the explosions theme). Saboteur 1 heads to the bridge with a backpack full of explosives and some timers. But when she goes to the bridge, she finds Saboteur 2 planting mines on the bridge so that it will explode the next time a vehicle passes over it. Saboteur 1 trusts Saboteur 2 to do a good job, so she goes home. The next morning an unsuspecting truck sets off the explosives, and the bridge collapses. It seems clear that Saboteur 2's planting the mines was a cause of the bridge collapsing. But it is not true that if Saboteur 2 had not set the mines, the bridge would not have collapsed. This is because Saboteur 1 would have destroyed the bridge if Saboteur 2 had not been planting mines. The bridge's collapsing was brought about *redundantly*, since there were two separate processes that by themselves would have led to the collapse of the bridge.

So while the bridge's collapse does not "causally depend" on Saboteur 2's mine-planting, in our technical sense of "causally depend", there is a chain of causal dependencies that lead from the mine-planting to the bridge collapsing. The truck hitting a mine causally depended on the mines being planted (Saboteur 1 planned to blow up the bridge directly, so if she had her way there would not have been any trucks hitting mines), and the collapse of the bridge causally depended on the truck hitting the mines, since by that stage if the truck had somehow avoided the mines, Saboteur 1 had gone home and would not have done anything about it.[6] So by finding intermediate steps, Lewis can provide for causation where there is not direct causal dependence, and that seems like a good thing in this case, since we do want to say Saboteur 2's mine-planting did cause the bridge collapse.

Unfortunately, there are other cases of redundant causation that Lewis's theory could not deal with so easily. There are cases of so-called "late pre-emption", when one causal process is cut off by the effect itself, rather than cut-off halfway as in the Saboteur case.[7] (In the Saboteur case, the mine-planting causes Saboteur 1 to go home, which is different from the case where Saboteur 1 turns up to find the bridge already blown). I find that these sorts of cases are the ones that most naturally come to mind when I try to think of examples of one causal process being pre-empted by another. If I am chopping wood, and one swing of my axe makes a piece of wood split, it is not true that if that swing had not connected the block would not have split; if I had missed with that swing I would have just swung again until I split the wood. (The later swings at that piece of wood are pre-empted by the earlier successful swing.) If I toss a fragile vase on to a busy road and it is hit by a passing truck, the truck causes the vase to shatter, but the vase would have shattered in pretty short order in any case, when it hit the road or when another vehicle hit it. Again, the shattering would have happened eventually, and it is only the shattering by the truck that stops the honours going to the road or other vehicles. Here a sequence of stepwise causal determinations terminating in the splitting or shattering cannot be found. For any point along my axe swing, there is no dependence of the wood splitting on that part of the swing. Take away the entire swing and hit, and the wood still gets split (by a later swing). (This is unlike the Saboteur case, since taking away late steps of the process, such as the truck hitting the mines, would result in the bridge *not* blowing up.)

Lewis obviously would not want to deny that, for example, I cause the wood to be split in the case described. The desire to account for this sort of case, and some others like it, led to Lewis's late view (2000b). This late view relies on a notion of one event, *C*, *influencing* another event *E*. Event *C* influences event *E* if there is causal dependence of "how, when or whether" *E* occurs on a "substantial

David Lewis

range" of not too improbable variations of *C* (*ibid.*: 190). In short, *E* is influenced by *C* if a range of changes in how *C* takes place result in changes in how *E* takes place. Event *C* might influence event *E* by making it happen earlier, or later, or by making it happen differently to the way it would have happened. (Saboteur 2's mine-laying *influences* how the bridge collapses. The bridge would have collapsed anyway, because of Saboteur 1, but not in the way it did when Saboteur 2 blew it up.) Instead of steps of causal dependence, on Lewis's new view, one event is a cause of another if there is a chain of steps of *influence* from the cause to the effect. There does seem to be this sort of chain of influences in the cases of late pre-emption mentioned in the previous paragraph: the truck hitting the vase *influences* the breaking, because it makes a difference to exactly when it happens, and exactly how it happens. So the truck hitting the vase causes the vase to break, according to the "causation as steps of influence" view, even though it was a counter-example to Lewis's original view.

Lewis's late view also explicitly deals with part of our talk about causation that I have so far been neglecting. As well as one event occurring affecting another event that occurs, absences and preventions are mentioned all the time when we talk about what causes what. Lack of food causes death by starvation. Failure to take hygienic precautions causes food poisoning. An absence of company can be caused by someone's being obnoxious too often. Absences and lacks can be both causes and effects (or even both at once; the non-delivery of a message can result in someone's not coming to a meeting). Absences are puzzling. It is not always clear where and when they are supposed to be. (Is the lack of dinosaurs found everywhere dinosaurs are not? Or only far enough away from them?) And it is not clear we should believe in them. Why suppose there genuinely are absences and lacks, rather than just interpreting this talk as a way of denying the presence of things? (Some places have elephants, some places do not. Do we need anything else besides elephants *not* being around to get an absence of elephants?)

Lewis is inclined to not admit the existence of absences and lacks, either as entities in their own right, or as being identified with presences of various sorts (2004c). Perhaps you could identify my absence at a meeting with my presence somewhere else. Maybe my sitting at home *is* my absence from the meeting. But this means saying some odd things about absences: my absence from the meeting is in my house (you'd think it was at the meeting, if anywhere), and there will not necessarily be anything very similar between my absence from

94

the meeting and another colleague's, if that colleague is out scuba-diving. If I had been driving around instead, would that have meant there would have been a very different absence of me at the meeting?

If we do not have absences to play with, though (rather, we will not take talk of "things" like absences and lacks at face value), what are we to do about absences as causes and effects? Lewis thinks the thing to do is to say that sometimes there is causation without an event as a cause or an effect: so causation is not always a relationship between events. When we say that "the lack of light caused the plant to wither", this is true just in case there are the right sorts of counterfactuals about there being little light and the plant's withering. Strictly speaking, though, the withering is not caused by a specific event called "the lack of light" (although there may be genuine events that do cause the withering as well). If it is true to say that had there been plenty of light, the plant would not have withered, for example, or alternatives to "the lack of light" would have resulted in differences in the withering of the plant (more light, less withering, for example, or the withering would have happened later, etc.) then there would be an influence-like pattern in place. Lewis does not want to say that the statements or propositions in the counterfactuals do any causing (e.g. "there was no light" or "there was less light than there might have been" are not associated with causes), but he is prepared to say that sometimes things are caused, or are causing, even though there is no event that is the cause or the effect (since they do causing by bringing it about that there is *no* event of a certain sort).

Although Lewis's counterfactual analysis of causation has to be tweaked to allow for causation involving events *not* happening, it handles these cases better than many rival theories, which are committed to identifying some feature of the causing event and the effect event, or something about their relationship, to be causation.[8] Taking causation to be a special relation between two events, or a matter of certain patterns of correlations between properties of the cause and the effect, or something like that, runs into problems when one of the supposed "events" to be related is missing. These rival theories can, of course, include absences and lacks as events in their own right, and postulate that these absences have the right sorts of features or stand in the right relations, but to the extent that this is unappealing, Lewis may have an advantage here.

Many other sorts of cases that bring with them their own challenges – "symmetric overdetermination", "trumping", "double prevention", and others – are discussed in the literature on counterfactual theories of causation, but I will not try to capture the entire to-and-fro here. There are also complications when we consider "chancy" causation: cases where an event does not guarantee another event, but brings with it some chance the later event will occur. The interested reader is, of course, invited to explore these discussions further.[9] The other half of Lewis's counterfactual theory of causation, however, concerns the causal counterfactuals themselves: how they are to work, and what facts they are sensitive to. One of the traditional suspicions about counterfactual theories of causation is that we cannot have an independent enough grasp of these counterfactuals. In so far as we can judge which are true it is by relying on our knowledge of causation. Since Lewis wants to run the analysis in the reverse direction – understanding causation in terms of counterfactuals – he needs to capture the right counterfactuals without in turn bringing causation into the analysis.

We have already seen (in Chapter 3) that Lewis gives an account of counterfactuals in terms of similarity between possible worlds: "if p then q" is true, provided that in all the sufficiently similar worlds where p is true, q is true as well. Which sorts of similarity are particularly relevant is a matter of context. Because of this, there seem to be contexts where we utter counterfactuals that do not line up with causation but, if anything, go in the opposite direction. "If the bottle had fallen off the table, something would have pushed it" could easily be the sort of thing we might say (in reconstructing a crime scene, or discussing whether it was a good idea to leave a certain bottle on a certain table that close to the edge, or in many other contexts). Does the bottle's not falling off the table cause the bottle to be not pushed? Presumably not. If anything, it is the other way around. However, if we let C be "the bottle does not fall off the table" and E be "nothing pushed the bottle", we have the counterfactual being true that if C had not happened, E would not have happened. (Cancelling the double negatives, this is just the counterfactual we started with: "If the bottle had fallen off the table, something would have pushed it".)

The problem here is that there is a class of counterfactuals known as *backtrackers*; many of them have antecedents involving some effect, and consequents involving something that would have been a cause of that effect. Another example is: "If I had arrived late to lunch, I would have been delayed by something important". The consequent talks about some cause of the antecedent's obtaining. If we let these counterfactuals into the account of causation, we shall get the wrong results all over the place. It will turn out that my not arriving late for lunch caused me to not be delayed beforehand, which is exactly backwards (if anything, my not being delayed was a cause of my making it to lunch in time). Lewis said we should ignore backtrackers when it comes to causation. (Causation is to be analysed in terms of *non-backtracking* conditionals.) At one point he offers a characterization of a backtracking counterfactual as a "counterfactual saying that the past would be different if the present were somehow different" ([1979b] 1986b: 34). This is intended only to be a characterization of the "sorts of familiar cases that arise in everyday life" (*ibid.*: 35). Something else would be needed if Lewis wanted to allow for the possibility of causation running from the present to the past in unusual cases (which is something he does want to allow; recall that he believes in the possibility of time travel, discussed in Chapter 2).

Assuming we had some adequate way to characterize the trouble-making "backtrackers", more still needs to be said about the relevant respects of similarity that govern when one world is "closer" to actuality than another. Lewis illustrates with another explosion example (*ibid.*: 43). A universe where there was an all-out nuclear war in the 1970s is in many respects quite a different world from our own (especially in respects we care about). Consider two worlds where Nixon "presses the button" to begin a full nuclear exchange between the USA and the USSR. In one, nuclear war results, with the catastrophic differences from our world that would entail. In the other, some electrical malfunction occurs and the order is not transmitted, and furthermore Nixon and his aides forget all about it and go on as before (perhaps repressing the memory because of the trauma of being so close to the brink, or because they tried to start the war after drinking heavily and forgot the next day, or some other rather unlikely circumstance). The world where Nixon presses the button but it does not work is different from ours in some noticeable respects, but most of its post-Nixon history is much more like ours than the one where all-out nuclear war follows Nixon's button-pressing. Now consider the counterfactual "If Nixon had pressed the button, there would have been a nuclear war" and the conditional "If Nixon had pressed the button, it would not have happened and not much else would have been different". The first seems true, the second doesn't; Nixon's order to fire the missiles would have resulted in the missiles being fired. (If you are sceptical of the example, choose some other occasion when someone has apparently had the power to make a huge difference to the world from the way it actually is.) When we are working out which world is "most similar" to the actual world in this case, we do not choose some standard of similarity where the absence of a nuclear war is more important than things going as they usually do when presidents give military orders.

Lewis attempts to specify which respects of similarity between possible worlds are the ones that typically matter to the counterfactuals relevant for causation in "Counterfactual Dependence and Time's Arrow" ([1979b] 1986b: 32–51). The discussion gets rather involved, but Lewis thinks that several criteria are important. The first and most important is that a world does not have "big, widespread, diverse violations" of our actual laws of nature (*ibid*.: 47). Sometimes an antecedent will force us to go to a world where the laws are very different ("If gravity obeyed an inverse cube law, then ..." or "If there really were wizards and dragons, then ..."), but in general we only consider worlds that conform to our laws of nature. When we evaluate "If Nixon had pressed the button, there would have been a nuclear war", the worlds where all the missiles spontaneously wink out of existence are not among the relevant counterfactual worlds.

Of second importance is keeping large areas of the world picked exactly the same as our world (well, exactly the same intrinsically, in any case). One of the main effects of this is to keep the past (or the time earlier than the one specified by the antecedent) mostly fixed. This makes sense once we are setting aside "backtracker" conditionals, and in general when we ask about causal counterfactuals we do not expect that what happens now would make a difference to what happened yesterday. Again, there might be some particular counterfactuals where we allow the past to be wildly different – ordinary backtrackers, and extraordinary ones about time travel, for example – but for the most part having an exactly similar past is important. Everything else being equal, one would want to keep the present and the future the same as well, but not at the expense of violating the laws, and if there is a difference now, then the future will have to be influenced by a present change.

Notice that Lewis's standards are slightly qualified. He does not say that normally there must be *no* violations of law, or ensure that the past is completely the same. This is to solve a tricky problem when we come to specify what things would be like if an antecedent were true. Take a conditional that has an antecedent about an event at a particular time: for example, "If I were in Sydney this morning, I would have gone to a cafe for breakfast". Suppose we keep the laws of nature the same, and the past before this morning the same as in this world. This morning, in the actual world, I was not in Sydney, but in Brisbane. So in the counterfactual world or worlds we are imagining, how did I get there? It looks as though we have two options: either we just have a discontinuity, where I suddenly disappear from Brisbane and reappear in Sydney, or we mess with the recent past enough to get me there in a more sensible way (perhaps we allow that I had a last-minute impulse and caught a plane late last night). It looks as though we either need a law-violation (for instance a case of teleportation), or we need to tinker with the immediate past (so that late yesterday also diverges from the actual world).

If we have a divergence in the recent past, we may still need to have some sort of law violation if the world is sufficiently deterministic. If the world is completely deterministic, then how the world was ten years ago determined how it was yesterday evening, including determining that I wouldn't rush out to the airport for an unexpected trip to Sydney. If that is to vary, we would need some kind of exception to the laws of nature, some "jump" in my brain, for example, which made me suddenly go to Sydney. Lewis wants his account of causation to work whether or not the world turns out to be completely deterministic, so he wants to allow that a violation of law might happen at the relevant close worlds. The alternative would be to have a ramifying set of changes flow all the way back to the Big Bang, just to produce my neural difference, and that does not seem very appealing.

So in normal circumstances we keep the laws and most of the past fixed, except for what Lewis calls a "small miracle", if necessary. We should not have more "small miracles" than needed, since we do not want gratuitous law violations in the most similar worlds. (This is his third condition on similarity: no more "small miracles" than needed.) If Lewis has the similarity conditions right, then we shall be able to explain things like the "Nixon pressed the button" conditional discussed earlier. "If Nixon pressed the button, there would have been a nuclear war" is true provided that the worlds most similar to ours in terms of the past leading up to Nixon's button-pushing, plus conforming to our laws of nature (except perhaps for some "small miracle" that produced the divergence required for Nixon pressing the button), are ones where Nixon's order travels out through the command and control systems in the usual way, resulting in missiles getting launched, and the tragedy of nuclear war. The world where some unlikely occurrence (or "small miracle") also serves to frustrate Nixon's order and otherwise isolate the changes produced by his decision is one where there are many more "miraculous" happenings to erase the traces of his button-pushing. So that is why the "most relevantly similar" world where Nixon presses the button is one where there is a war, not a spontaneous misfire of the button followed by a miraculous cover-up.

If the world is chancy, there may be less need for "small miracles" in the most similar worlds (although there may occasionally be some, when the difference specified by the antecedent requires too great a shift in how the world is). There may have to be something similar, though: a series of events with extremely low chance (but not ruled out by the laws of nature). Lewis calls these "quasi-miracles", since they play a very similar role to the role that "small miracles" would play if determinism was true.

Another, more serious modification to the account is needed once we deal with chancy causation. Take a probabilistic system, such as a plutonium atom decaying. A plutonium atom normally has a low, but not entirely negligible, chance of decaying in any given minute. That chance becomes much higher, however, if it is struck by a neutron. (Plutonium is dangerous in atomic bombs because if enough plutonium atoms are together, when some decay they spit out neutrons that trigger the decay of others, and soon a very large number of them decay in a short time. That decay releases energy, producing the characteristic explosion.) Suppose we have a plutonium atom that is struck by a neutron and immediately decays. We would be inclined to say that this could well be a case of causation. (You can *make* a plutonium atom decay by bombarding it with neutrons; you *cause* a nuclear explosion by bringing enough plutonium together fast enough.) Unfortunately, it is not clear that the conditional "if the plutonium atom had not been struck by the neutron, it would not have decayed" is true. For even if the plutonium atom were not struck by the neutron, there was a chance it would have decayed anyway. If it was not struck, it might have decayed, and so it does not seem to be true that if it were not struck, it *would not* have decayed. Once chance is in the mix, sometimes something we want to classify as an effect would have had some chance of happening anyway.

Lewis's suggestion is to count something E as causally depending on an event C if the chance of E would have been significantly lower if C had not occurred (1986b: 175–84) (again, with all the complications mentioned above). Causation is a matter of chains of causal dependence, as before. So the neutron collision counts as the cause of the plutonium decay, because the chance of the decay would have been much lower without it. If the decay caused by a collision has different features from a spontaneous decay, Lewis's "influence" story could be used instead; the neutron collision would count as causation because the decay would have been somewhat different without it. But I suspect Lewis would not want to use this instead of the probability-raising story, since there might well be cases where an event would not have been different whether it was probabilistically caused one way or another.

Lewis's theory here is similar in some respects to other probability-raising accounts of probabilistic causation, though his is distinctive in relying on counterfactuals about chance rather than other sorts of notions of probability-raising. The most common notion in the literature is defined in terms of conditional probabilities rather than counterfactuals about probabilities. Lewis's theory here is similar in some respects to other "probability-raising" accounts of probabilistic causation. One classic presentation of an account of probabilistic causation in terms of the conditional probability of the effect given the cause is by Suppes (1970).

The details of Lewis's story are controversial, but if we are to explain counterfactuals in terms of "relevant similarity" of worlds at all, we need to account for the fact that we do readily permit some things to become quite different, but other things not to. Nixon's button-pressing can wipe out most life on earth, which is a big change, but it cannot turn him into a giraffe, or produce an intervention by aliens (unless there were actually aliens standing by to prevent a war, of course). Furthermore, this story about what is kept the same and what is allowed to differ cannot appeal directly to causal facts if we are going to have a counterfactual analysis of causation, since the counterfactual analysis of causation explains causes in terms of what counterfactuals hold, rather than the other way around. Whether Lewis's understanding of the counterfactuals associated with causation, and his understanding of causation itself, is correct is still a matter of debate. But Lewis has at the very least brought out some interesting ways in which the puzzles of counterfactuals and the puzzles of causation might be linked, which is no mean achievement.

Dispositions

Another topic connected to laws of nature and causation is the topic of *dispositions*. Many of the ways we have for classifying objects are in terms of what those objects *do*: they are fragile, soluble, impenetrable, or explosive. Other characterizations may well be dispositional, although slightly less obviously. Being heavy, for example, is a matter of what a thing is disposed to do (exert a good deal of force in a gravitational field – or perhaps a good deal of force for its size). Our characterizations of people are also often in terms of dispositions. Some people, for example, are courageous (disposed to have courage, or if courage is itself a disposition, then being courageous is probably a matter of being disposed to have certain reactions to danger). Some people even think that all we can know about objects in the world is information about what their dispositions are (dispositions to change the dispositions of other objects, presumably). Dispositions are a large part of our picture of the world.

Dispositions can be had by objects that never manifest them. A particular salt crystal might be soluble in water even though it never comes in contact with water between its creation and its destruction. Most of us may be disposed to break under sufficient torture, but I hope that you will never have to find out the hard way whether this is true of you. An obvious account of dispositions would be a straightforward *counterfactual* analysis – an object is disposed to Φ if it *would* Φ were some activating condition to obtain. For example, an object is soluble (in water) if it would dissolve were it placed in water. Something is disposed to burn if it would burn in appropriate circumstances. We could also state this analysis with an explicit reference to conditions:

> An object is disposed to Φ in circumstances C if, and only if, it *would* Φ in circumstances C.

Mary is disposed to get angry in the circumstance of someone setting fire to her house if, and only if, Mary would get angry if someone set fire to her house.

This analysis is very appealing. It may even seem so obvious that it is not worth discussing. The problem is that it seems to face counter-examples. Some dispositions are "finkish": they go away just when you would expect them to be activated.[10] Suppose Mary is a very angry person, and has the disposition to get angry and violent at very little provocation. Because of this, Jane follows Mary around with a tranquillizer. Whenever Mary is put in situations of stress, Jane immediately tranquillizes her, which makes her very calm and sleepy. So while Mary has a very angry disposition, it is *not* true that were she to be stressed, she would get angry. So it looks as though

Mary can have the disposition without the corresponding counter-factual being true, because the conditions in which her angry disposition would manifest are ones that cause her disposition to go away (since Jane alters Mary's reactions in those situations).

Another example is Mark Johnston's "shy but intuitive chameleon" (Johnston 1992). This chameleon has the standard chameleon ability to change its colour to blend in with its background (at least for the backgrounds it usually finds itself on). However, this chameleon is very shy, so whenever it thinks it is being looked at it blushes a bright pink. Furthermore, it is amazingly sensitive to whether people are likely to be looking at it, and so the only times anyone actually sees it, it looks an embarrassed pink. Consider the chameleon on a day when nobody else is around, and it is sitting on a green leaf. The chameleon is green, and being green is plausibly in part a disposition to look green to people with normal sight, in good lighting conditions. (That is why something's looking green is a guide to its being green). However, while the chameleon has the disposition to look green (since it *is* green), it is not true that were someone to look at it, it would appear green. Were anyone to look at it, it would blush bright pink, and so it would look pink. Its disposition to look green is finkish: it goes away whenever it would otherwise be manifested.

Once the scheme of the counter-examples is established, it is not too difficult to think of cases either where something has a disposition, but something stops that disposition from manifesting, or it lacks a disposition, but would come to have it were the triggering circumstances to come about. (A man who does not have the disposition to be a big spender would satisfy the appropriate counterfactual if a mind-controller stood ready to turn him into a big spender whenever he faced the opportunity to spend money.) Does this mean that we have to give up trying to understand dispositions in terms of counterfactuals?

Lewis thinks that we *can* analyse dispositions in terms of counter-factuals, we just need a slightly more complicated account. Here is Lewis's final account ([1997b] 1999a: 149):

> Something x is disposed at time t to give response r to stimulus s if and only if, for some intrinsic property B that x has at t, for some time t' after t, if x were to undergo stimulus s at time t and retain property B until t', s and x's having of B would jointly be an x-complete cause of x's giving response r.

Ignoring some of the complications,[11] the idea is that when an object has a disposition, it has some intrinsic property that would go together with the relevant stimulus to give the relevant response. A grenade has an internal structure such that when the pin is pulled, the make-up of the grenade together with the pin-pulling produces an explosion. That's why we say the grenade has a disposition to explode when the pin is pulled. The problem in finkish cases, according to Lewis, is that sometimes this intrinsic property is removed by the stimulus itself, or by something that happens when the stimulus is present. To work out whether the object really has the disposition, we see whether there is an intrinsic feature of the object that is such that *were the object to continue having it*, that feature (together with the stimulus) would cause the object to manifest the appropriate response.

Consider one of Lewis's examples ([1997b] 1999a: 138). A delicate glass vase is protected by a watchful sorcerer. The vase is just like many other fine glass vases: fragile, and disposed to break when dropped or hit. The sorcerer's vase is the same intrinsically, so we are inclined to call it fragile. However, the sorcerer keeps constant watch over it. Should anyone hit it or drop it, the sorcerer would immediately turn it into some unbreakable substance. Lewis thinks that in this case the sorcerer's vase is fragile, it is just that the *sorcerer* has a disposition that means that the glass will not break if struck.

Lewis, in effect, defined dispositions in terms of a double counterfactual: what would be caused *if* the basis for the disposition remained through the stimulus (and a claim about what is caused by what is itself to be analysed as a counterfactual claim, for Lewis). His analysis, unlike the simple counterfactual analysis, also explicitly links dispositions and causation. An object has the dispositions it does because of what its intrinsic properties would cause in the presence of stimuli.

Two features of Lewis's account are worth noting. They will strike some people as counter-intuitive, but perhaps a defender of Lewis's account could mount replies. The first is that, according to Lewis, all of an object's dispositions must ultimately depend on its *intrinsic* properties, the properties it has by itself, considered in isolation from other things. Many properties we are interested in are extrinsic, and it seems that we are sometimes prepared to ascribe dispositions to something on the basis of how its extrinsic properties work. Someone who is disposed to be laughed at because of their name apparently has a disposition to have something happen to them, but what one's name is is a matter of what one is called, not a matter of some intrinsic feature. So when people laugh at Ocelot Dirtyshirt, it is not because of her intrinsic features. If she is frequently called that behind her back, or in official documents filled out by her parents that she does not have access to, she may not even realize that it is her name and people are laughing at her because of it. When someone is disposed to go bankrupt, that may not be because of their intrinsic features. Financial facts about someone depend on how society as a whole functions, and not always and entirely on that person's intrinsic features. (You could imagine two people exactly alike intrinsically, but differing in their disposition to go bankrupt because of the differences in how their financial communities are organized.) Dispositions will often involve intrinsic properties, but these may not be the most important ones involved, and if the examples in this paragraph work, they may sometimes not be involved at all.

The other challenge Lewis's account might face is that it does not say anything about *how* the intrinsic property, together with the stimulus, causes the response. Perhaps when the intrinsic property does the causing through some indirect or non-standard way, we would not want to ascribe the relevant disposition to the object. Here is a slightly modified version of Lewis's sorcerer example. Suppose we have a sorcerer who is very possessive of trees in general, so possessive that whenever someone touches a tree, the sorcerer makes it explode. (I am assuming that "being a tree" is an intrinsic property. If it is not, there is some property like it that is intrinsic, and let us suppose for the sake of the argument that this is the property that the sorcerer is responding to.) That would make it true that were someone to touch a tree, it would explode. And it would be because the object's having the intrinsic property (being a tree), together with the stimulus (the touching), would cause the explosion (via the jealous response of the sorcerer). Would we want to say that, in this case, trees had the disposition to explode when touched? It seems to me that we would want to say the same thing about this case as we did about the vase case. If we want to say that the vase is fragile, but would cease to be fragile when hit, then we should want to say that the trees are not explosive, but at best would become explosive when touched. (And maybe we should not even want to say that. It looks as though the sorcerer's disposition is what is responsible for the explosions, not any disposition of the trees.)[12]

Whatever the precise details of the analysis, the thrust of the theory is clear. If some sort of counterfactual analysis will work, then the dispositions of objects will not have to be an additional part of the story of the world. Ultimately, that will be settled by what causes what (which in turn will be settled by the laws of nature and the history of particular matters of fact). Dispositions, too, fit into Lewis's project of constructing a picture that respects "Humean supervenience".

Chance

Often our information about the world comes in the form of information about probabilities. We do not know whether an eight will be rolled on the next roll of some fair pair of dice, but we do know there is a 5/36 chance that it will be rolled. We often cannot predict the future with certainty, but an expert predicting the weather, or the currency market, or the course of a chemical reaction, may be able to estimate chances of different outcomes. Despite being very common and being mathematically well-understood, philosophical questions about what probabilities and chances *are*, and how they relate to other phenomena (e.g. to frequencies, causation, what it is rational for us to believe, and so on), are still a matter of philosophical controversy. Lewis's work on the philosophy of probability has been quite influential. This is not the place for a discussion of the more technical aspects of Lewis's work on probability,[13] but it is worth discussing some of Lewis's more philosophical contributions.

Lewis thinks there are two distinct notions of probability that we should employ. He calls the first "credence". Credence is a subjective notion. The credence a person has in a proposition is the "degree of partial belief" the person has in that proposition. Some things we are certain about, or close to certain about: that we are thinking creatures, for example. Our credence in claims like these is 100 per cent, or close to it (if we use the percentage scale) or 1, or close to it, if we assign credences between 0 and 1 inclusive. A coin that we are confident is fair, and that is about to be tossed, is one where we will have equal credences in the propositions "the coin will come up heads" and "the coin will come up tails": it will be 50 per cent, or 0.5 credence for each (at least roughly). And there are some things we are sure, or close to sure, are false. "I am an elephant" is something to which I assign close to 0 credence.

We can represent people's degree of confidence in various propositions by assigning strengths of credence, between 0 and 1. A theory of probability, interpreted as a theory about credence, will tell us how our credences should behave if we are rational.[14] For example, one of the theorems of probability theory says that for any proposition A, the probability of A (written $P(A)$), plus the probability of not-A ($P(\text{not-}A)$) will add up to 1. Interpreted in terms of credence, this means that the more sure that I am of A, the more sure I should be that not-A is false. (If I assign 0.8 credence to "Mike will have pizza for dinner", I should assign 0.2 credence to "Mike will not have pizza for dinner", for example). Lewis thinks that *subjective probability* is a measure of reasonable credence: the probability a proposition has for a person is equal to the credence that person *should have* in that proposition, given their evidence. My subjective probability for the toss of a coin that I know is fair *should* give roughly 0.5 to heads and 0.5 to tails, although my credence might vary from this if I am irrational. (I may have bet a large sum of money on it coming up heads, and wishful thinking makes me assign 0.7 to heads and only 0.3 to tails, for example.)

It is not entirely clear how credences should be related to the question of whether someone just plain believes something. Philosophers disagree about whether flat-out belief can be understood in terms of having a credence above a certain level, or whether the relationship between credences and plain belief is more complicated. Fortunately, we do not have to settle this question for many purposes. Often we can work out what someone will do with information about their credences rather than their beliefs. If someone thinks it is 0.9 likely that it will rain, they will probably carry an umbrella. Whether or not someone counts as believing that burglars will try to break into their house, if they assign 0.8 credence to the proposition that burglars will try to break into their house, they will probably take precautions. Indeed, much of contemporary decision theory[15] models rational behaviour with credences and utilities (utilities for an agent are a measure of how valuable an agent thinks various outcomes will be); questions about what people flat-out believe or flat-out desire need not directly arise.

If we take probability theory to be about the rational principles that govern credences, it provides a useful tool for theories of evidence and decision-making. But it may not capture all of what goes on when we ascribe probabilities to propositions.[16] Consider some of the probabilistic statements in science: a claim in genetics that an offspring of parents with particular genes has a probability of 0.75 of being brown-eyed, for example, or a claim in physics that a plutonium atom has a probability of 0.5 of decaying during a specified period. We often think of these as facts that are independent of what any particular person does or should believe. The principles of genetics were in operation long before there were geneticists to come up with theories about them, and whether an atom has a certain chance of decay does not seem to depend on whether theorists happen to be correct in their claims about it. There seems to be some more objective conception of probability at work in these cases. Lewis labels this more objective notion "chance" or sometimes "objective chance" (since in ordinary usage the words "probability" and "chance" are sometimes interchangeable).

At one time, it was possible to think that statements about chance were only interim statements that reflected our ignorance. We may think that some state had a certain chance of obtaining or not obtaining, but that just meant that we did not know enough about the determining factors behind it. Contemporary physics suggests otherwise. Quantum mechanics, for example, strongly suggests that certain fundamental physical processes are ineliminably chancy; radioactive decay is one example. When we are considering isolated radioactive atoms of the same element (and isotope), there may be no difference between the ones that will decay in the next five minutes and the ones that will not decay in the next hundred years. Which ones decay is just a matter of chance. This chance sometimes gets "washed out" when we get up to the macroscopic level, at least for practical purposes. Put a couple of kilograms of plutonium together, for example, and even though which atoms will decay is a matter of chance, it is almost certain that enough will decay to trigger a chain reaction. But the chances do not always get washed out. How many times a Geiger counter clicks in a minute when put near a radioactive substance is, to some extent, random. It may click 30 times in the first minute and 28 times in the second minute, and the only way to explain the difference is in terms of a different number of chancy atomic decays. Even when the chances do not get washed out, it may well be that the chances of something unlikely get very small rather than disappear altogether (or go down to 0). Most atomic physicists would believe that there is some positive, non-zero probability that there will be no atomic decays in a given minute in a kilogram of plutonium, it is just that this probability is incredibly small, so small that, for example, we should expect to never observe such a thing.

If there are chances in this sense, it looks as though there will be *single case* chances; some particular occurrence will have a chance, all by itself. Some people who believe in objective probabilities reject the existence of single case chances. They think it makes sense to ask about the chance of certain proportions of events in large enough samples, but not about single cases. So it might make sense to ask what the chance is that cars manufactured by a certain factory will break down within two years, but it does not make sense to ask what the chance is of *this car here* breaking down in the next two years (except to the extent we can reinterpret a question of this second sort as a question of the first sort). One reason for this suspicion is that we might have different answers to questions about different general types of thing, and no way to put these answers together. For example, suppose we believe, as a result of statistical analysis and some engineering theory, that 20 per cent of cars from the Fnord motor company break down in the first two years. Suppose we also believe, on the basis of some statistics from large samples, that 30 per cent of cars driven by teenagers break down in their first two years. We are presented with a particular car, that is newly made by the Fnord motor company, and is driven by a teenager. What is the chance *it* will break down? Is it 20 per cent or 30 per cent? Believers in single case chances will believe there is some answer to this question (although it might not be one that we have enough evidence to be able to give). People who are more sceptical might think the question does not have an answer. They can tell you something about the chance of "a Fnord motor car breaking down" or "a car driven by a teenager breaking down", but there is no single answer about a particular case. (There might be relative answers. We might be able to say "It has a 20 per cent chance of breaking down, *qua* Fnord" or "It has a 30 per cent chance of breaking down, *qua* car driven by a teenager".)

In any case, Lewis is not sceptical about single case chances. He believes that contemporary physics tells us there are such things, so we had better be able to make sense of them. (At the very least, we should not be able to show that there are no such things just by philosophical argument. Science might do away with them eventually, but philosophy should not rule them out by itself.)[17] For Lewis, objective chances should be part of our understanding of the world, along with the credences we ascribe to people (and the rational credences we say that people *should* have).

Lewis thinks the objective chance of an event can change over time. That a nuclear reactor will melt down at 5pm may have a small chance at 12pm, but a sequence of unlikely reactions between 12pm and 2pm may make it much more probable that the nuclear reactor will melt down at 5pm, and a usually unreliable engineer happening to notice what is going on and reporting it properly at 3.30pm may

David Lewis

make it less likely after that time that the reactor would melt down at 5pm. When we talk of the chances increasing and decreasing over time, sometimes we might just be talking about our credences: our confidence in a given proposition can go up or down as we learn more. But it seems that sometimes we can talk about the chances of some outcome changing over time even if our credences are not involved. (Some specific propositions about tomorrow might be more or less likely now than they were ten years ago, even if nobody has a clue about them happening.) After the time of occurrence or non-occurrence, Lewis thinks the chance becomes either 1 (if the proposition was true) or 0 (if the proposition was false). In this sense, Lewis agrees with the intuition that the past is fixed. Propositions entirely about the past either have no chance now of being false (if they are in fact true), or no chance now of being true (if they are in fact false). Of course, many of them *did* have a chance of being true (or false). For example, the chance that a coin comes up heads, once it is finally tossed and comes up heads, becomes 1, even if it was 0.5 until the toss. (It is not now still open that the coin might come down tails.)[18]

One challenge now is to say what these two notions of probability have to do with each other. Is it just a fluke that they both are called "probability", and that they both obey the probability calculus? Lewis thinks they have an important connection, and the important connection is a conceptual truth about the link between what the objective chances are and what our credences rationally should be. Lewis thinks that objective chances are the sorts of things that justify rational credences, or, rather, since we can hardly be blamed for not having credence in something we have no evidence for, the important conceptual connection is that *evidence* of objective chances is a particularly good guide to what our credences rationally should be. In fact, we can define objective chance as whatever it is about the world such that evidence for it is, in a certain strict sense, the best rational constraint on credences. Chances are the things about the world that make it appropriate, even when fully informed of the evidence, to have a partial belief to a certain strength. In a certain sense they are "objectified credences" (1986b: 98). Lewis suggests that this connection is best captured by what he calls the "Principal Principle":

$$C(A/E) = P(A)$$

where C represents rational credence and P represents objective chance.[19] That is, the rational credence in a proposition A, conditional on the "total admissible" evidence E, is equal to the objective chance of A. The idea is that an event has a specific objective chance, say, 0.5, just in case someone would be rationally obliged to assign 0.5 credence to that event occurring, given the total evidence. This principle should be indexed to a time, since the chance of A can change over time. So Lewis's principle says that the credence we should give to A at a time, given all the admissible evidence about A at that time, should be equal to the chance of A at that time.

What is the "total admissible evidence"? It had better not be all the possible evidence. Seeing the outcome, for example, should be ruled out (even if a fair coin has a 0.5 chance of coming up heads, your credence that it came up heads should be much less than 0.5 if you just saw it land tails). But it had better cover a great deal, if it is enough to guarantee that a rational person will be able to use it to match their credence and the objective chance. Lewis suggests that two kinds of information are admissible. The first is particular facts about what has occurred in the past: information about previous frequencies, how similar trials have gone, and so on. If all we know about a radioactive atom is its history, in minute detail, we are unlikely to know anything that will help constrain our credence more than information about the chance would. The same is not true of information at the time of the decay or afterwards. If we know how the coin landed, for example, then regardless of what chance it had before the flip, our credence should track how it landed, not the chance it had beforehand. Likewise, if we could find out something causally "downstream" of the coin flip – how it looked when it landed, or what an observer who was there says about how it landed – then we might have good reason to think it landed heads even if the chance of it landing heads beforehand was quite low.

The other component of admissible information is how chances depend on the history. Lewis called this a "theory of chance", and says we can represent it as a set of conditionals linking possible histories to assignments of chances (at a time). Together with information about the history, a "theory of chance" in this sense will enable us to tell what the chances are. At first pass Lewis's Principal Principle says that if we were certain of a total history and a theory of chance, we would be rationally obliged to set our credences as equal to the chance, for any proposition that has a chance associated with it.

In fact, in unusual situations, this will not be quite right. If I have good evidence that I am receiving letters from a trustworthy time traveller, who tells me how chance events are going to turn out, then information about what those letters say should be ruled "inadmissible", for the same sort of reason information directly about the future is inadmissible. So information about history is not always "admissible". But in ordinary cases, where information is not flowing from the future to the past (by means of precognition, time travel, wormholes, or anything like that),[20] the story as it stands tells us something important, Lewis believes, about why chances and rational credences both get called "probability". Objective chances have a sort of "to-be-believed" status; ideal evidence for objective chances constrains our partial beliefs, on pain of irrationality.

Of course, if the Principal Principle only told us how to constrain our beliefs when we had complete evidence about the admissible history and a complete theory of chances, it would be very little use in practice. But it has implications for what my credences should be when I am unsure of what the objective chances are. To take a rather idealized case, suppose there is some material in front of me and I have a 0.6 credence that it has a 0.3 chance of decay in the next minute, and a 0.4 credence that it has a 0.7 chance of decay. (Suppose I am not quite sure what it is made up of, but these are the only two alternatives left.) Suppose further that I know nothing "inadmissible" about the substance in front of me; I do not have letters from time travellers, working extra-sensory perception, or anything else. The Principal Principle tells me that if my credences were rational to begin with, I should have a $(0.6 \times 0.4) + (0.4 \times 0.7) = 0.52$ credence that it will decay in the next minute. The Principal Principle helps to tell me this because it tells me, among other things, that if I am rationally certain of the chance (and have no inadmissible information) my credence should match that chance, so it tells me what my credence ought to be if I am certain that the chance is 0.4, and what it should be if I am certain that it is 0.7, and that is why I can tell what my credence should be when I assign non-zero credences to each.

Lewis goes on to illustrate how the Principal Principle can be used to get credences in frequencies from credences in single case chances, how it helps to illuminate what evidence for single case chances could be like, and so on. The Principal Principle tells us a little about what objective chances must be like, if there are such things, but of course it leaves many questions unanswered. For example, is there some illuminating way to describe not just how objective chances are related to credences, but what they *are*? Lewis suggests a regularity theory of chances, one that is closely related to his theory of laws ([1994a] 1999a: 233–5). According to Lewis, in some worlds the simplest, strongest set of principles that describe the behaviour of objects are sometimes of the form "*F*s have a 50 per cent chance of being *G*". In a world with reliable half-lives for radioactive materials, but no further interesting frequencies about how those materials decay, the simplest, most informative thing to do might be to give the chance an atom of a certain sort will decay in a given time. The chances described by the law may be the same as overall relative frequencies (e.g. exactly half of the plutonium atoms in existence decay within the first *X* years of their existence), or the relative frequencies may be close enough to some round number that it is simpler, or more natural, to give a round figure.

If Lewis is right that some story like this is correct, then objective chances can be accommodated in the framework of Humean supervenience; they emerge out of the frequencies of behaviour (together with principles about simplicity and strength). Unfortunately, Lewis's theory has a technical problem, serious enough for Lewis to label it the "big bad bug" (1986b: xiv; [1994a] 1999a: 224). On the regularity analysis, what the chances are depends on the entire pattern of regularities in a world. (What goes on later can make a difference to what the simplest, strongest description of the whole turns out to be.) But because of this, information about the chances (e.g. of the sort that one can get from the history plus the "theory of chance" that gives the chances, given the history) brings with it information about the future. The details are a little complicated (they can be found in Lewis (1994a)), but the upshot is that the basic Principal Principle, together with Lewis's regularity theory of chances, yields inconsistent rational credence assignments.

To resolve this problem, Lewis adopts a modified version of the Principal Principle,[21] rather than giving up his regularity theory of chance (and with it Humean supervenience). This is partly because he has trouble seeing how any alternative story could explain the connection between objective chances and frequencies. Lewis thinks that this is not something that should remain unexplained, and the regularity theory has the beginnings of a story about why relative frequencies line up with objective chances. Lewis's willingness to modify the Principal Principle also illustrates his attitude to conceptual analysis. Statements of conceptual connections between different things (credences and chances, or mental states and behaviour, or colours and physically described surfaces of objects, or whatever) are almost never an "all or nothing" matter; it is as if they come with an implicit clause saying "... or close enough". The Principal Principle does not quite get the connection between chances and rational credences right, but it is close enough. Likewise, we will see that principles about beliefs and desires may only be about how they *typically* behave (Chapter 5), and principles about values may not quite match the things Lewis identified values with, but they fit them close enough to count as values (Chapter 8).

Laws, causes, dispositions, chances and Humean supervenience

Giving accounts of laws, causation, dispositions and chances are four of the central challenges in contemporary analytic metaphysics. A theory of each should make some reference to the others. What causes or dispositions or chances each have to do with the laws of nature, for example, are questions that deserve answers. Lewis's theories are obviously thus interconnected, but to an extent you could believe one without believing the others. One could adopt a counterfactual theory of causation without having a regularity theory of laws, for example. You may well need *some* story of what the laws of nature are to make sure the right similarity relation is invoked for causal counterfactuals, but stories other than regularity theories would presumably work. Or the Principal Principle might be taken to be a useful insight into the connection between rational credences and chances, even if you prefer a different theory of what chances are.

Taken as a package, however, they present a coherent picture of the functioning of the world: one where the world's behaviour is not to be explained by some extra metaphysical postulate, but in a sense the regularities of occurrences are fundamental. Things just happen, one thing after another, and it is out of this underlying distribution of "local, particular matters of fact" that some of the most general things we are familiar with – causal processes, chance events, dispositions of objects – arise. Lewis provides a distinctive conception of the natural order, which stands behind many of his specific proposals. Almost despite himself, Lewis became a system-builder, in a climate where system-building was often seen as suspicious. Lewis's understanding of these central metaphysical topics deserves its place in the options metaphysicians should consider and, indeed, they have informed contemporary debates on all these issues. Whether theorists of laws of nature, causation and so on agree or disagree with Lewis's conclusions, their appeal and the strength of his arguments, for his own view and against rivals, mean that they are theories metaphysicians working on these topics feel obliged to take into account.

Chapter 5

Realism and reductive materialism about the mind

One of philosophy's central puzzles is the question of how mental aspects of reality relate to the physical aspects of reality. On the one hand there are things such as thoughts, beliefs, experiences, consciousness, representation and meaning. On the other hand there are sensory stimulations, bodily movements and the location and nature of objects such as molecules and cells and mountains and stars. Very roughly, there are three philosophical approaches to this question. One is to take the mental as fundamental, and account for the rest of the world as a projection of our experience, or a creation of mind or spirit, or something that only has a nature relative to our concepts, or practices of investigation, or something else that seems equally mental. This approach has traditionally been known as "idealism", although some contemporary idealists prefer to identify themselves as "anti-realists".[1] The second approach is to take the mental and physical aspects of reality to be equally fundamental, with neither to be accounted for solely in terms of the other. In this approach, one of the important jobs of philosophy is to chart the relationships between the two. This sort of approach is often labelled "dualism" about the mind, since traditional versions of this view held that mind and matter were the two fundamental aspects of the world.[2] A final approach, often known as "materialism" or "physicalism" about the mind, takes only the material or physical to be fundamental, and takes it that all the mental aspects of the world are to be accounted for in material or physical terms.[3] Lewis, as a materialist about everything in our world, is a materialist about the mind as well.

In so far as there is a contemporary philosophical orthodoxy about this question, it is materialism. Inspired by the success of cognitive science and the information sciences, most contemporary philosophers of mind would subscribe to some form of materialism about the mind, although, of course, this materialism comes in a wide variety of shades, and with greater or lesser concessions to dualism. This was not so in the 1960s, when Lewis first began defending materialism about the mind. Then, dualism was much closer to being orthodoxy among Anglo-American professional philosophers (as it might still be in the population at large, when you consider that many people claim to believe that our minds continue a spiritual existence after bodily death). Even some of those who resisted dualism, such as Gilbert Ryle (1949), did not want to be materialists about the mind, but rather thought that the whole question about the connection between the mental and the physical was nonsense (*ibid.*: 22–3). It was in this climate that Lewis wrote "An Argument for the Identity Theory" (1966).

Lewis's materialist theory of mind

Lewis defends the view that every mental state is a physical state. (In "An Argument for the Identity Theory" (1966) he identified mental states with neurochemical states.) Lewis argues for this from two premises: one about the physical explanations of physical phenomena; and one about what we mean by our mental-state terms, expressions such as "belief", "desire", and all the rest. The claim that physical events have only physical causes is part of Lewis's materialism, but by itself it is not the same as materialism. You could believe that the physical is entirely explained by the physical, but that there are also non-physical aspects of the world, with their own non-physical explanations. What is distinctive about Lewis's argument is the claim he wanted to make about the meaning of mental vocabulary; once we understand what our mental words mean, we are on the way to discovering what the mind is.

Lewis discusses the case of experiences. What does an expression such as "the experience of drinking a cup of tea" mean, for example? (This is my example, rather than his.) Lewis claims that it ascribes a "causal role" to a state that a person has. For a state to be an "experience of drinking a cup of tea", it must be something that is normally produced by drinking a cup of tea, and it must typically cause things associated with that experience, a belief that one is drinking a cup of tea, for example. Names for mental states come in families,[4] and a theory of the mental tells us about beliefs, desires and all the rest, by telling us how they are typically causally related, and how they causally relate to physical events. Experiences are typically caused by certain physical interactions with the world, and at the other end of the internal causal process, decisions and mental events typically produce specific bodily movements; the decision to stand up typically produces a certain kind of straightening of the body, for example. If Lewis is right, it is part of what we mean by "the experience of drinking a cup of tea" that it is the sort of thing caused by ingesting a cup of tea, which is a physical state. Furthermore, the experience of drinking a cup of tea is supposed to be able to cause further physical states (e.g. a tea cup moving when it is returned to the table). Given Lewis's claim that the "true and exhaustive account of all physical phenomena" is given in terms of physical phenomena, then once we have established that mental states must be able to at least partially explain and be explained by physical phenomena, we have an argument that we must think mental states are physical states.

Where do these characterizations of mental states come from? Lewis thinks they come from "folk psychology": the everyday set of opinions we have about the mind. This understanding of the mind is "common knowledge", but it may well be tacit. We might not be able to rattle off a set of doctrines about belief and desire, but we are in a position to recognize the truth of claims of folk psychology when we come across them. "Someone who is in a lot of pain tries to get the pain to stop" is something we can recognize to be true because of our ordinary understanding of pain. It may have exceptions (and our ordinary understanding of the mind gives us a guide to some of those exceptions), but it is typically true, and we've known psychological generalizations like this since the Stone Age (or considerably earlier).

Folk psychology gives us a lot of information about what it is we are looking for when we are trying to work out what experiences, beliefs or decisions are. (Notice that folk psychology probably has some slack built into it. Most generalizations about experiences, beliefs, desires, pains or whatever will be generalizations about what these states do "typically" or "for the most part". But that information is still very useful as a starting-point). Folk psychology cannot answer all the questions about the mind by itself. Lewis thinks we have a two-stage process here. The first is to discover the causal roles associated with mental terms by folk psychology: what the theory says typically produces a state, and what that state typically leads to, often in conjunction with other mental states. The second step is to discover what states in the world play those causal roles. That is a job for science. The brain sciences will tell us what physical state inside us is caused by various kinds of impacts on our senses, which states go together to produce bodily movements of various kinds and so on. Together, with the information about causal roles we get from folk psychology, and causal information about which physical states cause which physical states, we shall be able to discover which neural state is which mental state. (Of course, we do not know enough about how our brain works to be able to do this, and maybe the complexity of the story will stop us ever knowing the exact story. But, according to Lewis, we already know enough to be confident that each mental state will be some sort of brain state).

An important thing to notice about these roles is that they will be largely "interdefined". According to a popular construal of folk psychology, for example, what a belief causes depends a great deal on what other beliefs someone has, and what desires that person has.[5] How anger will cause someone to react depends on what they take their situation to be, and other mental facts about them (what other emotions they have, their temperament and so on). This means that we would have real difficulty in identifying a state as a belief or desire in isolation. Fortunately, we can consider the role of all of them together. There are non-mental causes that feed into the whole system (impacts on sensory organs, for example), and non-mental effects at the other end (bodily movements, including making noises with our voice boxes and mouths). Given someone's dispositions to respond to inputs by producing outputs, folk psychology gives us a way of describing them in terms of beliefs, desires, emotions, decisions and all the rest. (In practice, we rely on a tacit grasp of folk psychology to guess at the psychological states of others. Nobody explicitly goes from a list of all of someone's behaviour and behavioural inputs to ascribing to them a complete set of beliefs and desires all at once.) While we may talk about the folk-psychological role of pain or a belief about tables, if this is to help us sketch an account of mental states in terms of other states, we shall need to appeal to the overall specification of the roles played by mental states in combination.

Indeed, strictly speaking, Lewis does not seem to believe in individual beliefs and desires as separate entities with their own causal roles. It may be that "beliefs" is a "bogus plural" ([1994b] 1999a: 311). We have a system of representation that represents our entire belief state and desire state, but whether it can be carved up in any psychologically interesting way into individual "beliefs" is something Lewis said folk psychology is agnostic about (*ibid*.: 311), and Lewis seems agnostic about this too. It may instead be that believers and desirers represent in the way a map does, or a hologram, or a connectionist network; a map represents many things, but for much of the information it contains you cannot cut out the piece of the map that represents just that information. A map of the world will show that New York is closer to Los Angeles than it is to Tokyo, but there is no way to erase just that piece of information, without erasing other information as well. Lewis certainly thinks that there are believers, and that they represent things – they do believe that penguins are birds, that ice melts, and all the rest – but whether this is because they have individual pieces of mental life called "beliefs", or whether they have larger representations that encapsulate a lot of information together, is something that Lewis at least wants to remain uncommitted about. Despite this qualification, in much of Lewis's writings he does talk as if there are individual fine-grained mental states, like pains or beliefs with specific contents, so I shall leave this qualification implicit. It will come up again in Chapter 6, when we look at what Lewis has to say about the *content* of beliefs and desires, how they come to be *about* the things they are about.

In the jargon of philosophy of mind, Lewis defends a "type–type" identity theory, and not merely a "token–token" one. A token–token identity theory of mind says that the things that have mental states are physical, but it does not necessarily identify a mental state (like pain) with any *type* of physical state. A type–type identity theory, on the other hand, says that certain types of mental states, or properties, are identical to certain physical ones. Saying that someone has a certain mental feature is just attributing to them a certain physical feature, although under another description. The talk about types and tokens comes from a distinction between general features, or properties and relations, on the one hand (the types), and individual or particular things on the other (the tokens). Where talk about "states", like mental states and physical states, fits into this distinction is a bit hard to tell. Sometimes we seem to talk about states as if they were types (so that different people can be in the same state, or one person might be in the same state at different times), and other times we seem to talk about mental states, for example, as if they are particular objects. The pain *I* have after crouching from too long is a different thing from the one *you* have; it is not as though we can share them or swap them, or that you can literally feel mine or I can feel yours. Lewis tends to talk about states as types (so a certain state of pain would be a type of pain sensation, rather than the sense in which a particular pain only exists on a particular occasion of having such a sensation). So I shall talk about states in that way here, but it is worth keeping in mind that this is not the only way people use the expression "mental state".

One reason why people (even people sympathetic to materialism) stop short of identifying mental properties with physical properties is that they think a mental state (like being in pain, or believing that there is a cup of tea on the table) can be shared by different things that have very little physically in common: a human being and an advanced robot, for example, or a possible creature with very different insides. Lewis addresses this concern in "Mad Pain and Martian Pain" (1980b). In that paper, Lewis addresses two kinds of challenge that a theory that identifies mental states with physical states has to face. Lewis presents the first challenge with the example of a "madman". We think that some people behave atypically; someone who is insane or deranged may not behave the way someone normally would with a given set of mental states. For example, we think it is possible for someone to be in pain but have none of the usual dispositions to act that go along with that; in principle, someone could be in pain but show no discomfort, or even behave in some quite different way, by giggling, perhaps. (It would be very strange, but people who are insane or deranged can behave in very strange ways, we think.) There might be less far-fetched cases as well; someone who is completely paralysed after an accident may not be able to signal that they are in pain, or engage in the usual pain behaviour such as flinching or screaming, but for all that they may still have mental states, be in pain, and so on.

On the other hand, we are somewhat inclined to think that creatures that are very different inside could have mental states. An alien might not have nerves like ours, and might have a very different way of processing information about its environment. (Maybe it does not even have a centralized system like a "brain".) Lewis uses the case of a hypothetical Martian to discuss this possibility. Nevertheless such an alien creature could be in pain, it seems, especially if it engages in pain behaviour in the way we might expect. For example, if it screamed or drew back if unexpectedly burnt or cut, or favoured injured limbs (or whatever) and so on, then we would consider that such a creature could be in pain, even if we knew it was very different from us inside. The point might be generalized. If a spaceship lands and alien creatures come out and hold conversations with us, seem to want things and have beliefs in not-too-dissimilar ways, and discuss mathematics, physics and interior decorating with us just like a fellow human being, then we will probably think the aliens have minds, even if we discover that they have a very different internal arrangement for processing information.

The challenge is to admit both of these intuitions at once: to allow that someone could be in pain while having a state that did not play the usual role, but on the other hand allowing that something could be in pain without having any physical state in common with us. A classic identity theory – that said that pain was such-and-such a neural state, for example – handles the first sort of case but has trouble with the second. This is because once we find out what the neural state is (by finding out what state is normally produced by cuts, burns, etc. and which also normally produces screaming, complaining, favouring the injured limb, etc.), we can say that someone is in pain if they have that neural state, even if *in them* the neural state does not produce the standard behaviour. This theory has trouble with the Martian, though. If pain is such-and-such a neural state, then a creature without that sort of state (and maybe without neurons altogether) is not in pain. On the other hand, some sort of behaviourism, defining mental states entirely in terms of their role in behaviour, would handle the case of the Martian, but not the case of the madman. The Martian is disposed to behave in the right way, so it is in pain (or has a belief about where a cup is, or whatever), but the madman (or the totally paralysed person) does not, so the behaviourist will find it difficult to agree that the madman or the paralysed person does have the relevant mental states.

So, how does Lewis's theory allow us to say that both the madman and the Martian are in pain, even though the madman does not have a state that works the way pain is supposed to, and the Martian does not have any neurophysiological states in common with us when we are in pain? For Lewis, pain is the physical state that occupies the pain role; that is, it is the physical state that is typically caused in such-and-such ways, and typically has such-and-such effects (where this role may need to make reference to other mental states, as discussed above). Different features can fill the role in different sorts of creatures: a certain neural firing in human beings, but some quite different process in aliens (and different processes again in artificially intelligent robots, angels, or whatever). Despite the fact that there are many different properties or states that can play this role, the properties and states in creatures like us and the hypothetical Martians are still physical ones. It is as if everyone comes to a party wearing their favourite colour, and they all count as wearing their favourite colour, even though John wears blue and Bill wears red. It is not as though there is some additional colour property, "favourite", that should go on a list of colours along with red, blue and the rest.

How does Lewis make room for the madman, then? Remember that his account of what mental states are is in terms of what they *typically* cause and what they are *typically* caused by. These qualifications seem to be built into the folk psychological understandings of these states. Nobody thinks that pain *always* causes people to cry out or to avoid its source, and generalizations about more sophisticated states are even harder. (For example, what exceptionless generalizations are there about people who believe that there is a table in the room?) Before this can help us, though, we need an answer to the question: "typical" relative to what? A state that works some ways in one situation might work other ways in others. Lewis thinks that one way to restrict this is to restrict it to a claim about what that state mostly does "in an appropriate population", and one way to limit appropriate populations is by species. So if the madman has a state that mostly has the right causes and effects to be pain *in human beings*, we could say that it counts as pain in the madman, even though it does not do the right causing in him. A paralysed person might count as being thirsty, even though she has no disposition to get up and have a glass of water, because (in part) the state she is in mostly makes human beings seek out liquid to drink.

In fact, Lewis's full story about what the "appropriate" group is will be one with some vagueness. He mentions four criteria, which may often conflict:

> Perhaps (1) it should be *us*; after all, it's our concept and our word. On the other hand, if it's *X* we are talking about, perhaps (2) it should be a population that *X* himself belongs to, and (3) it should preferably be one in which *X* is not exceptional. Either way, (4) an appropriate population should be a natural kind – a species, perhaps. ([1980b] 1983a: 127)

Since the madman has a state *we* have, and belongs to the same species, we rightly take that into account when we think the madman is appropriately grouped with us, and so his states are behaving atypically. For a Martian that is like most Martians, criteria (2), (3) and (4) pull us sufficiently strongly so that we are inclined to take what role states ordinary Martians have as the appropriate standard when we are trying to work out whether to say the Martian is in pain.

When we get to sufficiently unusual cases – creatures that are distantly related to us, but typically behave in very inhuman ways, or Martian sub-groups, or one-off creatures (say, which are produced when a mad scientist's lab explodes, or come into being for a few seconds as a result of an incredibly improbable cosmic accident) – Lewis predicts that our concept will give us much less guidance about what to say. This may well be right. When we try to apply a concept to a situation that is very different from the ones we usually have any reason to think about, we are often inclined to think that there is no determinate fact about how the concept applies.

Lewis's identity theory, then, turns out to identify a mental state with a physical state *relative to an appropriate population*. In human beings, pain is such-and-such, but in Martians, it is something else. There may even be empirical questions about how populations are similar or different; it is a matter for biologists whether birds have the same (or similar enough) neural structures as we do for pain, or perception, or beliefs and desires. (No doubt the "higher" mental functions will be less likely to be shared. A pelican is unlikely to have anything that would count as believing in the Marxist theory of labour value, or preferring detective stories to romances). For Lewis, it is even contingent what pain is for human beings. He would have agreed that in principle it would be possible for human beings to have evolved so a different neurological structure played the pain role. In a sense, then, the identity between mental states and physical states is "contingent", but that is only because some other physical state could have fit the required description, and not because there is a state that could have failed to be identical to itself. (There is a sense in which there is a "contingent identity" between John's favourite colour and blue, if by that all we mean is that "John's favourite colour" could have been some other colour than blue if John had preferred something else.)

So while Lewis had a type–type identity theory, it is not an unrestricted one. There is not a single type of physical state we can point to and call pain, but rather there is pain-in-human-beings, pain-in-lizards, and (perhaps only in other possible worlds), pain-in-advanced-robots, pain-in-Martians and so on. One challenge to this sort of view is the thought that being in pain should be a property that is in common to everything that is in pain; it should be one and the same thing in human beings, lizards, robots and everything else. (Likewise for believing there is a cup on the table, or being in love or any other mental state). One thing that all of the creatures in pain

David Lewis

have in common is a certain functional characterization: they all have *some state or other that plays the pain role* (i.e. some state that has such-and-such typical causes in their population, such-and-such typical effects in their population, and so on). Why not say that it is this functional characterization, which they all share, that is pain, and not the physical states that are different in different kinds of creature?

Identifying mental properties (or states) with the having of some property or other with certain causes and effects is sometimes called "functionalism". Many contemporary philosophers of mind would describe themselves as functionalists, although people mean slightly different things by the expression. Some people say that everyone who has a property with a certain causal or informational role counts as being in pain, and they identify the property of being in pain with what is in common to everyone who has a state that plays that role. These people would endorse the objection in the previous paragraph and, in one usage of the term, this is the only sort of view that counts as "functionalist".[6] Others distinguish two sorts of functionalists: ones who say that mental properties are what everyone who has a state with the right sort of role have in common (sometimes called "role functionalists"); and others who say that the mental property is the property that plays that role, so it is different in human beings, robots, Martians and so on (called "realizer" functionalists, since they say that the mental properties are the properties that play the roles, or that "realize" the roles). Lewis counts as a "realizer functionalist", according to this distinction. Lewis himself said that he was not sure whether he should count as a functionalist ([1994b] 1999a: 291, 307) because he was not sure whether when most people used the expression "functionalist", they meant just "role functionalist", or whether they used it in the second, broader way.

Lewis rejected "role functionalism" in favour of "realizer functionalism"; pain in human beings is a neurophysiological state, not the state of having-a-property-with-a-particular-causal-profile. One reason for this is that the realizer state, but not the role state, is the one that does the right sort of causing. It is the neurophysiological state that causes the screaming or flinching, not the more abstract functionally specified property. Another, related reason[7] is that folk psychology tells us that pain is what *occupies* the pain role. Folk psychology tells us a lot about what pain is and how it works, and not about what pain's realizer is and what it does. (Folk psychology might not say anything about pain's realizer, if it even has one.) Lewis thinks that there is the role property too, of course, and that everything that can be properly described as being in pain does have something in common. The dispute is about which property is the one our ordinary mental terminology picks out. So in terms of an overall theory of the mental, the difference between role functionalism and realizer functionalism does not seem so great.

Another challenge is that Lewis's theory leaves too much as hostage to empirical fortune. Lewis assumes that there are natural groupings of occurrences of states, so that an occurrence of a state can be "atypical" relevant to the "appropriate" category. Some philosophers have worried about whether there is any useful commonality that can be described in physical terms, even for human beings. What if each one of us has rather different states that play causal roles in our brains? (There is, say, some random element in our brains' "training", so that different neural structures appear in different people depending only on some small, insignificant differences in early childhood.) What if, even more worryingly, there is not much commonality in each person over time? What if my neural structure "resets" itself each night when I am asleep, so it is as if the same program is run on a quite different architecture? One worry would be that if it turned out that this is how the brain works, then, according to Lewis, people like us would not have mental states at all, since there would be no state that *typically* played the right sort of role in an appropriate population. But, the objection might go, that's absurd. We already know enough about people like us to know that whatever it takes to have a pain or have a belief, we have them, regardless of how brain science turns out. (If you don't agree that we already know enough to know that we are sometimes in pain, get someone to hit your thumb with a hammer.)[8]

I am not sure what Lewis's response to this objection would be. Some would welcome the theoretical space for folk psychology to turn out to be wrong in the light of further investigation, but I doubt this would have been Lewis's response; he was not particularly sympathetic to eliminativism about the mental being a live possibility.[9] Lewis might have been happy to narrow down the "appropriate population" as much as was needed to have it turn out that we do have mental states. He suggests there could be variation between human beings ([1994b] 1999a: 305), and this willingness to draw the lines of the appropriate population as narrowly as needed ([1989b] 2000a: 83–5). Or perhaps he would just be prepared to say that we know enough, already, to know that it cannot turn out that different human beings have very different physical structures underlying their behavioural dispositions, and that we do not have the sorts of brains that process-information with very different physical states at different times. This might seem to prejudge questions that should be left to the neuro-physiologists, but presumably we knew some things about how the mind works all along, and maybe those things do imply limits on how our brains must be structured.

The analytic status of Lewis's theory

Folk psychology gives us the role a state must play to be a belief, or a pain, or whatever; and scientific investigation of the world tells us what states play those roles. As it turns out, according to Lewis, they are physical, neurological states (at least in human beings). There are two ways someone could take this remark. You might think that it is only epistemological or heuristic: this is how we work out what the mental states are. Or you could take it as definitional: to be in pain is, *by definition*, to have a state that does such-and-such. Lewis wanted to make the stronger, definitional claim: folk psychology is not just a starting-point for finding out what mental states are, it defines the meaning of our mental discourse. There could not even possibly be mental states that our folk psychology was largely wrong about. Many of the claims of folk psychology about the roles that mental states, then, are *analytic* rather than synthetic,[10] according to Lewis. For this reason Lewis's style of philosophy of mind is often called "analytic functionalism".

Why suppose that the roles specified by folk psychology have any analytic connection to the meanings of our mental vocabulary? After all, with many theories, we think whether or not they are right is a matter mostly of how the world is, not how the theories are. If we have a theory of bananas, even if it proved to be a very good guide to bananas, that would not prompt us to think that *by definition* bananas are grown in warm climates, weigh less than ten kilograms, and so on for the rest of the claims of our theory. Why should folk psy-chology be built into the meaning of mental terms, any more than "folk banana-ology" should define the word "banana"?

This question touches on a central part of Lewis's philosophical methodology (and as such it will be discussed further in Chapter 9). Lewis thinks that terms in a theory are *implicitly defined* by the content of that theory.[11] What we mean by calling something a such-and-such is that it behaves enough like a such-and-such in the theory we hold. So not only mental terms but all the expressions in our language (or nearly all of them) get the meanings they do by being part of characterizing theories. (There is some reason to think Lewis would apply this claim to the whole of language. At any rate, he was prepared to apply it not just to new theories that introduce new vocabulary (1970b), but also to our folk theories of psychology and persons ([1974a] 1983a: 111; [1972] 1999a: 259–61).) Lewis's claim about words getting their meanings from the theories in which they figure is a distinctive philosophical claim, and not one that should be taken for granted, but there are three things to point out that make the view slightly less extreme than it might initially seem.

First, it is not the entire theory that is analytically true, according to Lewis; rather, the theory supplies us with what would be true by definition of the things described by the theory *if there are any*. So it is not analytic that people have beliefs that, together with desires, often cause actions; rather, what is analytic is that *if there are any beliefs and desires and actions at all*, then beliefs and desires sometimes go together to cause actions. So while the terms in theories pick out things that, by definition, work more or less as the theory says, this does not make the whole theory true by definition. (That would make discoveries all too easy.) It just means that if the theory is too far wrong, then none of the objects it supposedly picks out with its distinctive vocabulary really exist. For example, if I come up with a theory of a new sort of supernatural angel-like entity (call them the Orgons), and construct a theory according to which every Orgon has an office in the celestial hierarchy, and has powers *vis-à-vis* other Orgons depending on which office they possess (e.g. Orgons in the office of celestial harmony are allowed to kill Orgons in the office of the lesser servitors), I shall not have defined Orgons and their offices into existence. All I have established as true by definition with my theory is that *if* there are Orgons and celestial offices in my sense, *then* every Orgon has an office, some offices bring the power of life and death over other Orgons and all the rest of it.

Secondly, Lewis allows for some slack in what is true by definition when some group of terms appear in a defining theory. For something to count as a belief at all, it must behave in a close enough approximation to how beliefs are supposed to behave in folk psychology. But the match does not need to be perfect; "imperfect deservers" of the name "belief" may do well enough to deserve being called beliefs. Here's a (perhaps simplified) example that philosophers use to illustrate one case. At one stage, people had a theory of sea creatures that included creatures called "whales". Whales were large sea creatures, were hunted for blubber and other things, could sometimes be seen washed up on shore, were big fish, and so on. One day (according to the example), people realized that a significant part of the folk theory of whales was mistaken. It turned out that the large, whale-shaped sea creatures that were hunted for blubber and so on, were in fact mammals, and not fish as the theory had said. If the definition given by the folk theory of whales was very strict, people should have said that it turned out there were no whales; there were things much like whales, which people had been mistakenly labelling "whales", perhaps, but since those big things were mammals and not fish, they didn't fit the folk theory. But, of course, that's not what people said. Instead, they treated it as a discovery about whales. The things everyone called "whales" were not quite the way folk theory had thought they were. "Whale" had some flexibility, and something could count as a whale even if it did not fit the theory perfectly.[12]

It might be the same with beliefs, desires, pains or whatever. Maybe they do not fit our pre-theoretic understanding perfectly, but as long as a group of states do the job well enough, they will count as what we were talking about all along. However, if it turned out that we had no states at all that were anything like what beliefs or desires or pains were supposed to be, then it would have turned out that we did not have beliefs, desires and so on.

Thirdly, recall the nature of folk psychology. Folk psychology, according to Lewis, is something we may be able to deploy on a case-by-case basis, but is something we cannot just articulate. In some earlier work, Lewis had suggested that articulating folk psychology is something we could do just by gathering "platitudes" or commonplaces about the mind ([1972] 1999a: 257–8), but he later rejects this view (*ibid.*: 298). I suspect this later rejection is not to be read as saying that in principle someone could not articulate folk psychology, but it seems at least to say that we should not expect any individual to be able to just reel off everything about our common-sense understanding of the mental.

The analyticity provided by a term's role in a theory is conditional (when something is analytically true about beliefs, it is a statement of the form that *if* there are any beliefs, they behave in thus-and-so manner), and flexible (a belief has to behave only more or less as the theory says it does). And the analyticity of claims about the mind comes from an *implicit* theory, one that we may only dimly grasp explicitly. So Lewis's argument to the challenge offered above – Why should folk psychology be built into the meaning of mental terms, any more that "folk banana-ology" should define the word "banana"? – would be to say that "banana" *is* defined implicitly by the theories we have about bananas as well (although the definition of "banana" also yields conditional truths, has a fair amount of flexibility and may not be explicit). Lewis's approach to the mind generalizes, as we shall see in later chapters.

Much of Lewis's argument for the identity theory of mind could survive even if we rejected the claim that folk psychology's contribution is largely analytic or definitional, however. Provided folk psychology is largely *correct* about what beliefs, pains and other mental states do – how they are caused, and what in turn they cause – then Lewis's argument identifying mental states with physical states could still be used. Provided the mental state is the thing that does such-and-such, and the thing that does such-and-such is a particular brain state, we can infer that the mental state is the brain state without worrying whether the claim from folk psychology about the mental state is analytic or synthetic. Of course, if what folk psychology says about the mind is just a synthetic claim about matters of fact, and in no way definitional, it might provide us with less guidance about what a mind could be like in conditions very different from the ones folk psychology is used to. Folk psychology might just be thought to be silent about aliens, angels, robots and so on. (At the very least, we would want some extra justification for extending our theory of ordinary human minds to the states of other creatures that apparently have minds.) If we take folk psychology to be a source of interesting analytic truths, then that might be useful epistemologically (if we are discovering definitions, which might be easier than checking factual claims about how human beings work), and it might be useful in other ways as well, but the central argument for Lewis's materialism seems to be able to survive without it.

Experiences and qualia

One challenge to materialist theories of the mind, particularly functionalist theories, comes from those who do not think these theories do justice to the felt quality of our experiences, how things feel, for example, or the character of sensation. Capturing the typical causes and effects of pain is one thing, but some think this leaves out another aspect: how it *feels*. Lewis resists this charge:

> Pain is a feeling. Surely that is uncontroversial ... A theory of
> what it is for a state to be pain is inescapably a theory of what it
> is like to be in that state, of how that state feels, of the phenom-
> enal character of that state. Far from ignoring questions of how
> states feel ... I have been discussing nothing else!
>
> ([1980b] 1983a: 130)

Experiences are the things that we feel, that are experienced in a
certain way. "What it is like" to have a state like being in pain is just
that: the state of being in pain. That is what we are aware of, that is
what produces the reactions in us. There is no need to have an extra
non-physical sensation-aspect to capture what it is like "from the
inside".

Philosophers of mind who worry about this experiential, phenom-
enal aspect of experiences (and of other mental activities with associated "feelings", like emotions, jolts of recollection, etc.) often call
these aspects of mental life "qualia". For various reasons some
philosophers suspect that materialists cannot do justice to qualia.[13]
Perhaps this charge was justified against the philosophical behaviourists. With their focus on behaviour and their neglect on the inner
workings of subjects, they would have little to say about the nature of
experience, a paradigm inner state. Lewis discusses two of the arguments anti-materialists have offered based on qualia.

The first is discussed in Lewis's "Should a Materialist Believe in
Qualia?" (1995). He suggests that there is one part of our folk-psychological attitude towards the character of experience that materialism
about the mind does not accommodate (or at least his version of materialism does not). Lewis thinks that it is part of our folk psychological
opinions that we can *identify* the subjective characters of experience
in a particularly strong sense; we know all there is to know about the
intrinsic nature of a quale, when we have it. That is, there is nothing
hidden or mysterious, or any way that what we know about "what it's
like" falls short of the full story of the qualia we experience. That is
not to say that we could *articulate* all of this knowledge. It is very difficult sometimes to put into words what our experiences are like. Nor
is it to say we automatically remember what we know when we
experience qualia. We might have forgotten exactly what sort of
experience it is when we are asked later whether another experience
is the same or slightly different, for example. Lewis called the thesis
that we are in a position to know our qualia in this strong, nothing-
left-unknown sense, the "identification thesis".

Materialism, Lewis argues, should reject the identification thesis. My current experience of blue or my current pain in the back may in fact be identical to some particular neural firing, and have the features that neural firing has, even if I am completely unaware of anything about neurology (and even if I am convinced that I am an immaterial soul, or otherwise completely reject materialism). So our having an experience doesn't tell us everything about the intrinsic properties of our experience, or put us in a position to distinguish the feeling of one sensation from any other. Nevertheless, Lewis thinks a materialist can believe in qualia, in the felt quality of experiences. It is just that qualia do not behave quite like folk psychology claimed they did. For a feature of experience to count as being a quale, it has to play enough of the role folk psychology assigns to qualia. But the material goings-on in our heads do play enough of the role to be experiences, even if the "identification thesis" is not true of them. They are what we are aware of when we reflect on our experiences, they are what we remember when we remember how we felt, and so on. ("Qualia" itself is, of course, a term of art, and it is difficult to say concisely exactly what they are supposed to be in an illuminating way, but Lewis thinks that our ordinary conception of the mind includes belief in them nevertheless.) Lewis admits there may be some vagueness or "semantic indecision" here. If a philosopher really wants to reserve "qualia" for supposed features of experience for which the identification thesis is true by definition, she may be within her rights, and if someone does so insist, Lewis will say *in that sense* there are no qualia. But in so far as there is an ordinary notion of qualia, Lewis thinks that what the materialist offers is good enough to satisfy it.

Some philosophers stress the identification thesis strongly: that what we know about pain "from the inside" exhausts what is to be known about its nature.[14] Some may think that Lewis does not do enough justice to this intuition, in which case they will think that qualia continue to be a problem for materialism. Other philosophers might well be sceptical that folk psychology is committed to anything as strong as the identification thesis. It may well be true that folk psychology tells us we can know a fair bit about the subjective nature of our experiences just by introspection – if I see green, I know what that seems like to me straight away – but many people will think that folk psychology is close to silent about how mental states are ultimately to be explained, and silent about what, if anything, is true about them that goes beyond the immediately obvious. If this is right, then Lewis has conceded too much to the "friends of qualia".[15] Theories

David Lewis

about qualia are speculative philosophical doctrines, not part of the common-sense understanding of the mind, these critics will charge. Of course, while these critics will disagree with Lewis's view of qualia, they are likely to be sympathetic to his defending materialism. If the identification thesis is merely a piece of speculative theory, then it does not matter so much if materialism rejects the existence of any objects that are supposed to satisfy the "identification thesis" by definition.

A more famous argument involving qualia that is supposed to cause trouble for materialism is Frank Jackson's "knowledge argument" (1982, 1986). We are supposed to discover some new fact when we have a new kind of experience, a fact about how that experience feels to us, or "what it's like". That new fact, according to this argument, is not one that can be communicated in other ways, or, at any rate, we could be informed of all the physical facts without having any knowledge of that fact. So qualia are a distinctive part of reality, not reducible to anything physical.

The example used by Jackson to motivate this argument is now famous in contemporary philosophical circles: "Black and White Mary", or Mary the colour scientist (Jackson 1986). Mary is brought up in a black and white room, and never sees any colours besides black, white and shades of grey. On the other hand, she is given as exhaustive an education in colour science as you like, through books and black and white television screens, with instructors, cameras placed wherever would be helpful, and all the rest. Mary eventually knows an incredible amount about human brains, optic nerves, optics, light reflection from objects, and all the physical facts relevant to colour. (Maybe no ordinary person could know all the facts in sufficient depth, but, for the sake of the example, we can assume Mary is superhumanly good at learning about the physical basis of colour and colour vision.) Then one day Mary is allowed to leave her black and white room, and sees a red apple. The intuition is, according to Jackson, that when Mary sees the apple for the first time she learns something new: she learns *what red looks like*. And that is something she could not have learnt in her room. Since she learned all the relevant physical facts in her room, the fact she learned is a new one. So there are facts about experience that go beyond the physical ones.

Lewis needs to deny that Mary learns some new fact: that there is some extra aspect of the world (or human experience) that is revealed to Mary when she first gazes on a red thing, and that is not described by a complete physical description of the occasion. (Lewis points out that this is a problem not just for materialists. Mary can read up as much as she likes about spirits, and non-physical aspects of reality, and anything else a non-materialist might believe in, and that still will not help her (Lewis [1988c] 1999a: 280–81).) Lewis's response[16] is to say that what Mary gains is not awareness of new facts, but a new set of *abilities*. Lewis says that here he is following Laurence Nemirow,[17] and this sort of response became known as the "Lewis–Nemirow response". She gains the ability to discriminate colours by sight. Before she may have known in theory which thing had which colour, but now that she has seen red, she can tell whether something is red just by looking. She also gains the ability to imagine and remember certain sorts of seeing, with a new way of representing that to herself. The basis for imagining a room visually might be different from the basis for imagining a room in terms of a linguistic description of the scene, even if the facts about the room would be the same in both cases. She also gains the ability to imagine similar sights. After a few different colour experiences, she may be able to imagine seeing arrangements of combinations that she has never in fact seen. This ability to use visual imagination in this way is something she lacked in the black and white room (although she could imagine in monochrome well enough, I expect), but this is a piece of know-how, and not a discovery about some previously hidden quality of the world.

In another place (1983a: 131–2), Lewis uses the analogy of a machine that has a database with information about shapes and also a pattern mould. The pattern mould stores templates of shapes that are presented to it in the right kind of way, and can stamp out copies of that shape. It could turn out that the machine does not share all the information between the database and the pattern mould; it may have records in the database that it cannot use to create new templates, and conversely it may have templates for shapes that were never entered into the database. Storing information about a shape in the pattern mould gives it an ability that it does not possess when the information is only in the database; it can stamp out copies with the mould, but not directly from the database. Nevertheless, it is tempting to say that the machine is storing the same information (shape information) in two different ways, and not that there is some special extra-physical aspect of shape that one of the machine's subsystems can recognize but the other cannot. A straightforward application of this analogy is that experience (visual experience of colours, experiences of tastes, or whatever) presents physical facts in distinctive ways. In principle we could find out what we find out from looking at a coloured scene by engaging in intensive lessons in physics and neurobiology, but the appearance of learning something qualitatively different comes from the information reaching us in a very different way. Lewis himself seems more cautious about explaining away the plausibility of Mary gaining new information by appealing to the "same information, different way of presenting it" story. In "What Experience Teaches", Lewis seems to treat this explanation as a speculative supplement to the "new abilities" explanation:

> If the causal basis for these abilities [the new ones gained by experience] turns out also to be a special kind of representation of some sort of information, so be it. We need only deny that it represents a special kind of information about a special subject matter ... Treating the ability-conferring trace as a representation is optional. What's essential is that when we learn what an experience is like by having it, we gain abilities to remember, imagine and recognize. ([1988c] 1999a: 290)

Lewis's theory of mind, then, treats minds as complicated physical phenomena. What is essential to a mind is what it does: the dispositions to behave that it has, and how it causes behaviour as a result of causal inputs. Furthermore, a crucial part of Lewis's argument for his theory is conceptual. It is something like an analytic truth that mental states have such-and-such roles (or perhaps have such-and-such roles in typical members of a population), and it is this analytic truth that gives us the starting-point for determining which states in fact are mental states for creatures like us. There does not need to be any trace of the supernatural or irreducibly mental in Lewis's picture of our mental states, including the felt nature of our experiences.

Chapter 6

Representation and mental content

Chapter 5 dealt with Lewis's theory of what the mind is, and how to identify mental states with physical states. This chapter also deals with part of the theory of mind: what is it for a mental state to *mean* something, to be *about* an aspect of the world? What makes my belief that dolphins live in the ocean *that* sort of belief, rather than a belief that dolphins live in mountains (or, for that matter, rather than the belief that there are eggs in my fridge)? In turn, armed with an account of what it is for a mental state to have a "content" (that is, a meaning, or a specification of what it is about), we shall be in a position to tackle the question in Chapter 7: what is it for a piece of language, or some communicative act, to have a meaning or be about something? What makes the pattern of ink marks "wombat" be about a certain kind of small mammal rather than about the ocean or cosmic radiation? Some people try to tackle the question about language and public meaning first, and only then turn to the question of mental content. Lewis's account of language use, on the other hand, relies on being able to make antecedent sense of the beliefs, desires and intentions of speakers; so it relies on there being an adequate answer to questions about what gives these beliefs, desires and intentions their content.

A central kind of mental representation according to folk psychology is the kind of representation that is called a "propositional attitude". Central cases are the kinds of beliefs and desires that are specified by "that" clauses. One example would be the belief that dolphins live in the ocean. Another would be the desire that December be warmer than July. These "beliefs that" and "desires that" seem to have contents that can be true or false. A belief that dolphins live in the ocean is *true* if and only if dolphins live in the ocean. We do not talk about desires being true or false in this sense, but there is an equivalent, some kind of notion of satisfaction of a desire. The desire that December be warmer than July is *satisfied* if December is warmer than July, and *unsatisfied* otherwise. (This satisfaction may not necessarily bring with it any kind of emotion. In this thin sense of satisfaction, having one's desires satisfied does not necessarily involve any *feeling* of satisfaction.) So while it may not make much sense to say a desire is true or false, the content of the desire can be assessed for truth or falsehood.

We have many other words that describe propositional attitudes besides "belief" and "desire". I can hope that it will rain, or fear that a snake will bite me, or pretend that I am the King of Mars, or think that elephants are big, or intend that I will not get wet, or judge that I will get wet and so on. Perhaps all of these other propositional attitudes can be analysed in terms of beliefs and desires, perhaps sometimes in combination. We also have ways of talking about many mental states that describe them as being about something but not by supplying "that" clauses: I can want an ice cream, or believe my informants, or feel heat on my arm. Ice cream, informants and heat are not the sorts of things that are true or false (in the sense that propositions are, at least), but nevertheless we seem to have mental states that are about ice cream, informants and heat here.[1] Again, perhaps we can understand all of these in terms of propositional attitudes (wanting an ice cream might be desiring that I have an ice cream, to take a relatively easy example). Lewis does not deal at any length with the question of whether all of this variation could be dealt with through analyses into beliefs and desires. He leaves it an open question ([1994b] 1999a: 308), although his focus on beliefs and desires suggests he thinks these two are the primary content-filled states he is concerned to explain.

What is a mental content?

The contents of these propositional attitudes represent ways the world can be or fail to be. From this comes the popular idea that we specify the meaning of a belief or a desire by supplying a *truth-condition*: by specifying the conditions under which the content is true or not. There are a variety of attempts to explain what a truth-condition is. One of them is the idea that a truth-condition is a function from possible worlds to truth-values. That is, we have two truth-values, true and false (which we may represent as 1 and 0, or, as I shall represent them here, T and F), and a function that associates each possible world with either T or F. The truth-condition associated with "some dogs bark", for example, would be a function that took each possible world where some dogs bark to T, and all of the rest of the possible worlds to F. My belief that some dogs bark is somehow associated with this truth-condition rather than another one, some other truth-condition such as the one associated with "some cats bark", for example. Whether a belief is true, then, would depend on two things: which truth-condition it expresses, and also which world it is in. The truth-condition for "some dogs bark" associates the actual world with T, but (as far as I know) the one associated with "some cats bark" associates our world with F.

A truth-condition, on this way of thinking, is just something that is true according to some worlds and not according to others. Once we have specified the function from worlds to truth-values, we have completely characterized it. It simply draws a distinction between possible worlds: the ones associated with T, and the ones associated with F. Equivalently, we could specify a truth-condition just by providing the set of worlds associated with T. If the divisions are exhaustive, then all and only the worlds not associated with T will be associated with F. In fact, if we characterize a truth-condition just with a set of worlds, then T and F can drop out of the picture; we do not have to find some special object to be "the true" and another to be "the false". This is one way of introducing the notion of a proposition as a set of possible worlds. The proposition that "some dogs bark" is the set of possible worlds where dogs bark. We can represent the contents of thought as being sets of possible worlds: intuitively, the worlds where the relevant belief would be true, or the relevant desire would be satisfied.

There are some advantages to representing the contents of beliefs as sets of possible worlds, rather than, for example, sentences in some privileged language. One advantage is that there may not be a sentence for each content of our thought. English, for example, seems badly equipped to capture every possible shade of opinion or nuance of desire (even if we somehow had enough self-knowledge and were so articulate that we could try to express all the detail of our thought in words). Another advantage is that it makes relationships of implication and compatibility easy to describe. The contents of two beliefs are compatible, for example, if they overlap. That is, there is some world included in both of the contents, so some world where they are

David Lewis

both true. The content of one belief *implies* the content of the other if the first is a sub-set of the second. The content associated with "some dogs bark and some cats howl" is the set of worlds where dogs bark and cats howl, and that set will be a sub-set, for example, of the set of worlds where some dogs bark. Making a proposition more informative, in this way of thinking about propositions, is a matter of ruling out possibilities. The more worlds I can exclude from the content of my beliefs, the more opinionated I am.[2]

Another advantage of treating content this way is that it is neutral on the question of what form the actual mental representations must take. A linguistic model of mental representation lends itself to thinking that there is a "language of thought", that representations in the brain themselves have linguistic structure. While Lewis thinks that the "language of thought hypothesis" is a respectable empirical conjecture,[3] he does not think it is part of the analysis of content. While one can have a linguistic conception of content without endorsing the language of thought (Donald Davidson is one example), a non-linguistic conception of content might seem more neutral.

Treating the content of beliefs and desires as propositions, and treating propositions as sets of possible worlds, is the starting-point for Lewis's theory of mental content. (This is a conception of propositions Lewis shares with Montague (1974), Stalnaker (1984), and many others.) However, these propositions do not have quite the range we want contents to have. The problem is that they leave out a "point of view" on a world, which can make an important difference.

For illustration, imagine that you are locked in a prison cell with two doors.[4] Through one door is freedom and through the other the hangman awaits. Since you are cautious when facing such a decision you look around the cell for any hint about what lies outside. You are in luck. You find a huge encyclopedia (or maybe a computer workstation with a "Total World Encyclopedia" installed). Hungry for information you begin to look through it. You find out that it is describing the entire world in very fine detail, and you are excited when you read about a prisoner, with your name, in a prison cell just like yours, and you find the encyclopedia tells you that for that prisoner, freedom is through the door on the left and the hangman through the one on the right.

Unfortunately, when you read further, you find the story of another prisoner, at the other end of the same prison. He or she too is in a prison cell just like yours, and also faces two doors. That prisoner (who also has your name) will be free if they go through the door on the right and will be hanged if they leave by the door on the left.

138

No matter how thoroughly you scan the encyclopedia, you cannot find an asymmetry between the two prisoners (the other prisoner is also frantically perusing an encyclopedia, trying to work out which cell is which). Even if you find out every objective fact about the world, there is still one piece of information missing: which prisoner is *you*? You can find out as much as you like about the prisoners, and your duplicate is described in the same terms by the encyclopedia. You could, in principle, know the complete objective description of the world – where every prisoner, hangman, prison cell, and everything else is – but it would not be enough to tell you which twin is which. What you need to know is more than what is true of the world you are in. You need to know where you are in the world.

There are other examples that show that knowing something about someone is often different from knowing something about yourself. If you know that Subject 17 of a certain experiment is about to develop cancer, you may well feel sorry for them. But if you find out that Subject 17 is *you*, your reaction may well be quite different. There are other examples where ignorance is a matter of one's location, and not anything about what the world is like. Suppose when you went to bed at 10pm you knew you were in for a bout of insomnia from 2am to 5am. You wake up in your darkened room and lie awake, futilely trying to get to sleep, or trying to think of something to do about your insomnia, or whatever. After a while you wonder what time it is. What kind of fact do you want to know, when you want to know what time it is? For Lewis, there is no "privileged present". Different stages of a person exist at different times, and the "present" for a stage is the time it exists at. So in principle you could know everything about how your night of insomnia will go. Perhaps your thoughts will circle fruitlessly, or perhaps you will keep trying to count sheep and lose count after a while. Nevertheless, in the early hours of the morning there will be something important that you do not know if there is no way to check the time. (Have you just thought the thoughts you were going to think at 3am, or have you thought them again at 4.20am? You wish you had not lost track. And you also wish you were at 4.20am rather than 3.00am, so the sleeplessness will be over sooner.) You could know everything about what order events will occur in and still not know when you are in that order.

This extra information, besides objective information about what the world is like, is what is called *de se* information ("of the self") (see Lewis 1979a). When I discover something "*de se*", I discover something about how I am located, or what I am like. Most information we gain through sensation is *de se* in the first instance. Not only do I notice that there is a cup on a table, but I notice that there is a cup on a table in front of *me*. A plane passes overhead (over *me*, or close to over me); a smell of smoke means there are traces of smoke *here*, that is, traces of smoke where *I* am. When I feel a pain, I do not just discover that there is some pain out there, I discover that *I* have it. A lot of information we get is also associated with a time ("*de nunc*" meaning "of now"): it is raining *now*, or I am standing *now*. (Or a pain is past, before *now*, or an expected show has not yet happened, it happens after *now*.) Lewis's own view of people allows us to understand *de nunc* information as a special case of *de se* information. Since we have different time slices at different times, finding out what is happening now is like what is happening at the same time as *this* time slice: which time slice *I* am, if we think of momentary thinkers as time slices rather than long-lived people. For those who do not believe people are made up of short-lived time slices, *de nunc* information needs to be included in the "location" information along with *de se* information.

So we need to be able to represent an opinion not just by providing a set of worlds, but also a location in each world, and not just a range of possibilities for how the world as a whole is, but also who in that world is me. (In the case of the unlucky prisoners above, they may be very sure which world they are in – they know enough to rule out nearly every other possible way the world is – but unfortunately they have no way to choose between two alternative individuals in that world, to be able to tell which individual is them, and which is the other prisoner.) Lewis thinks the way to do this is to represent mental content with a set of individuals – a set of what he calls "doxastic alternatives" or "doxastic counterparts" – the set of people one could be, given a belief. So my belief that I am more than four feet tall has as its content the set of possible people taller than four feet in height. My belief that I do not have red hair has as its content the set of non-red-haired people. My total opinion about myself can be represented by a set of possible individuals as well: the set of possible people who are all as I think I am. They will still differ in all sorts of ways that I have no opinion about; some will have an even number of hairs, some an odd number, and since I'm a bit hazy about where in my torso my liver can be found, different doxastic counterparts will vary with respect to where their livers are. Likewise, the total of my desires of how I want myself to be can be represented by a set of possible individuals, one that does not overlap with the set associated with my belief, alas! Nobody's perfect, and I don't even *believe* that I am perfect.

Lewis argues that this "location" information can serve all the purposes we want. We do not need to characterize some beliefs with a set of doxastic alternatives, and another kind with a set of possible worlds. For any belief about the world can be represented as a *de se* belief (Lewis 1979a). The belief that elephants never forget, for example, can be represented as the *de se* belief that *I exist in a world where* elephants never forget. Beliefs about specific objects (*de re* beliefs, meaning "of a thing") can also be represented, Lewis thinks, as *de se* beliefs. The belief that Henry VIII had six wives can be represented as the belief that I am in a world where someone who is related in thus-and-so ways to me had six wives. The relations may well include such features as there being a causal transmission of names from Henry's baptism, to historians' reports about him, to my use of an expression "Henry VIII". If Lewis is right, *de re* attitudes can be viewed as special cases of *de se* attitudes.

This enabled Lewis to give a unified account of the contents of "propositional" attitudes such as beliefs and desires. Instead of sets of worlds, Lewis uses sets of individuals to be the contents of beliefs and desires. The belief that I am hungry is represented by the set of possible individuals who are hungry. The belief that monkeys climb trees is represented by the set of possible individuals who live in worlds where monkeys climb trees. The desire to be famous (i.e. that the desirer be famous) is represented by the set of famous possible individuals. The desire to own the *Mona Lisa* is given by the set of people who own an object with such-and-such relations to them (e.g. is a painting in their world, has a causal chain running from its naming to their use of "Mona Lisa", etc.). The advantage of doing things this way is that it handles *de se* beliefs and desires in a unified way with other beliefs and desires, something that the content-as-sets-of-possible-world account has trouble with. If many beliefs (e.g. perceptual beliefs) and many desires ("self-centred" desires in the usual sense) are *de se*, having a single account that handles them and other beliefs and desires is very convenient.

Sometimes Lewis characterizes his view of mental content as a view according to which mental contents are *properties* rather than propositions. After all, for Lewis, properties are sets of possible objects (see Chapter 3), and so the set of individuals who are associated with one of my beliefs, or with one of my desires, gives us a property. In the case of belief, I self-ascribe the property (I think the property is one that *I* have, whether it is being hungry or being in a world where monkeys climb trees), and in the case of desires, I desire that I have the property in question (the property of being famous, or owning a painting related thus-and-so to me, or whatever). This can provide the material for an alternative account of mental content for those who adopt some alternative account of properties. They could say that mental contents are properties as conceived of in their account, rather than as conceived of in Lewis's. This will only be feasible if the conception of properties is *abundant* enough: if there are enough properties to go around. Conversely, Lewis's theory of mental content gives him another good reason to think that there must be abundant properties, and not merely sparse ones (see Chapter 1 for the distinction).

Impossible contents

If we construe the content of mental states as sets of possible worlds, or as sets of possible individuals as Lewis does, there is a natural story available about what our beliefs taken together *implicitly* represent. Whatever the storage medium in the brain, almost certainly there are many things we would want to say someone believes that they do not have explicitly coded in their head. You probably believe that penguins are shorter than zebras, although I suspect you had never consciously considered the question until you read that sentence. It is also very plausible that you believed that penguins were shorter than zebras even before you read that sentence. Even if you had never considered the question before, it is not as if you reasoned your way to a new discovery, or that you would not have been able to make judgements about what a black-and-white animal was that you had a quick glimpse of. You would not have judged something zebra-height to be a penguin, or vice versa.

It may be that ordinary belief attributions typically ascribe contents that are only implicit in the brain's storage. Some methods of information representation allow for division into pieces, each of which represent discrete pieces of information on their own, but others are limited in this respect. Maps cannot be cut into sentence-sized pieces of information for some sorts of information they convey (such as relative distances), and holograms are very difficult to break into topic-demarcated chunks. The unit of representation in the brain may not be able to be divided into sub-representations particularly easily. The more this is so, the more we need a story about how there can be more propositions represented than there are representationally significant physical pieces of brain. (In this section I shall talk about propositions for simplicity, rather than the properties/sets of possible individuals, which are Lewis's preferred contents. A similar story will work for these, but it is harder to present succinctly.)

The natural thing to say is that a set of beliefs implicitly represents any proposition that is entailed by the set of beliefs together. If we take propositions to be sets of worlds, and say that what it is for a proposition to be true at a world is for that world to be a member of the proposition, then, for example, the proposition that trees have leaves is the set of all worlds where trees have leaves, and so it is true at just those worlds in that set; that is, it is true at any world where trees have leaves, and no other worlds, which is what we would have expected. One proposition p will thus entail another proposition q just in case p is a sub-set of q. The set of worlds where trees have green leaves is a sub-set of the set of worlds where trees have leaves, and if the first is true at a world (includes a world), the second is true at that world too.

While this story is simple it has a few odd consequences. One is that we implicitly believe *every* proposition that necessarily follows from the ones we believe. This can seem psychologically implausible, since it is often true that people do not seem to realize things that in fact follow from everything else they believe; logic puzzles are not that easy to solve. A related odd consequence is that propositions that are necessarily equivalent – that is, that imply each other – count as the same proposition. When two propositions are necessarily equivalent, after all, then in any world where one is true the other is true as well, so they will be identical to the same set of possible worlds. It does seem possible, though, to believe that something is a triangle without believing that it is a polygon with internal angles that add up to 180 degrees; while either implies the other, not everyone who believes one believes the other. Things are even worse when we come to the "necessary a posteriori". It may be a necessary truth that water is composed of H_2O molecules, or that Karl is Charlemagne (since both "Karl" and "Charlemagne" are names of the same man, and that guy is necessarily self-identical). Lewis had things to say about *de re* belief, but they are complex (1981b; [1979a] 1983a: 152–6; esp. 1986a: 32–6). So I merely note the problem here as one that calls for an answer.[5]

Another odd consequence concerns impossible beliefs. An impossibility, such as the contradiction that it is both raining and not raining in the same place at the same time, is true at no possible worlds at all. It corresponds to a set with no worlds as members: the null set. It is a sub-set of any other set of worlds, and so entails every other proposition in this system. But it seems that we can believe something impossible without implicitly believing everything. Someone who is in a hurry and confused might both believe it is raining outside (they may be able to hear it, for example), but also believe that it is not raining outside (they leave their umbrella on the table because they think they will not need it). But this person is not so confused that they implicitly believe everything.

Other cases make it even more plausible that we sometimes have mutually inconsistent beliefs. Lewis cites an example of his own. He used to believe that the railway line and Nassau Street in Princeton were roughly parallel, but that the railway line ran north–south and the street ran east–west ([1982] 1998: 103–4). He held these beliefs separately, and one day realized that they did not make sense together, but before he realized and revised them, he had beliefs that were mutually inconsistent. However, that did not mean that he believed any proposition whatsoever.

There are also inconsistent beliefs that take a good deal of work to demonstrate. Sometimes a mathematical conjecture is believed, but then eventually proved to be inconsistent. Sometimes a complicated physical theory, especially one that blends theories from different areas, is inconsistent as formulated. The discovery that there was a lurking inconsistency prompts revision, but it does not usually lead the theorists to suppose that those who accepted the theory believed every proposition whatsoever.

Lewis's suggestion for dealing with impossible beliefs is "fragmentation": representing someone's beliefs with two or more assignments of content. So, for example, in the Nassau Street/railway line case, we can partition Lewis's beliefs into two consistent chunks: one according to which the railway line runs north–south and Nassau Street east–west, and another according to which they are parallel (but that does not say very much about the common direction the two take). We may even find it convenient to divide them further. If he had no inclination to put the direction beliefs together to conclude that the street and railway line were orthogonal, perhaps the belief about the street's direction, the belief about the railway line's direction, and the belief that they were parallel should all be assigned to different total assignments of content. Suppose we have some agent whose beliefs are "quarantined" in this way. There are several total assignments of content we can offer, each of which is inconsistent with its rivals. What are we to say about what the agent believes?

Anything that the agent believes according to *all* the assignments of content should count as something they believe. According to all the alternatives we could ascribe to Lewis, he counts as believing that Nassau Street is in Princeton, so that is something we can safely count him as believing. If we wanted to be restrictive, we could insist that these are the only things he counts as believing, and any of the contested propositions could be counted as things about which his beliefs were indeterminate. But on a more generous conception, we could count among the things he believes anything true according to *at least one* of his alternative belief contents (1982). On that conception, he counts as having inconsistent beliefs. He believes that the street is east–west, the railway line is north–south, and that they are parallel (plus some obvious things about how directions work and what it is to be parallel). For some believers, there might be quite a lot that differs between their partitions. Someone in the throws of a conversion, for example, might behave rather erratically. If Kristy both believes that many of her pastimes are innocent pleasures, *and* that they are corrupting influences controlled by the devil, it may be hard to know how she will react when, for example, she is in the room with the television, or has a choice between gardening and praying, but her behaviour may still be explained by assuming that she has these two inconsistent ways of looking at the world simultaneously. I suppose we could try explaining her behaviour – throwing away the television remote control, but later watching television, dramatically burning gardening catalogues, but still watering her plants – as her having rapid changes of belief. But in the sense in which we normally ascribe people beliefs even if they are not currently doing anything relevant (the sense in which I believe I own leather shoes, even when I'm not wearing them or thinking about them), we may be inclined to ascribe to her both sets of views, and say rather that which beliefs get *manifested* can switch rapidly. After all, we are accustomed to thinking that some people have blindspots or inconsistencies in their political or religious beliefs, and we often want to think their beliefs are inconsistent (even if the different parts of the inconsistent whole tend to manifest at different times) rather than say that they are consistent, but just rapidly shifting between consistent total alternatives.

This conception of belief allows that someone can have inconsistent beliefs without thereby believing everything. On this conception, someone can even have inconsistent beliefs without believing their conjunction. In Lewis's example, he does not believe that Nassau Street and the railway line are parallel and not-parallel. The belief that they are "parallel and not-parallel" is not one that is true according to any of the fragmented contents. (The logic for belief that corresponds to Lewis's conception is "non-adjunctive", according to which "*p* and *q*" does not automatically follow from the two premises *p* and *q* together).[6] Our beliefs might consist of several different consistent sub-systems (why suppose our brains always integrate every piece of information we have with every other piece?), and as well as helping deal with inconsistent beliefs, this story may also help explain some of the cases where we do not believe every entailment of our beliefs, even when our beliefs are consistent.

Suppose we are solving a murder mystery where we have a long list of clues. We have a list of suspects, a list of pieces of information about the murder weapon, and perhaps a list of locations where the murder could have taken place (this sort of puzzle will be familiar to people who have played *Cluedo*). Even after we have enough information to rule out all the suspects but one, we may not immediately realize who the murderer must be. It takes considerable thought and care to realize how all the evidence fits together, and to make sure we have not overlooked an option. If the clues are represented in different sub-systems of our overall beliefs, then that could explain why we do not effortlessly put the information together. We may know that the professor did not do the murder with the rope, and also that if the murder happened in the kitchen it was done with the rope, and that the murder happened in the kitchen, but miss the fact that this means that the Professor did not do the murder. While we have each piece of information in some sub-system, until we integrate them into one their joint implication is not believed. This fragmentation story can be part of the story about why we are not "logically omniscient": why we do not automatically believe everything that follows from our beliefs.

The fragmentation story does have its limitations, however. While it deals with someone who has several beliefs that are not jointly consistent reasonably well, it does not seem to handle cases of single explicitly self-contradictory beliefs. Some people believe that some liar paradox sentences ("This sentence is not true") are both true and not-true. (If the sentence is true, it's not-true, and if it's not true, since that's what it says, it had better be true.)[7] Regardless of whether this view of the liar paradox is correct, it is believed, and believed by people who do not thereby believe everything. (They do not believe that they are ten-metre tall walruses, for example.) However, it is difficult to divide their beliefs into consistent sub-beliefs. (Consider their belief "some propositions are both true and not-true".) Another problem is that sometimes people seem to act in a way that is explained by the mixture of their beliefs, but which cannot be broken into sub-actions each of which can be explained by one of the sub-systems. Take Kristy, the woman torn between believing that her pastimes are temptations from the devil and that they are healthy innocent pleasures. Suppose we find her deciding to watch the television, but only for half an hour. The system where she is convinced the television is the devil's work does not explain why she is watching the television, and the system where she thinks watching television is a harmless pleasure does not explain why she would restrict herself to half an hour, so we may suppose. Perhaps this example could be explained away in other ways. Maybe we could postulate a third system where it did make sense to watch television, but only for half an hour, or maybe we could invoke some sort of irrationality or weakness of will to explain how the action made sense on one of the fragments or on the other. But if the fragments regularly interact to produce actions and further beliefs that do not make sense according to any of the fragments taken individually, we may need something stronger than Lewis's "compartmentalization" story. A final point to note is that the compartmentalization story will not help with some kinds of logical omniscience. Automatic belief in all necessary truths, for example, will not be able to be avoided by compartmentalization, since a necessary truth is implied by any proposition whatsoever, and so all the necessary truths will be implied by any compartmentalization, no matter how impoverished.

Attitudes that come in degrees

As I mentioned in Chapter 5, Lewis allows that we have "degrees of partial belief", or *credences*. Obviously, desires can also come in degrees. We want some things more than other things, and we can hope to measure this by assigning *values* to desired contents. Credences, as was mentioned in Chapter 5, are typically assigned a number between 0 and 1 (inclusive). A credence of 1 is assigned to things that are absolutely certain, and 0 to things that are absolutely certainly false. (Whether we *should* ever assign credences of 1 or 0 is an interesting point. Perhaps we are never entitled to be that dogmatic. But standard probability theory says we should assign these extreme credences at least to logical truths and logical falsehoods, respectively.) Values also get assigned numbers, but usually these are allowed to take any finite value, positive or negative. That is, we can *disvalue* an alternative by giving it a value less than zero, and there

David Lewis

is no assumption in general that values only get figures between 0 and 1; values of 10, 1000 or 10^{500} might be assigned to different propositions.

Lewis wrote several papers on decision theory,[8] but his decision-theory framework was for the most part fairly orthodox (e.g. as in Jeffrey 1983). There are a few differences worth noting, however. One is that Lewis allows for *infinitesimal* credences: credences with a non-zero value that are, however, so small that they are smaller than any positive real number (see, for example, Lewis ([1980c] 1986b: 88)). This is to cover cases where there are infinitely many alterna-tives, and someone thinks they all deserve some non-zero credence. Lewis does not ever give the details of how this modification would be carried out, and it faces significant technical and philosophical concerns. A more interesting departure is that Lewis was one of the defenders of a variant of normal decision theory called "causal deci-sion theory". Orthodox decision theory says that what decision is rational for an agent depends on their credences about what will be true if they pick one of a range of alternatives, and how much they value what will happen when they pick one of the options. The agent should pick whichever option has the best "expected utility". The expected utility of an action is the sum of the expected utility of each possible outcome of that action, which in turn is generated by multi-plying their credence in each possible outcome, given a decision, with the value of that outcome, given the decision. Causal decision theory differs from this by saying that when we calculate the value to maxi-mize (which they may call expected utility, as in ordinary decision theory, although Lewis prefers to call it expected value, to avoid confusion), instead of evaluating the overall expected utility of an outcome, we should only calculate the expected utility of what the action will bring about, or cause. The difference is that sometimes an action will be *evidence* of something outside the agent's control and, when it is, its performance will be "bad news" for the agent, even though it does not make things any worse for that agent.

Consider an example. Bob wakes up one morning with partial amnesia, shards of glass on his clothing, and cuts on his hands and arms. Both hands are injured, but the left one is particularly painful. Bob assumes that he has been in some sort of accident, and is under-standably puzzled. In automatic pilot, he goes and turns on the radio and his coffee machine. He is just about to wash the blood off his hands, when he hears on the radio that last night security cameras caught someone punching the windows of shops in Bob's neighbourhood. Bob

148

panics. Could he somehow have been doing that? His mind races. Had he been drinking, or taking drugs, or is he ill? He wishes he could remember. Listening further, he hears that analysis of the security camera footage reveals that whoever smashed the shop windows was right-handed (and looks male, and roughly Bob's height), although the police have not yet worked out who it was. At this stage Bob *very much* wants it to not be him who broke the shop windows. He would feel terribly guilty, and he could be caught, which would be humiliating and might lead to him losing his job. Bob is scared. He returns to the sink to wash his hands, and faces a decision.

This is probably not a very significant decision, but Bob has to decide which hand to turn the tap on with. He cannot remember which hand he normally uses. He does remember the tap requires some coordination to operate and he does not want to use his "off" hand, especially with his hands injured. If he turns out to be ambidextrous (or if handedness didn't matter), though, he'd slightly prefer to use his right hand, since it is less badly injured. It seems that he should try his right hand first, right?

There is a problem, though. There is some tendency for right-handed people to use their right hands for tasks like this, and if Bob is right-handed, then it makes it more likely that he broke the shop windows last night (in the sense that if he discovers he is right-handed, he would be rational to give a higher credence to the claim that he broke the windows). Using his right hand on the tap would be some evidence that he broke the windows, and that would be *very bad news*. The expected utility of his using his right hand might be lower than using his left, since it is more likely he broke the windows if he is right-handed, and using his right hand makes it more probable that he is right-handed. Orthodox decision theory says that this should be part of the considerations when we decide what would be rational for Bob to do. It makes a difference to the expected utility of using his right hand versus using his left.[9]

However, this line of reasoning seems very odd. While evidence about Bob's handedness makes a difference to what credence he should have that he was the window-breaker, it seems silly to risk hurting himself more than he needs to (by trying his left hand first) just to avoid this bad news. Whether or not he broke the windows is not *causally* influenced by what he does this morning, so whether or not an action will make it more plausible to Bob that he did the breaking should not make a difference to his decisions in the same way that, for example, taking a risk of a future window-breaking might. Causal decision theory says that when Bob is choosing between his alternatives, he should pay attention only to the comparative value of the outcomes that can be *caused* by his decision and how likely they are. Whether the decisions are *evidence* of something now out of his control (such as what he did last night) should be irrelevant.

Causal decision theory makes a difference in some real-life cases. For example, when some behaviour is correlated with having a disease. If the behaviour is a cause of the disease people have a good reason to stop it, although if it is a mere symptom they do not have the same reason to avoid it, even though, in both cases, the probability that they have the disease given that they engage in the behaviour is higher than the probability that they have the disease if they do not engage in the behaviour. It also sheds light on some philosophical puzzles in decision theory, such as Newcomb's paradox and the prisoner's dilemma.[10]

The final way Lewis extends standard decision theory is that he thinks that the degree of credence associated with a belief (or value associated with a desire) can often be indeterminate, to a limited extent. Many people have thought it was artificial to ascribe exact numerical values to credences. (What's the difference between believing something with 0.3033 credence and 0.3034 credence?) Even some of the qualitative judgements about strength of credence or value can seem artificially precise. Perhaps there is just no fact of the matter about whether I'm more sure that the Lincoln car is still in production than that Ecuador produces silver (two things I'm currently not very sure about). Sometimes there seem to be determinate relations between different credences that in themselves seem indeterminate. Mary may be pretty unsure whether Jane (her friend in another city) is asleep, and also pretty unsure about whether Jane's eyes are currently shut, but confident that the conditional probability of Jane's eyes being shut, given that she is asleep, is very high. Similar points can be made about what someone desires. Sometimes it will be definite which of two options someone prefers, although not very definite how valuable each of the options is compared with most of the alternatives; and in other cases there may be a great deal of unclarity both about whether one option is preferable to another, and whether either option is particularly desirable.

One way to try to capture this vagueness and indeterminacy is to adopt a weaker theory of credences and valuations, to give them much less structure than they have by being assigned precise numerical values. Another way to represent this indeterminacy is to represent someone's credences and valuations with a range of precise credence–valuation pairs, and say that something is true about someone's credences if it is true according to all the pairs associated with the person, false if it is false according to all the pairs, and indeterminate otherwise.[11] For example, suppose I am fairly confident that the light in the next room will go on if I flip the switch in front of me (but I cannot directly see the light). My credence that the light will go on next door when I flip the switch might lie in a range between 0.8 and 0.999 (I'm not so confident that I'd bet much money that I was right). If so, it is true that I give more than 0.5 credence, false that I give credence 1, and indeterminate whether I have a credence above 0.9.

Sometimes conditional credences will be determinate, or fairly determinate, even when the unconditional credences are not. Mary's confidence that Jane is asleep might be indeterminate in the entire range from 0.05 up to 0.95 (if she really has very little opinion), and her confidence that Jane's eyes are closed might be about as indeterminate. Nevertheless, perhaps every total precise assignment of credence to Mary may give her a conditional credence of 1 of Jane's eyes being shut on Jane's being asleep. (More realistically, there may be a narrow range around 1, if Mary is not dogmatic). Treating beliefs and desires this way is one natural way of fleshing out Lewis's rather more vague remarks in *On the Plurality of Worlds* (1986a: 30), where he discusses indeterminacy of beliefs (and presumably he would say something similar about desires). It is an application of the method of "supervaluations" to probability assignments.[12] We shall see this approach to indeterminacy of representation again in Chapter 7, where we come to the meaning of words and other linguistic items.

What counts as having one content rather than another?

Since Lewis is a materialist, whether or not someone counts as believing or desiring something (or believing or desiring to a certain degree) is a matter of how they are, specifiable, in principle, in physical terms. So what gives a belief or a desire one content rather than another must ultimately be determined by physical facts about a person and their environment. As we saw in Chapter 5, Lewis thinks that what mental states someone has is a matter of their functional organization. Mental states are physical states with the right sort of causal role; they conform, well enough, to what folk psychology implicitly tells us about what a pain is, or what it is to believe something, and so on.

Lewis tells the same sort of story about what it is for a belief (or partial belief) to have a specific content; a belief or desire counts as having a certain content because of what it is typically caused by, and what it typically causes. Since what someone will do, or how a sensation will affect someone, depends on a range of beliefs and desires they have, assigning content to beliefs and desires will be a somewhat holistic process. An agent will have an overall belief profile and overall desire profile (or more precisely, a set of credences and a set of valuations) in virtue of the agent's overall dispositions to behave, especially in response to causal inputs (such as sensations). In fact, the assignment of an overall distribution of credence and an overall distribution of utilities may have no particularly privileged division into particular items of belief or desire: "beliefs" and "desires" may be words that are "bogus plurals" (see Chapter 5).

One problem with trying to fix someone's beliefs and desires entirely in terms of their dispositions to behave (or the causal roles of their internal states) is that many different combinations of beliefs and desires might produce the same dispositions to behave. We may be able to map a sensible set of beliefs and desires onto a crazy set. Someone might buy a vanilla ice cream and take a bite because they believe that way they will eat vanilla ice cream, which is something that want to do; or someone might do the same thing if they want to eat a hotdog and believe that they are under hypnosis to see hot-dogs as vanilla ice creams; or because they hate eating vanilla ice cream and they want to punish themselves. And while we cannot fully explain someone's dispositions in practice, so it is hard to give examples of complete belief–desire combinations with different content but with the same dispositions to act, it may be that there is more than one combination of beliefs and desires that could be invoked to explain a complete range of dispositions.

Lewis allows that there may be some indeterminacy about what people believe and desire (the point is related to the point made about indeterminacy of someone's credence and value functions, above). But he also thinks there are constraints that can make a difference between assignments of content that would both explain the same behaviour. One is a constraint Lewis called the "rationalization principle" ([1974a] 1983a: 113). Assignments of content to beliefs and desires are to be preferred when they make their bearer largely rational. So an assignment of content is preferred if, according to it, the person typically attempts to satisfy their beliefs given their desires instead of, for example, always choosing some less desirable outcome or ignoring what they believe, when trying to decide what to do. (People may fail to act rationally sometimes, especially when they are emotional, tired or sick, but not all the time.) Lewis thinks there are other constraints of rationality as well: there is a "modicum of rationality in our acting, believing and desiring" that would rule out, for example, "a bedrock craving for a saucer of mud" (an example Lewis cites from G. E. M. Anscombe in Lewis ([1994b] 1999a: 320)). There are principles of theoretical rationality about "which hypotheses we find credible prior to evidence, hence which hypotheses are easily confirmed when their predictions come true" (*ibid.*). A system of beliefs and desires must satisfy these criteria. If one satisfies these better than the alternatives, given a behavioural profile and all other things being equal, then the better one will be true of the agent instead of the worse ones (or instead of indeterminacy between the different assignments of content).

At one stage at least ([1974a] 1983a: 112), Lewis also followed Davidson[13] in thinking that an assignment could do better by the "principle of charity": everything else being equal, an assignment of belief contents should be preferred if it assigned beliefs closer to the truth than its rivals. That is more or less Davidson's version, but Lewis wants to allow for more error than that. Sometimes people are in situations where it would be more rational of them to believe something false (for example, if unbeknown to them they were being presented with misleading evidence). Lewis suggests that perhaps systems should be preferred that ascribe to people methods for coming to beliefs like ours. (This may be similar to the rationalization principle, if our methods are rational.)

Why are systems that are rational, or that tend to have correct beliefs, the ones that agents will have to have? Why, in other words, could we not have two agents with the same dispositions to act, but where one is highly rational and the other is highly irrational, but also happens to have such odd beliefs and desires that the craziness does not become obvious? I may behave like an ordinary citizen because I *am* an ordinary citizen, or because I am secretly terrified that all-seeing aliens will abduct me if I do or say anything out of the ordinary, no matter what the provocation. And we could think of stranger beliefs and desires to explain a range of behaviour. Of course, some systems of belief or desire might be more plausible than others. If someone with bizarre beliefs and desires acts like someone more normal, we may never have reason to suspect otherwise. But is there anything in principle to make it impossible? Lewis's justification of his principle of rationalization and his principle of charity would be, presumably, one based on his analytic functionalism. To be a believer and desirer is to have a group of states that stand in roles defined by folk psychology, and folk psychology not only has things to say about how beliefs and desires interact, but under what circumstances a person develops one belief or desire rather than another. If the principle of rationalization and the principle of charity come from folk psychology, and Lewis seems to think they do ([1974a] 1983a: 112), and the contents assigned are whichever best play the role for contents defined by folk psychology, then we have a justification for accepting that these principles do constrain content.

A qualification to the constraints mentioned so far should be noted. As discussed in Chapter 5, Lewis thinks that we should classify a mental state not in terms of how it behaves in an individual at a time, but how it would behave in a *normal* member of the relevant population to which the possessor belongs. So when we talk about how a state is disposed to behave, or what content a state would have if we assume that the possessor is rational and liable to be correct, we should really refer back to how that state behaves in normal members of its owner's population (whatever a normal member is; as we saw in Chapter 5, this can be difficult to settle).

A final constraint Lewis thinks is in place is that some assignments of content are more *natural* than others (in the sense of "natural properties" discussed in Chapter 1). Believing that Flossie is an elephant is a more natural belief than the belief that Flossie is one of a completely gerrymandered set of possible individuals. The belief that a table is round has a more natural content than the belief that a table is 437 metres from the Eiffel tower. It is not that we cannot ascribe unnatural properties and relations to objects – obviously we can, and do – but it is rather that when everything else is equal, a more natural content should be ascribed rather than a less natural one. Lewis puts the point in terms of "semantic eligibility" (which he defines in turn as a matter of degree of naturalness). Lewis argues that there needs to be some natural way of "carving up the world" in order to answer the anti-realist challenge that the mind-independent world would have very little to do with whether our theories were true or false, since there will nearly always be *some* way of mapping the terms of a theory onto the objects in the world so the theory comes out true. If we cannot somehow restrict which formally adequate interpretations count as genuine interpretations, we are left with the conclusion that the truth of our beliefs has very little to do with how the external world turns out to be, a conclusion that Lewis thinks would be absurd.[14] Lewis therefore adds the constraint that a more natural assignment of content to an agent's beliefs and desires will beat a less natural one, everything else being equal.

An appeal to brute eligibility (naturalness) can seem like a blank cheque, and many of Lewis's critics have been uncomfortable with the lack of detail in the principles of semantic eligibility. It is also not entirely clear where Lewis thinks this constraint comes from. He says that it is an "*a priori* ... constitutive constraint", and not a "contingent fact of psychology" ([1983c] 1999a: 55). I do not know whether he would think it is implicit in folk psychology as well, and so a constitutive constraint like other parts of the folk-psychological role assigned to mental content, or whether he would have thought it was a more fundamental constraint, perhaps one that is not to be further explained. At this point Lewis's metaphysics plays a key role in his philosophy of mind. It may be one of the best illustrations of why divisions of philosophy like the division into "metaphysics" and "philosophy of mind" are sometimes artificial.

While I have listed the constraints Lewis mentions in a certain order (conformity with dispositions, the principle of rationalization and principle of charity, and the requirement of semantic eligibility, or naturalness), this is not to indicate a hierarchy of constraints: I do not want to suggest that Lewis thinks that conformity with dispositions trumps the rest, or that assigning a sufficiently natural content is the least important constraint. Presumably some principles of balance will be required here. Indeed, assigning content is rather like finding a balance between simplicity and strength (and naturalness) for laws of nature, as Lewis himself notes (*ibid.*). We are not explicitly given principles about how to trade off these constraints in cases where there might be conflict. For example, a natural, rational assignment does not quite fit with dispositions to behave, or a more rational picture emerges if we assign slightly less natural content. Perhaps in hard cases different trade-offs result in indeterminacy about which content the believer really possesses, and perhaps there is something still to be said about the principles of balance.

Lewis's story about mental content addresses many problems in contemporary philosophy of mind and Lewis carves out a distinctive set of answers to important problems. Furthermore, if Lewis is successful, he manages to handle mental content without needing to add any fundamental resources over and above those supplied by his basic metaphysics: having a mental content is a matter of being related to a set of possible individuals, and what determines that content a believer or desirer has is a matter of the dispositions to behave that a person has, plus principles of interpretation drawn from common-sense psychology. One distinctive thing to note is that Lewis's story of the meaning of mental states is not dependent on the story of the meaning of sentences or other pieces of language. The two are not entirely independent, since what it is rational to say will depend to some extent on what someone means by one noise rather than another, for example; but in construing mental content in primarily non-linguistic terms, Lewis provides himself with a set of theoretical resources that will prove very useful in trying to explain the meaning of the spoken and written word. It is that challenge that must now be faced.

Chapter 7

Language, use and convention

In Chapter 6 I discussed the content of mental states: what states of mind *mean*. In this chapter I shall discuss the related question of meaning for pieces of language. Speech, writing and other forms of communication surround us and, since the "information revolution", dealing with publicly accessible systems of representation is more important for more people than ever before. Language also influences many of the most important aspects of human life. Our ability to think in the way we do in the first place may to some extent depend on being exposed to language as infants and children; without language human relationships would not be able to have the character or richness that they do, and economies, societies and cultures as we know them would be impossible. It is difficult to overstate its importance to us.

Here are three questions about language to get the ball rolling.

1. How do words and sentences in a language get their meaning?

It cannot in general be by a pre-established agreement about what the words are to mean, since that agreement would presumably have had to be formulated in language and be mutually understood already. (Explicit agreements may well be possible for some artificial languages, like Esperanto or COBOL, but this is presumably not what happened with English or Sumerian).

2. How does the meaning or content of pieces of language relate to the meaning or content of the beliefs and desires of speakers?

The study of language has tended to be bifurcated into two styles of theory. On the one hand, languages can be understood as a set of formal principles of generation of the meanings of complex pieces of language from the meanings of simple ones, together with an account of how meanings are connected to the truth and falsehood of sentences on occasions of utterance. On the other hand theorizing about language can centre on investigations of uses of language, and what circumstances production of one piece of language rather than another is appropriate. Given this:

3. How do we reconcile language construed as a formal set of principles generating sentences and their semantic values with language construed as a social practice of exchanges of utterances?

Lewis offers answers to all three questions.

Convention and language

Some of Lewis's earliest work was on convention: what is it for a convention to hold in a given population, and how can a convention be established, when it is often implicit (it may not even be obvious to the participants that part of their behaviour is conventional), and does not in general result from an agreement? Conventions can "spring up", and people can be part of a convention without ever having talked about it with others, let alone agreed to it. One example Lewis offers is of "contented oligopolists" selling a particular good. They may fix their prices at about the same amount, and tend to offer their goods at whatever the others do, but they may have been very careful never to talk explicitly about it with their competitors, for fear of being charged with collusion (and they may not be on speaking terms with their competitors in any case). And the oligopolists would be unlikely to think that their competitors were breaking an agreement or cheating if they suddenly put their prices up or down. (They may be annoyed that their competitors are rocking the boat, but they could hardly complain that a promise had been broken.) Nevertheless, there is a conventional amount that they all charge for their goods. Note that the conventions of language, for example conventions about how English is used, are likely to be both implicit and not as a result of an agreement, for the most part.

Lewis's theory of conventions begins by pointing out that people often have to solve "coordination problems": problems where the best results are gained by people coordinating their actions, and where it is in everyone's interests to do so. These might be cases where our only relevant priority is to coordinate, when a pair of friends want to meet for lunch, say, and none of them care very much about where, or when different actors would prefer different kinds of coordination (e.g. if I prefer to eat Korean food, but you prefer burgers), but still where coordination is what is most preferable. I would prefer to eat burgers with you to Korean food on my own, and likewise you would prefer to put up with Korean food rather than eat burgers on your own. Solving coordination problems is often a matter of getting good enough information about what other people plan to do. (If you normally go to the burger joint, and I'm trying to catch you for lunch, and I think you have no idea where I normally eat, I'll go to the burger joint.) Sometimes getting this information is by means of explicit agreement. If you say, "This time, let's have burgers", and I say "Okay", then, unsurprisingly, we both have pretty good evidence that the burger joint is the place to go for lunch together this time. But sometimes this coordination problem can be solved without an explicit agreement. I could just start regularly turning up at the burger joint. If I do this for long enough, you could quickly catch on that that's the place to go for lunch with me. Or I could say, "I'm going to eat at the Korean place whatever you do!" (Perhaps I am trying to play hardball, or bluff that eating Korean is more important to me than having lunch together.) If you come to the Korean place as a result, we have solved the coordination problem, but hardly through any agreement.

What gets complicated when we are trying to solve coordination problems is that each person must try to predict what the other is going to do, and the others' decision itself depends on what they think other people are going to do. Whether I drive on the left- or right-hand side of the road largely depends on what I expect about which side the other road users are likely to travel on. (Lewis makes the nice point that even if driving on the right, say, is made illegal, still that would be the side worth driving on if everyone else continues to drive on the right. It isn't worth driving into an oncoming truck to obey the traffic laws.) But most of the other people will be trying to decide what side to drive on by working out which side everyone else will drive on too. (They may just drive on one side by habit, but it is a habit formed by, and based on, continuing expectations about how others will drive).

Solutions to coordination problems often have an interesting feature. A group of people will prefer to do what it takes to achieve that

solution *conditional on everyone else doing so as well*. We both prefer
to eat at the burger joint, if the other person is going to be eating there
as well, and likewise we both prefer to be at the Korean place if the
other is going to be there. When driving on the road, people prefer to be
on the same side as everyone else going in the same direction (even if
they have other rather strong preferences too – they'll prefer to drive
on the side that they are used to and that their car is designed for, but
not at the expense of constantly ploughing into oncoming traffic).
When behaviour settles on one of these options – when an entire group,
or near enough, all act as they would wish to act provided the others act
accordingly, because they expect that the others will do so for the same
reason – it is called a "coordination equilibrium".

Lewis thought that *conventions* tend to arise where there are several available coordination equilibria, and people have settled on one
of them in their behaviour. In fact, behaviour in response to this sort
of situation is part of what it is to follow a convention. Lewis uses half
of his book *Convention* (1969) to explain and defend his particular
story about conventions, but the final version of his analysis of conventions is as follows:

> A regularity R in the behaviour of members of a population P
> when they are agents in a recurrent situation S is a *convention* if
> and only if it is true that, and it is common knowledge in P that,
> in almost any instance of S among members of P,
>
> (1) almost everyone conforms to R;
> (2) almost everyone expects almost everyone else to conform to
> R;
> (3) almost everyone has approximately the same preferences
>   regarding all possible combinations of actions;
> (4) almost everyone prefers that any one more conform to R, on
>   condition that almost everyone conform to R;
> (5) almost everyone would prefer that any one more conform to
> R', on condition that almost everyone conform to R';
>
> where R' is some possible regularity in the behaviour of members
> of P in S such that almost no one in almost any instance of S
> among members of P could conform both to R' and to R.
>
> (1969: 78)

This is quite a mouthful! A convention, for Lewis, is a regularity in
behaviour. You could instead say that it was something that *governed*
a regularity, in which case this should be recast as a definition of what

the regularity governed would have to be like. This would only be a terminological difference. This regularity is the sort of thing that provides the solution for coordination problems. If we have a convention of meeting at the burger joint for lunch, for example, the features of *R* will ensure we are able to coordinate. (Almost everyone conforming to the regularity is a good start; we will all at least go to the burger joint.)

For the regularity of behaviour to hold in a community, it should hold among most of the members. If it does not, then the relevant population for the definition should probably be smaller. It might be that sometimes we talk about a convention in a community that only some specified sub-group partakes in. Lewis suggests that we might distinguish a convention *within* a population (which may hold only of a sub-group) from a convention in a population or of a population ([1976a] 2000a: 140). Either way, something like (1) seems plausible: there had better be widespread conformity, to count as a convention that is in force.

Condition (2) is a condition of "common knowledge". One of the things that is special about a convention, rather than an accidental regularity of behaviour or a regularity that is explained by some quite different phenomena, is that people know others will behave in that manner. The best reason to drive on the right in the USA is that you expect almost everyone else will as well. So (2) is probably redundant, given that all the conditions must be common knowledge in the population *P*. For Lewis, when something is common knowledge, not only does everyone in the group believe it, but they all have good reason to expect each other to believe it, and expect that everyone in the group has good reason to expect that everyone has good reason to expect it, and so on *ad infinitum*. So common knowledge that almost everyone conforms to *R* will all by itself tend very strongly to produce the belief that everyone will conform to *R*, whenever it is relevant for a member of the population to give much thought to the matter.

Condition (3) seems too strong. Provided we have similar preferences about some important joint options, it should not matter very much if we vary a great deal in our preferences about other options (e.g. about what happens if you don't have lunch at all, or if we find ourselves separated at lunch). Lewis himself came to think this condition was too strong ([1975] 1983a: 171), and it seems that by 1974 he was happy to drop it.

Condition (4) captures the spirit of the requirement that there must be a conditional preference for the convention. If I did not want to follow a "convention", even if everyone else engaged in that behaviour, it is likely that eventually I wouldn't. And if I had some overriding external reason to behave in a certain way, then it would not really have the force of convention for me. If I went to a certain lunch place every day because I was marched there at gunpoint, I would not really be participating in a convention of going there (although perhaps my guards might be). If *all* of us were marched to lunch at gunpoint, then there would be a regularity all right, and one that we would expect each other to conform to, but it would not have the conventional force that, for example, starting a letter with "Dear so-and-so" has. Of course, for some conventions, we might hope that they would generally break down, or want to be free of them, but even if, for example, you feel constrained by our convention of wearing clothes in public, you probably prefer to continue wearing them if nearly everyone else does, so you won't be persecuted, laughed at or embarrassed.[1] Typically, conventions that we are party to are ones that we want others to conform to as well. If they are to serve as solutions to coordination problems, the regularity will serve better than everyone acting in an uncoordinated way.

Condition (5) states, in effect, that there must be an alternative possible convention. A forced "convention" is not really a convention at all, but is non-conventional and non-arbitrary. Speaking French in France would not be a convention unless there was some alternative that people could in principle do instead (e.g. speak in English, speak in German). The alternative R' might not be particularly convenient or satisfactory. In general, it is unlikely to be better than R, or people would switch systems. Nevertheless, without feasible alternative conventions, a regularity will not seem very conventional. Starting a letter with "Dear so-and-so" rather than "Salutations!" seems very conventional, but going upstairs by walking rather than on our hands and knees seems less conventional. What makes our practice of starting letters seem so conventional is partly that we could easily imagine how to adopt an alternative, conventional, system.

So we have a convention where there is a regularity of behaviour, it is common knowledge that the regularity obtains, almost everyone in the group prefers to continue it if everyone else does, and almost everyone prefers that way of doing things to some other way that would be conventional if it obtained. A convention, thus, need not be the result of an agreement. If a group of people start doing things a certain way, it may become conventional even if no group ever sat down and decided to do things that way. It is still more than a coincidence, and it is more than unconscious imitation or a regularity that holds entirely because of some external pressure (an authority, a feature of the environment, or whatever).

Lewis thinks that people speaking the same language share a convention for expressing meanings. The English-speaking community, for example, uses words a certain way, and prefers to keep doing that if nearly everyone else does (although if everyone else started speaking Estonian, presumably most of us would learn Estonian and switch). Of course, there are smaller communities with more specific conventions: those that speak a specific dialect, or those who share a specific body of slang. A convention like this could conceivably spring up without some official social agreement to speak English, or agreement about exactly what counts as English and what does not. In order to say what the content of the convention is, though, Lewis has to find some way of characterizing what it is people are doing when they produce sentences of English in the conventional manner for English-speakers.

Lewis approaches this by first establishing what a "signalling convention" would be. This is a rather simple sort of convention, where, for example, one party engages in some sign when they observe a certain occurrence. I might raise my hand when I see a light go on, for example. Another sort of signalling convention would occur where there was a convention of action in response to a signal: if we had the convention that you brought me a drink whenever I raised my hand, for example. In both of these cases, signalling conventions can be described in terms of Lewis's account of conventions, and it can be understood how such a signalling convention could convey information: for example, how a mutual convention about hand-raising could communicate information about a light going on. It can also explain the communication of simple imperatives. I can use the second signalling convention I mentioned to get a drink from you, if it should become established.

With these simple conventional signals as a model, Lewis goes on to develop a story about the conventions that govern the use of full-blown languages. Of course, language is much more complicated than simple conventional signals. Sentences are much less restrictive in when they can be used, we can do things besides make assertions or issue commands, and we build up entire assertions from components. Even if you have never seen the sentence "Some aardvarks eat wolves", you can work out what it literally means. One crucial thing about the meaning of a sentence, for Lewis, is that when it is uttered in a particular context it has a truth-condition; in a context, it determines a set of worlds where it counts as true. The conventions of language determine which language is being used by a given population, that is, which sentences are associated with which truth-conditions in a context of utterance. A truth-condition, for Lewis, is a specification of the conditions under which a sentence is true, and this is given by a set of possible worlds (see Chapter 6 for a discussion of this notion of truth-condition).[2]

If we characterize a language L in terms of the truth-conditions of its sentences (or, better, in terms of the function from contexts to truth-conditions associated with each of its sentences), then a population counts as speaking L if they have conventions of "truthfulness and trust in L". To be *truthful* in L is to try to not utter sentences of L unless you take their truth-condition (or truth-condition in context) to be satisfied. To be *trusting* in L is to expect that people who utter the sentences associated with L will be truthful-in-L with those sentences (Lewis 1983a: 167). The combination of these conventions, together with the assumption that people often know what they are talking about, will produce a reliable way to get someone to share your beliefs. If you and I are in a community that uses L, then you know that if you produce a sentence, I shall be able to tell that you believe the sentence is true, and since I trust you to try to tell the truth, and trust that you know the truth, I shall come to share your belief. Of course, language does not always do this – we do not always believe people, people do not always use language correctly, and people do not always try to tell the truth – but provided enough of these conditions *typically* obtain, we have explained how we can transmit our beliefs with language.

Notice that these conventions are specified in terms of beliefs (what truth-conditions a speaker or hearer believes to hold, or "takes to be true" in the language of the previous paragraph). The notion of following a convention invokes preferences and intentions, as well as beliefs ("expectations"). Lewis thus relies on mental states having content in explaining the meaning of expressions in language. It is a "head-first" strategy, rather than one where the content of mental states is analysed by assuming that we already have an independently meaningful language in play.

One challenge this theory faces is accounting for the meaning of very complicated sentences, the sort that are grammatical, but that no one could say or would say. (Consider a sentence with a string of a million adjectives, for example, or one with thousands of subordinate clauses.) For meaning to be conventional in the way Lewis suggests, we would need a convention of truthfulness and trust in these extremely long sentences. But, arguably, we do not. We do not have any regularity of saying such things, or trust that were someone to say such an absurd sentence, they would be speaking truthfully. If such a sentence was said at all, the speaker may well be expected to trip up somewhere and not say what they intended, or may be doing it merely as a stunt, or whatever. (This objection is discussed in Lewis ([1975] 1983a: 187; 1992).) To account for the meaning of these sentences, Lewis recommends we extrapolate from the meanings of sentences that are frequently used, or might reasonably be expected to be used. Of course, there will be many (perhaps infinitely many) ways of extrapolating from a finite sample to a complete language. However, Lewis trusts that some extrapolations will be more natural than others (in the sense of "naturalness" discussed in Chapter 1). Some general rules of language, or relations between sentences in use and truth-conditions, will be less gerrymandered or artificial than others, and the right principle of extrapolation will be one of the natural ones ([1992] 2000a: 149–51). Presumably, if there is more than one natural one for a given language community, this will be a source of indeterminacy of meaning for the very long, never-used sentences.

Some sentences may have the same truth-conditions whatever the context in which they are uttered (although this might always be an idealization). Some sentences, though, obviously have different truth-conditions depending on their context. "I am hungry" in one sense means something quite different when Bill says it from when Jane says it. In the first case, it needs *Bill* to be hungry in order to be true, and in the second it needs Jane to be hungry. In another good sense the sentence means the same thing when each of them say it: "I" is a single word of English. Context makes a difference to who is picked out by a use of "I". Other "indexicals" work like "I"; words like "here" or "yesterday" make different contributions to truth-conditions depending on where and when they are said, respectively.[3] *Tense* in language produces context dependence. "Shakespeare is writing *Hamlet*" would have been true if it had been uttered at the right time several hundred years ago, but would be false if I said it now; what I should say is that "Shakespeare was writing *Hamlet*", or, more strictly, "Shakespeare was writing *Hamlet* at such-and-such a time", if I want to express the same truth-condition. There is widespread agreement that for giving the meaning of sentences with indexicals or with tenses we need to say how context influences the truth-conditions expressed.

The extent of context-dependence

Other cases are more controversial. Lewis at one point suggests that sentences with proper names in them are thereby context-dependent ([1975] 1983a: 173); the causal history of the speaker's coming to use the name needs to be supplied by the context. If this is right, two communities with the same beliefs about the world might vary in who they pick out with a name ("Napoleon", for example), even if there is no difference in the communities' beliefs about the world. If there is a possible community just like our present-day one as far as their beliefs go, but who have a different history and are subject to a massive late-nineteenth century hoax, they might pick out a fictional character when they say "Napoleon", even if their word "Napoleon" is subject to the same linguistic conventions as ours is. Lewis can be interpreted as suggesting that this possible community might in one good sense mean what we mean by "Napoleon", although the different context will mean that their sentences will have different truth-conditions. Lewis's philosophical opponents would be inclined to deny that there is any good sense of "meaning" where the community imagined means what we mean by "Napoleon".

There has recently been some controversy about which parts of our language are context-dependent and which parts are not. Some think that proper names, and so-called "natural kind terms", such as "water" or "dog", can pick out different objects in different possible contexts of utterance. Others think that these English words essentially pick out the things that they in fact pick out. In other possible situations where they appear to pick out something else, it is not that English is interacting with context differently, it is rather that an alternative to English is being spoken.

Consider one example, due originally to Leibniz (minus the details about atomic chemistry). "Gold" is used in the actual world for a certain metal that, as it happens, is yellow, malleable, heavy and valuable, and is an element with atomic number 79. Consider another possible community that uses their word "gold" for a yellow, heavy, valuable metal with quite a different chemical composition. (It might be a compound, or a different element. Suppose, if you like, that this community lives in a possible world with different laws of chemistry.) Could that other community count as using the English word "gold", if they behave just like us in the sounds they make to each other? Obviously they use a word that gets pronounced and written "gold", but that does not settle it, any more than a Californian surfer and a

German speaker have the same word "rad", when the German uses that sound as a noun for wheels and the surfer uses it as an adjective for admirable things.

One side of the debate argues that the community we are considering can be using a word that means the same as ours. For example, if ours means something like "the actual heavy valuable yellow metal around here", then they can mean the same thing (although "actual" and "around here" are indexicals, so they will pick out a different metal). On the other hand, if ours is a non-indexical expression that has as its entire meaning the element with atomic number 79, then the alternative community just means something different with their word, and it is impossible that they are a group that uses the English word "gold" to pick out their valuable yellow metal. They must be using a different language. People sometimes call such a language "Twinglish", since this sort of thought-experiment is usually called a "twin earth" thought experiment, after Putnam (1975c).

This debate goes under various names. Sometimes it is called a dispute between people who think language has "narrow content" versus those who think it has only "wide content", and sometimes it is construed as a debate about "the interpretation of two-dimensional modal logic". As you might expect, it is caught up in many other disagreements as well. Lewis argues that there does not need to be any real disagreement here. In "Index, Context and Content" (1980a), Lewis points out that there are often two options when we come to say how a word plus the "meaning" of a sentence come to produce a truth-value. Lewis introduces the expression "semantic value" for something that does two jobs: it "must enter somehow" into the story of when a sentence is true in a given language on a given occasion, and it should be determined by the semantic values we associate with the sentence's constituents ([1980a] 1998: 25). "Semantic value" is a technical term that works like the word "meaning", but since "meaning" is used in so many ways by different people, Lewis thinks it worthwhile to introduce "semantic value" as a stripped-down expression with fewer potentially misleading associations.

Lewis points out that there are different things that can be properly called a "semantic value" without there being a genuine disagreement. This is because there are many features of sentences that somehow enter into the story of when a given sentence is true, and which are also determined as a function of features of parts of the sentences. In particular, we often have two general strategies: we can adopt a "variable but simple" option or a "constant but complicated" option when selecting which sort of "semantic value" we want to focus on and perhaps call "the meaning" of an expression.

Let me take the example of the word "here". One thing we could do is to say that "here" has a different semantic value depending on who is saying it; that is, "here" in my mouth on a given occasion can *have a different meaning* than "here" in your mouth. If we did this, we could make the semantic value of "here" on a given occasion rather simple; we could just identify it with a region of space, for example. We could have a simple theory where the semantic value of "here" in the mouth of someone on top of the Eiffel Tower is a particular region of space – the one at the top of the Eiffel Tower – and someone who says "here" when they are in the Taj Mahal picks out a region of space there.

Or we could focus on a more complicated semantic value for "here". We could, for example, say that the semantic value of "here" is a function from a speaker at a time to the place where the speaker is. Then both speakers use a word with the same "semantic value". One and the same function (the "here function", we could call it) maps Pierre onto the top of the Eiffel Tower, and Raj onto the inside of the Taj Mahal. These two theories assign different semantic values to Pierre's use of "here": the first assigns a region of space, and the second assigns a function from speakers (and times) to regions of space. But they need not be in conflict. Both the region and the function play a role in determining whether Pierre's sentence "It is windy here" is true. *Both* count as "semantic values". You could imagine a heated argument between philosophers or linguists about which counts as "the meaning" of Pierre's word "here". But if we're arguing about *the* semantic value of what Pierre said, the debate is pointless. Both sides can be right that their candidate is a "semantic value".

Lewis would want to say the same thing about the debate about "the meaning" of proper names, or natural kind terms, or other pieces of language. Our usage of the word "gold" to pick out a yellowish metallic element and the usage of a possible community who use the sound "gold" around a yellow compound metal have something in common, and something different. One way to describe our usage is to say that the semantic value of our word "gold" is the element, and their word "gold" is a compound; another way of describing us is to say that both groups use the same word which has as its "semantic value" a function from a speaker (or a speech community) to, for example, whatever yellowish, heavy, valuable metal is around that speaker (or whatever). This issue is one that philosophers argue about: what is "the meaning" of our word "gold"? Do the people on twin earth use *our* word "gold" or do they use a word with a different meaning? Lewis says there is a non-issue here, if what people are arguing about is semantic values. Both the metal and the function play a role in determining how my sentence "Wedding rings are often made of gold" gets to be true when I utter it on a given occasion. And both sides are likely to agree that it has something to do with the explanation. Those who think that it is not part of the meaning think the function is part of the "meta-semantic" story about how our word "gold" came to have the meaning it has.

If Lewis is right, much of the debate, which is still raging, is misguided. Arguments about whether we and the people on twin earth have "the same meaning" are largely the result of different terminological choices about what sort of semantic value the different sides want to focus on, and *not* necessarily substantive disagreements about the function of language. Of course, for one purpose or other it may be more convenient to pay more attention to one part of the story or the other, but we should not be confused into thinking that this makes one choice the once-and-for-all "right answer" about *meaning*. Both answers do the job well enough.

Since Lewis holds that it is often more or less indifferent whether we use "complex but constant" semantic values that allow for a large role for context, or "simple but variable" semantic values that give less of a role to context but have more meaning-variation, he feels free to appeal to context when describing the meaning of philosophically interesting expressions. The next section discusses some of Lewis's distinctive philosophical positions that this tendency allowed for.

Context and contextualism

Lewis often invokes features of context to explain the meanings of expressions. We have seen one example already. In Chapters 3 and 4, I discussed how counterfactual conditionals invoke a relation of comparative similarity ($A \mathbin{\Box\!\!\rightarrow} B$ is true provided all the most relevantly similar worlds where A is true are ones where B is true). What the "relevant similarity" is gets defined by context. In the case of counterfactuals relevant for causation, features such as the laws and exact matches of history count highly for relevant similarity, but features such as general similarity of the future do not count for very much. On the other hand, a so-called "backtracker" conditional allows for much more variability of the past, and takes other features to be more important. For Lewis,

> If I jumped out of the window, I would have broken many bones.

might well be true if I utter it in a tall building looking out through the open window. But the counterfactual sentence

> If I jumped out of the window, I would have been unhurt because I would have arranged for a safety net.

could be true if I uttered it instead, because what similarities are relevant in the two cases are very different. In the first, we hold the surroundings fixed – where the window is, my current state, and so on – but do not hold fixed that I'm a careful sensible person. In the second case, we allow for more variablity in what I might have done to prepare, or what might be different in the surroundings, and hold fixed that I'm not crazy enough to jump out the window if I'm going to get badly hurt. The difference is entirely in which sort of similarity is appropriate given the utterance.

Context supplies part of the truth-conditions of utterances in all sorts of other ways. Another way it can do this is by making some object or other salient. If I say "What was that?" out of the blue, you will be able to make sense of what I am talking about if there is some obvious thing of note in the context (e.g. if there has just been a loud boom, or a large animal has just run past, or something similar). You may also be able to work out what I mean by looking at my body language (if I'm pointing, or staring at a particular spot). If nothing stands out as particularly relevant, then I am unlikely to have successfully communicated a specific question, unless I supply some follow-up.

Another case where context plays a role is in definite descriptions (expressions of the form "the X"). "The" has some suggestion of uniqueness, but it is often uniqueness only relative to a context. If I say "the man has crossed the street", I am probably not indicating that there is only one man in existence, but what I have said will still make perfectly good sense when there is a particular man who is salient in the conversational context. For example, take the following piece of speech:

> I'm looking out through my front window, and there are three women and a man having an argument outside. I'm not sure what they're arguing about, but it looks as though two of the women are storming off. The other one is still shouting at him,

but I think he's trying to leave as well. The man has crossed the street, but the last woman is still shouting at him.

The previous course of the conversation has made it clear which man I'm talking about. This uniqueness can also shift during a sentence, as Lewis was one of the first to note (1973a: 111–17). I can report the goings-on in a scene of a movie by saying "So the man with a gun fires at another man, who also has a gun, and kills him". Obviously, whoever "the man with a gun" is, he isn't the only man with a gun in the scene, since the "other man" also has a gun. But what I said makes sense (and would probably be counted as true if, in the scene, there was only one man with a gun who fired, and he shot a man with a gun who was killed). We can do this often; you can make sense of things like "the king met with some other kings" or "the pig grunted at the other pigs", provided somehow you can work out which king or which pig I had in mind from the conversational context.

How does context supply these constraints (a salient object, or a respect of similarity, or one of the many other supplements that context can supply)? Presumably there are many ways, but one way Lewis points to is a "rule of accommodation" (1979d). Sometimes someone will say something that will not be true unless the context is a certain way. Consider the pair of counterfactuals about jumping our of the window. Since they cannot both be right in the same context, each can only be correctly uttered if the context selects the similarity relation relevant for it, rather than the other similarity relation. When that happens, then the listeners typically "accommodate"; if one of the ways of adding to the context would make what is said appropriate, then the saying itself brings that context into force. If I say either counterfactual out of the blue, it would sound acceptable, because each will bring with it the context it needs to be appropriately uttered.

Accommodation does not always happen. If one context is firmly fixed, or one conversational partner is particularly stubborn, then it will not happen. Another example of accommodation Lewis mentions is the example of "relative modalities" ([1979d] 1983a: 246–7). As we saw in Chapter 3, there are different senses or "grades" of possibility. Some, such as logical possibility, are very generous, and some, such as practical possibility, are much more restricted. It is logically possible for me to run a marathon, and even physically possible, but it is not an immediate practical possibility (because I would need to do a lot of running before I was fit enough). Context will often determine what grade of possibility is relevant. If I say "It is possible for me to run at the speed of sound, but not to run faster than the speed of light", that suggests I have nomic possibility, or possibility given the laws of nature, in mind. Other speakers, however, can change the context or the "conversational score". If you respond "It is possible to run at the speed of light, it would just require different laws of nature", then it looks as though you are making the standard more generous (maybe shifting the conversation to logical possibility) and if you say "You can't run a marathon, you can't even run ten kilometres!", then you are (unkindly) shifting the standard to something like practical possibility. I, in turn, could resist the shift ("That's not what I meant") or I could go along with it ("I can run ten kilometres on a good day"). What is interesting here is that people can say things that apparently conflict but do not really; "I can run at the speed of sound" uttered in one context can be true, and "I cannot run fast enough to do a mile in four minutes" uttered in another context can also be true, even though the statements apparently conflict (and would conflict, if uttered in the same context). This can lead people astray if they look for a single right answer to questions about what it is possible for me to do.

There is a lot of contextual variability and often it is fairly obvious when it is pointed out. The role of context can become philosophically interesting when it might shed light on difficult debates, especially if there might be context shift going on that people are unaware of. In "Scorekeeping in a Language Game" (1979d), Lewis makes two philosophical suggestions that have since become important positions in their respective areas.

Vagueness

What Lewis's views about vagueness were at different stages is a matter of some controversy. But at least in "Scorekeeping in a Language Game" (1979d), they appeared to be as follows. A vague term is associated with a range of different "delineations": precise boundaries for where the term applies and where it does not. "White" for example might be associated with a range of different sets of objects. Some of the sets will be more generous than others (some might include some rather greyish objects, or objects with small bits of other colours on parts of their surfaces, and other delineations might only include pure white objects). "The Sydney Opera House is white" is true in English on some delineations of "white" (probably most of them) and probably not for others (since it is not entirely flawlessly white). Truth in a language is assessed relative to an occasion of utterance, and relative to a world, and also relative to a delineation ([1970a] 1983a: 228–9).

When we assert a sentence that is associated with a set of different delineations (e.g. a sentence containing the predicate "is white"), Lewis thinks it is appropriate to assert if it is *true enough*: "true over a large enough part of the range of delineations of its vagueness" (*ibid.*: 244). How much is enough, of course, may depend on context. Sometimes standards are low. Under such circumstances it may be perfectly acceptable to say "France is hexagonal", to use one of Lewis's examples. On other occasions it may not be. The rule of admissibility means that the context may be determined by what is said. If I say "France is hexagonal" out of the blue, then that will normally be acceptable, unless I'm among pedants. On the other hand, were I to say "France is not hexagonal, because Brittany sticks out too far", then that would be assertable as well. Lewis notes that it seems to be easier to raise the context than lower it. It is much more acceptable to respond to the claim that France is hexagonal by saying that it isn't, than to respond to the claim that France isn't hexagonal by saying that it is.

Lewis thinks this feature of context is sometimes ignored, and so we might be led to think that there is a unique, very high standard (say, where almost no physical objects are hexagonal because they do not have exactly the same shape as a geometrical hexagon). He diagnoses this mistake in Peter Unger's argument that nothing is flat. Unger (1975: 65–8) thinks that a surface is not flat if there is some other surface that is flatter (you cannot have flatter than flat). So we can reason that almost nothing is flat. A field has grass and small rocks sticking out of it, and isn't as flat as a pane of glass; a pane of glass has micro-ridges and depressions, and so is not as flat as something else we can imagine; and so on. So virtually no physical object is flat. Lewis thinks this argument might be well and good when it is uttered, but it manages to be appealing because Unger is shifting to a context where there is an incredibly high standard for being "flat". Even if Unger is right to say at the end of his argument, for example, "a pane of glass is not flat", that does not mean that we are wrong in ordinary contexts when we say that a pane of glass or a tabletop or a writing surface is flat. We are just making our utterances with some more generous contextual standard for what counts as flat. Pointing out that a tabletop is less flat than a polished mirror does not show so much that we were wrong when we said the tabletop was flat, it just shifts us to a context where the mirror defines the standard for flatness.

Lewis does not say very much about how contextualism might solve the philosophical problems of vagueness. Later writers (such as Raffman (1994), Soames (1999) and Graff (2000)) point out that contextualism can help with the Sorites paradox. This is the argument that says that, for example, one grain of sand cannot make the difference between a heap and a non-heap of sand. Start with a heap of sand, remove one grain without disturbing the shape too much, and you will still have a heap afterwards. If you begin with a large pile (say, one million grains) and remove them one by one, repeated application of the principle means that you're always left with a heap afterwards. But that means you still have a heap even when you get down to ten grains, or five grains, or one grain! Many vague paradoxes seem susceptible to this sort of reasoning, and the reasoning must be going wrong somewhere, since one grain of sand isn't enough for a heap.

For example, contextualists can hold that a context is selected so that whichever sized heap we pay attention to, both one grain more and one grain less count as "heaps" according to that context. If there is a subtle context shift as we go through the million stages of argument, then in every context, the principle that one grain does not make a difference holds for the particular cases under consideration, and we never notice that each context allows for some sharp boundary, because the boundaries are always off where we are not paying attention. Contextualism about vagueness has its critics. It might be implausible that contexts draw sharp boundaries, even sharp boundaries that are "out of mind", and it seems odd that we cannot have a context that focuses on all the heap sizes at once. For example, if I say explicitly "I wonder whether it is true for all heap sizes that one grain more or less does not make a difference to whether a collection of grains is a heap?" Nevertheless, developing and testing rules about context shift may offer us new philosophical resources to tackle the problems of vagueness, problems that have plagued philosophy of language since the time of the ancient Greeks.

Epistemology

Lewis pioneered contextualism in epistemology ([1979d] 1983a: 247), a position that has subsequently produced a large literature (DeRose (1992), Cohen (1998) and many others). Lewis himself proposed a detailed version of contextualism in "Elusive Knowledge" (1996b). According to contextualists about knowledge, a claim that someone knows something depends for its truth or falsehood on the context of utterance.[4] Lewis's version is that on an occasion of utterance, a person S "knows proposition P iff P holds in every possibility left uneliminated by S's evidence; equivalently, iff S's evidence eliminates every possibility in which not-P" ([1996b] 1999a: 422). What makes Lewis's theory contextualist is that which possibilities count as among "every" possibility varies from conversational context to conversational context.

For example, suppose I say that Bob knows that the Chinese have launched someone into orbit. In an everyday context, that means that Bob has evidence that rules out the Chinese launch having been called off, or maybe rules out that the Chinese were hoaxing (e.g. Bob might have seen a newspaper report saying the Chinese have claimed to send a man into space, and checked to see whether NASA agrees that the Chinese sent someone into orbit). But perhaps Bob has not ruled out more far-fetched possibilities, that all the countries of the world are conspiring to make people think the Chinese have put someone in orbit, say, or that Bob's friends have all been playing a trick on him by faking a newspaper, changing the phone number next to "NASA" in his phonebook and having an accomplice ready to take his call, and so on. Bob may also not have enough evidence available, given his present experiences and recollection, to rule out the possibility that he is seriously delusional, and only *thinks* he remembers checking the newspapers and other information sources about the Chinese launch.

In philosophical contexts, there are more far-fetched possibilities still that may be brought up. Perhaps we are all being deceived by Descartes's omnipotent evil deceiver. Perhaps we have been put in an advanced virtual reality machine, and deceived into thinking we live in the early twenty-first century. Perhaps the world started 30 seconds ago (in just the configuration we thought it was), but nearly everything we believe about the world before that is false. And so on. Many people agree that it is plausible that our evidence does not rule out these hypotheses. If those things had happened, then our current evidence would in some relevant sense be the same as it in fact is. A sceptic would argue that this means that we know far less than we think; since we cannot rule out the possibility of an evil deceiver, that means that we cannot rule out very much about how the world is.

David Lewis

Lewis's response to the sceptic is to agree that in a situation where we are considering possibilities like evil deceivers or sudden insanity or whatever, we cannot rule out very much, and so the sceptic is right. But only in those contexts. In ordinary contexts, we "properly ignore" many of these far-fetched possibilities, so that the only possibilities we need to rule out are more mundane ones. In more mundane circumstances, the possibility that the Chinese rocket exploded on launch might be ruled out, for example, by Bill's memory that the newspaper had a headline "Chinese Launch Successful", together with his memory that the article was about China successfully launching a person into space. If Bill wants to rule out his having been an identical twin, his childhood memories or his mother's testimony ("No, you're not an identical twin. Do you get these crazy ideas from philosophy books?") might be enough.

Suppose a sceptic offers this argument:

You believe that there is a book in front of you.

But, there are possible situations where your evidence is the same (or relevantly the same) as you think it is, but where you don't have a book in front of you. Suppose a powerful demon is deceiving you.

So your evidence does not rule out the possibility that there is no book in front of you after all, so you don't *know* there is a book there.

If Lewis is right, what has happened here is that the sceptic has changed the context. By explicitly bringing up the possibility of deceiving demons, the sceptic has produced a context where the claim "You don't know there is a book in front of you" is true. But this does not mean that the sceptic has shown you were wrong when, for example, a few minutes earlier you thought, "I know there is a book in front of me". (An odd thing to think normally, but perhaps the sceptic started the conversation by asking you to give an example of something you knew.) We are usually entitled to ignore sceptical possibilities, and we usually do ignore them. If Lewis is right, then our ordinary judgements about how much we know might well be okay, even though once we start thinking about scepticism, we should say something quite different.

What makes contextualism so philosophically interesting is that if there is a context shift here, it is not one we are ordinarily aware of. We usually think (as the sceptic does) that when the sceptic argues that, for instance, we do not know if there is a book in front of us, then the sceptic is arguing that our ordinary judgements about what we know are *mistaken*. But if there is a hidden shift of context, then the sceptic has not shown that at all; she has only shown that we should say we do not know very much *in the context of discussing scepticism*, or "in the epistemology classroom". The fact that whenever we try to answer the general question of what people know this produces a context where the right thing to say is that people don't know much, would explain why the sceptic's arguments seem so hard to answer.

Contextualists about epistemology have different stories to tell about when we can and cannot legitimately ignore some possibilities of error. If legitimate ignoring is too easy, then we shall know more than we think (e.g. if someone comes to a belief carelessly and ignores something that should have been obvious that counts against it). If legitimate ignoring is too difficult, the sceptic may win after all. (If, for some reason, we have to always keep in mind that there is a possibility of insanity or deception by conspiracies, then there will usually be possibilities of error uneliminated by the evidence we have available.) Lewis gives his account of when it is permissible to ignore possibilities of error in "Elusive Knowledge" (1996b).

Of course, contextualism about knowledge is controversial. Some people want to say that we can, even in a discussion of scepticism, show that there is no possibility of error, given our evidence (e.g. Williamson 2000). Others will want to say that Lewis concedes too much to the sceptic when he says that knowledge is a matter of having no possibility of error. "Fallibilists" will say that the *possibility* that evidence leads to error is not always enough to block knowledge when we believe something on the basis of that evidence. The error has to be in some sense *likely* or *plausible* or something similar before knowledge is blocked. (Even if we grant that it is possible for my mother to not tell me the truth about whether I'm an identical twin, I can still know that I'm not an identical twin on the basis of her say-so, provided she's sufficiently reliable, or trustworthy, or somesuch.) And the sceptic may not be happy with the contextualist story. A sceptic will probably argue that the contextualist story does not go far enough. So it is unlikely that contextualism will definitively settle debates about the nature of knowledge, but it is certainly one of the options that should be taken seriously.

Chapter 8

Values and morality

Lewis's views about ethics and values are not as well-known as his views about metaphysics, mind and language. Lewis addresses several different sorts of questions in ethics and value theory. He proposes a theory of what moral values are, and how they can play the distinctive role that moral values are supposed to. He has views about the right form of an ethical theory: he resists consequentialism in favour of an alternative closer to virtue ethics. In this chapter I shall discuss both Lewis's metaethical views and what can be extracted about his general ethical theory. Lewis also has interesting things to say about a range of applied ethical issues, including topics as wide-ranging as the morality of nuclear deterrence and what a theist should say about the problem of evil. I shall discuss two examples of Lewis's contributions to applied ethics: his writings about punishment, and his liberal defence of the value of tolerance.

The nature of value

One common challenge for materialist philosophies is to give an account of truths about morals and ethics. In fact, this is a difficult challenge for anyone. It is not easy to explain what morality is, how it has force for us, and what it is for an action to be right or wrong, or an outcome to be morally good or morally bad, regardless of your general philosophical position. (Coming up with some explanation or other might not be too difficult, but coming up with the correct one and showing it to be correct is very hard.)

It might seem particularly challenging for Lewis's view, for Lewis has also given us an account of desire and decision that does not leave any obvious room for ethics. The rational thing to do is to satisfy one's desires given one's beliefs. Where is the room for morality in this? Furthermore, there is a great deal of flexibility in what one can desire. There does not seem to be much room for hidden necessities that will draw us in a certain way, or irresistible moral features of actions that will draw us to them. Different possible agents can want very different things, and be entirely rational to pursue them. Why should an agent who wants things that are extremely different from what we want behave in a moral manner?

A non-materialistic worldview could, I suppose, just take value to be a fundamental feature of the world that some things have value and other things do not. It might be puzzling how we could detect it (unless the theorist also supposed we had special extra-physical value detectors, or supposed that value could make some sort of difference to our perceptual systems). But a materialist will want to explain in physical terms how an entirely physical piece of the world could count as valuable, unless the materialist wants to be a nihilist about value, and say that everything is as worthless as a random clump of sub-atomic particles. Anti-materialists sometimes raise nihilism as a spectre against materialists, but it is in fact rare for materialists to be nihilists.

One starting-point for a materialist would be to start with us, as valuing creatures. Perhaps if we had a story of what it was for one of us to count something as valuable we could work back and discover what about the world produces that reaction in us. We could then identify valuable things and properties of things in terms of their effects on us, or alternatively in terms of our attitudes towards them. A broad class of such theories have been labelled "dispositional theories" of value, and it is this approach that Lewis takes (most clearly in his paper, "Dispositional Theories of Value" (1989b)).

Lewis's theory of value (including moral value) is that what is valuable for us is what we would value in ideal conditions, which seems reasonable, provided we can spell out what it is to value something, and what it is to be in ideal conditions for valuation. (We do not want the specifications of ideal conditions to make the claim trivial – by saying for instance that the ideal conditions of valuing are when people appreciate what is truly valuable – since that will not help us get any closer to an informative story about what is valuable.) As for the first part of the story, Lewis thinks that what it is to *value* something is to desire to desire it. That is, when someone values a certain kind of situation, they want to be the sort of person who desires it and

seeks to bring it about. Valuing, for Lewis, is not an infallible indicator of what is really valuable, since someone might value something
when they are not in ideal circumstances (they are ignorant or confused or upset or unimaginative or whatever). Lewis only says a little
about why he things valuing is desiring to desire. He does not think
that valuing something is merely desiring it. He gives the example of
addicts, who cannot help desiring more of a drug even though they
hate this desire and would eliminate it if they had enough self-
control. (Harry Frankfurt is well known for arguing that unwanted
desires should be seen as not expressing a person's values; see Frankfurt 1971.) Lewis also thinks that there is no particular reason to go
higher up the chain. We may have desires about what we desire to
desire, and desires about those desires and so on. He also suggests
that we only take into account *intrinsic* second-order desires rather
than *instrumental* second-order desires (Lewis [1989b] 2000a: 71, n.
4). Instrumental desires are desires we have for something only as a
means. I might have an instrumental desire for a train token, only
because I have the desire to travel by train. (And that desire may
itself only be an instrumental desire. I might want to travel by train
only because I want to get somewhere, and so on). An example of an
instrumental second-order desire might be a desire to like the current fashion, when a person has that desire only because they want to
fit in; they desire to desire some particular piece of clothing, for
example, because wanting that sort of clothing is a way to think like
the "in" crowd.[1] "Intrinsic" desires are non-instrumental ones. (It has
little if anything to do with the notion of "intrinsic" used in the literature on properties.)

The second part of the account is to specify the ideal circumstances
for valuing: the circumstances where someone's valuing is not
warped or clouded in ways that we recognize can lead to error. After
all, we are inclined to think that people can make mistakes about
what is valuable, and even though Lewis was a "subjectivist", and
thinks that what has value is ultimately settled by our dispositions,
he does not want it to turn out that whatever anyone's opinion is
about what is valuable, that is automatically correct. (Some people do
have this more extreme subjectivist position, but most of us think it
is a mistake to find torture or sadism or sexual violence valuable,
even though some people value them.) Lewis thinks it is important to
do justice to our ordinary conception that we leave room for "mod-
esty"; we do not usually think that you can "just decide where you
stand, then you may judge of value with the utmost confidence!"

(*ibid.*: 79). Lewis claims that the ideal condition for valuing is "full imaginative acquaintance" with the state or feature in question. Why this and only this is what is needed is not clear (although how we would work out what is needed, exactly, is a tough question). Lewis does reject some other components of an ideal situation that some might suggest. For example, he rejects the common suggestion that an ideal valuer is fully informed, because he thinks some kinds of information would only interfere: perhaps information about the inevitability of death or the evolutionary history of our desires would serve to lessen their force; or knowledge of the cost of something, or the tragedies that have struck people down in seeking it, would be discouraging. While costs should be taken into effect when we are balancing our pursuit of different values, Lewis thinks knowledge of cost only gets in the way if we are trying to work out what is valuable in the first place. Others might think one or more of these things are crucial: if something could only be valued in ignorance, they might doubt that it was truly valuable.

Depending on what gets packed into ideal imaginative acquaintance, there might be other suggestions one could have about what makes a situation ideal for evaluating. Perhaps we should not allow any limitations of cognitive processing to be relevant. Maybe we cannot think about things for very long or keep many considerations in our head at once. Or maybe there are things required for ideal evaluation that would be very difficult to discover. Of course, if it is a matter of ideal evaluation by our actual standards, we should hope that we have at least some sort of implicit, know-it-when-we-see-it grasp of what conditions are needed.

We probably do not, in fact, judge what is valuable by getting into ideal circumstances first, recognizing that we have made it to ideal circumstances, and then judging. Lewis recognizes this, as you might expect. Instead, Lewis suggests, we find out about values in a fallible and sometimes piecemeal way. We start from what we in fact value, try to correct for any reprehensible biases or other distorting factors, try to improve our imaginative acquaintance with the thing we are interested in (perhaps through direct experience, perhaps through the testimony of others, perhaps through reflection) and trust that we have come close enough to the same judgement that we would have in ideal circumstances. His theory thus leaves room for moral enquiry and investigation, and gives us comparatively tractable questions of fact to seek out in order to improve our beliefs about what is, in fact, valuable. (In all likelihood, many of these questions will be psychological questions.) There are matters of fact about which things have value, on this theory, even though these matters of fact are largely facts about us and what we would do (in particular, what we would desire to desire in circumstances of ideal imaginative acquaintance). The moral and other aspects of value reduce to psychological matters of fact (albeit ones that may be tricky to discover).

One feature of subjectivist theories that some people find welcome and others find a serious drawback is that they are often "relativist": what is a value for one person may not be for someone else. For some sorts of things (which is the best colour, or which is the best football team to support), relativism might seem very plausible. But many people think that it is less plausible when it comes to morality. Cultural mores, or conventions about how to behave, certainly differ. But we don't think all conventions of behaviour are equally okay for the people who follow them. Slavery and genocide were wrong, even when most people (except maybe some of the slaves and victims) thought they were acceptable or even morally admirable. Many of us are not inclined to think other people's moral beliefs are as acceptable as our own when we encounter people who torture others, or practise human sacrifice, or do any of a wide variety of other things. Of course we might, and probably should, think there is some degree of permissible variation; the point is that when it comes to morality, most people think there are limits to permissible variation.

Subjectivism can lead to relativism if the relevant subjective states can be different from person to person. And certainly what someone desires to desire when they have the necessary imaginative acquaintance looks as though it is the sort of thing that could vary between people. Lewis believes that it is certainly possible for someone to be so constituted that what they value in ideal circumstances is very different from what we would value. He uses as an example a world where, in ideal circumstances, the people value "seasickness and petty sleaze" ([1989b] 2000a: 89). And it may even be that there is variation between different people in this world as to what we would desire to desire. It may depend on culture or temperament or other things. Does this mean that Lewis's view leads to relativism? And if so, how do we make sense of moral disagreements, if different things are moral for different people?

Lewis recommends a sort of "wait-and-see" relativism. For all we know, human beings (at least actual human beings) are all disposed to value the same things given the right imaginative acquaintance, or so Lewis claims. Perhaps we all do ultimately share the same standards of value, in which case we do not need to be relativist (except when it comes to comparing our values with the values of non-actual people). Or we might differ along cultural lines or along individual lines. Then value claims are tacitly relativized to "the speaker, and those somehow like him" (*ibid.*: 83), and the "somehow" might get filled out differently depending on how much in common there is in our dispositions to value. Of course, as we have seen, it is possible for someone to be mistaken about what is valuable, since what one values may not be what one would value in ideal circumstances. So much of our moral disputes and investigations might still make sense even if relativism was true. We might, for example, be assuming that people we argue with are like us in the relevant respects, or at least we are prepared to presuppose this in particular disagreements. And, after all, many people do come to the point where they think it is not worth continuing to argue about values with someone. This might be for all the usual sorts of reasons we give up on argument, but it may also sometimes be that they think the argument reduces to a "clash of values" that there is not much more to say about.

Lewis suggests that his account best fits our practices of evaluating, arguing about value, and acting on value (*ibid.*: 87). Indeed, Lewis thinks he is giving us the meaning of our word "value", and words like it. His theory is meant to be an analytic truth (*ibid.*: 86), in the same basket as "all parents have children". He admits, of course, that it is an unobvious analytic truth. Someone could be able to use the word "value" without agreeing with his analysis. He also says that his account is "equivocally analytic". Actual use of the expression "value" might leave it somewhat ambiguous or undetermined what people mean, and if so Lewis's theory would be a cleaning-up of the expression; it aims to fall "somewhere near the middle of the range of variation and indecision" (*ibid.*: 86–7). Philosophers have not yet come to any agreement about the best way to tell whether a proposed philosophical analysis gets it right or misses out on crucial aspects of the concept to be analysed, although in practice many philosophers do seem to think that in doing "philosophical analysis" they are engaged in the pursuit of unobvious analytic truths, and their success or failure is judged on the basis of how well the analysis they come up with fits our pattern of usage of the expression in question.

One aspect of our ordinary opinions (or some ordinary opinions) about moral value that Lewis's theory does not capture is the intuition that many people have that moral values and norms are "objective" in some sense; they apply to someone regardless of what they would prefer to do, and regardless of what sort of person they would like to be. Even if we did come across someone who wanted to be a bloodthirsty torturer, and wanted to be like that even after proper imaginative acquaintance with that lifestyle choice (perhaps they have had a few years' experience, have thought about it a lot, have a sense of what their victims experience, etc.), we think that would still make no difference about whether or not it is morally valueless and evil to be a bloodthirsty torturer. For better or worse, we do not take this belief of ours to just be a report of our own preferences either. Certainly, we want to be the kind of people that dislike bloodthirsty torture in the world, but that is not all there is to our condemnation of the torturer. There are two aspects to this belief we have (or some of us have): a certain anti-relativism that has already been mentioned – what is fundamentally morally valuable does not vary from person to person (at least not to the extent of making bloodthirsty torture okay for people who endorse that choice); and a feeling that the truths of ethics are necessarily true – there could not be variation depending on accidental facts of human psychology.

Lewis's position is consistent with thinking that all human beings have the same fundamental valuing dispositions (so someone who appears to be a thoughtful torturer is mistaken or irrational or has some other imaginative defect).[2] He does take the point, though, that his theory makes what is valuable for us contingent. We could have had other desires to desire under ideal circumstances, and so other things could have been valuable for us.[3] Or perhaps we could say that those other valuers are talking about something else – maybe what is valuable is what we *actually* are disposed to value in ideal circumstances – but this does not eliminate the worry that they would be in relevantly the same position as us, and be correct in what they used the word "value" for, even though they called very different things "values" ([1989b] 2000a: 89). Lewis admits that it would match some of our strands of thought better if there were something that necessarily every thinking thing, actual or possible, would be drawn towards if they considered it: that is, if there were something that, necessarily, every valuer would value in ideal circumstances. Unfortunately for that strand in our thought, there is no such thing, as far as Lewis can see. This realization may be disturbing, but he thinks we should not go so far as to say that there are not values at all. Rather, what we have is something that did not quite measure up to what would have been ideal, and we should believe that values are not quite what we might have expected, rather than conclude that there are no such things at all. (This is a case of an "imperfect deserver", the sort of case that will be discussed further in Chapter 9.)

If Lewis is right, then even the realm of value and ethics can be accounted for in a materialist system (and one based on a fairly sparse conception of the material, at that). Or at least the start of such an accounting has been given. One problem is that while Lewis tells us a story about moral value, it is not explicitly a story about what we *ought* to do. A natural story is that what we ought to do is maximize moral value, or maximize some balance of moral values. This is even what is suggested by the role of moral value structures in Lewis's semantics for deontic logics (the logics of obligation) (Lewis 1973a, 1974b), but other things Lewis said suggest that he might not endorse this consequentialist thesis about the connection between moral values and obligation (and for Lewis's anti-consequentialism, see the next section). Nevertheless, presumably with moral value in place, we are in a position to start developing a theory of obligations without needing too much more in the way of fundamental resources.

Of course, other psychologistic theories of value would also be compatible with Lewis's materialism, provided they did not require that we have new mysterious mental faculties not allowed by Lewis's philosophy of mind. If such approaches do not work, though, and ethics or values generally require us to recognize another, extra-physical, aspect of the world, then this would be an area where we would have to develop a non-materialistic understanding of our world. The challenge then would be to explain how these non-material aspects of our world affect material states such as bodily movements (as when we act or talk morally) and other material systems. It is very hard to see how a story like this will work, so, after all, some story along Lewis's lines may serve to unlock very puzzling questions about value and its place in the world.

A plurality of values and the faults of consequentialism

Lewis's dispositional theory of value is an answer to "metaethical" questions: for example, what is moral value and what connection does moral value have to motivation? The distinction between metaethics, on the one hand, and ethics or morality, on the other, is drawn differently by different people, but the idea behind the demarcation is usually that moral or ethical theories offer answers to moral problems, whereas metaethics answers questions about the nature of morality and moral theorizing (What is it about? Why does it matter? How do we discover answers to these questions?) The boundary can be somewhat fuzzy, but let me turn to Lewis's ethical writings: what Lewis has to say about which moral principles are correct, and which are not.

Lewis never advances a complete ethical system, and perhaps he thought that ethics may not be very systematic. Why should our desires about what we desire not be a mass of unsystematic preferences? So remarks about Lewis's ethical views have to rely on piecing together fragments. Some themes can nevertheless be discerned.

Different systematic ethical theories tend to operate with one of three basic notions. "Consequentialists" typically focus on the value of outcomes, and evaluate actions in terms of how they contribute to outcomes, or how they are reasonably expected to contribute to outcomes. A basic example is utilitarianism. One simple version, for example, concentrates on the maximizing of pleasure. Actions are right or wrong in so far as they contribute to the total of human pleasure or avoid adding to the total of human suffering (and maybe the pleasure and suffering of other creatures is to be taken into account in the calculation as well). Another simple version would focus on what an agent *expected* the effect on human pleasure and suffering to be. This second version might say an action was morally right even if it unforseeably led to disaster. "Deontologists" tend to think the basic moral concept is that of duty or obligation. A simple deontological theory may have a list of hard-and-fast rules of conduct, to be pursued for their own sake, regardless of the cost. (Other versions might have ways of ranking different rules of behaviour, and might have rules that look less like a code of conduct and more like a set of priorities.) "Virtue ethicists" think the fundamental notion is what sort of person one is. Actions are correct or incorrect in so far as they flow from the right traits of character. (In a simple virtue theory, something might be correct if it is done from a sense of honesty or justice, regardless of what the action itself is or what consequences it has.) Actual ethical theories may have more qualifications and aspects than the simple ones I have sketched, or may be combinations of these theories, but this should serve as a guide to common styles of ethical systems for those unfamiliar with contemporary philosophical ethics.

Those familiar with Lewis's approach to rationality and decision-making might expect Lewis to be some sort of consequentialist. Since rational decision-making is a matter of maximizing the amount of expected utility caused by an action (its expected value), then presumably right action would be a matter of maximizing some expected utility produced by an action as well. Not, however, for Lewis. Lewis had several criticisms of standard consequentialism, and instead suggested that moral considerations were more pluralistic and messy than traditional consequentialism suggested. Whether Lewis's views were consequentialist in some wider sense is not a straightforward matter and is a question I shall return to.

Several times Lewis makes the point that some forms of consequentialism, for instance "radical utilitarianism", are distant from moral common sense. Here is a representative passage, in a discussion of "radical utilitarianism, stark and unqualified":

> It is no easy matter to accept the strange doctrine that nothing at all matters to what ought to be the case except the total balance of good and evil – that any sort or amount of evil can be neutralized, as if it had never been, by enough countervailing good – and that the balancing evil and good may be entirely unrelated, as when the harm I do to you is cancelled out by the kindness of one Martian to another. ([1978] 2000a: 34)

It is not that consequences do not matter morally, especially when they are extreme enough. Lewis at one point writes "Consequentialism is all wrong as everyday ethics, right as a limiting case" ([1984a] 2000a: 214), where the limiting case he has in mind is when the stakes are high enough: whether military personnel should obey commands to launch nuclear strikes. It is rather that they have a limited weight, a weight that is all too easily outweighed or otherwise overcome by other moral considerations, at least in everyday cases.

There are several respects in which Lewis thinks consequentialism departs significantly from common sense, to the detriment of consequentialism. The first is that it is too impersonal. To value the welfare of strangers to anything like the same extent we value our own welfare and the welfare of those around us is a "betrayal of our particular affections" (1986a: 128). We somehow just do not have the obligation to assist the poor and starving in the third world to the same extent we would if they were nearby and well-known to us, even if the amount of effort in the two cases would be the same (1996c). Some may find this a distasteful moral view to defend, but Lewis does at least seem to be right that neglect of stranger's suffering is part of our ordinary moral practice, whatever we may tell ourselves in our theoretical moments about our obligations to all of humanity. With few rare exceptions, we do not do as much as we could for others, not even the little extra it would take to do great good. (At least this is true if it is true, as it is widely believed, that donations to third-world charities do great good in individuals' lives with the expenditure of comparatively little of the resources of a first-world donor.) Lewis proposes taking common-sense moral sentiments seriously on this point. If we are inclined to think that it is permissible to ignore the easily avoidable suffering of strangers, maybe this is because it *is* permissible to ignore that suffering.[4]

Another respect in which Lewis's opinions can be contrasted with many mainstream views is that he was always careful to leave room for "a plurality of incommensurable values" (2000a: 98). There might be various moral values, in conflict with each other. Not only may it not be possible, even in principle, to achieve a result that is ideal with regard to all of them together ([1993a] 2000a: 103), it may even be that it is psychologically impossible to appreciate all the aspects of moral value at once ([1989b] 2000a: 82). It may not even be possible (at least for beings like us) to take them all into account when making a moral decision.

Associated with this, Lewis resisted the idea that we could give unified moral evaluations of character. Some people (maybe most people) have a mixture of virtues and vices, and these virtues and vices may interact (as, for example, a virtue of patriotism or friendship could be inextricably linked to inappropriate partiality or vengefulness). There may be no way to issue a general overall judgement of whether someone is a good person or not. As Lewis says, in his usual style, in answer to the question of what to think of a man in an example who displays a mixture of admirable and regrettable traits:

> Well – I've told you what to think ... He is a strange mixture of good and evil. *That* is what to think of him. Isn't that enough? Why do we need a simple, unified, summary judgement?
>
> If there were a last judgement, it would then be necessary to send the whole morally mixed man to Heaven or to Hell. *Then* there would be real need for one unified verdict. I would be very well content to leave the problem of the unified verdict to those who believe in a last judgement. And they would do well to leave it to the Judge.   ([1984a] 2000a: 207)

In many respects I get the impression Lewis was inclined to think of morality and ethics in terms of virtues of character. He once identified himself as one of those "who think of morality in terms of virtue and honour, desert and respect and esteem, loyalties and affections and solidarity" (1986a: 127), which suggests more of a virtue-theoretic conception of morality than a consequentialist or deontological one. (My guess is that had Lewis tried to articulate a complete view, it would have contained elements of each, and he would have resisted the attempt to reduce all the different aspects of moral behaviour and evaluation to any single one.)

One last point should be made about Lewis's thinking, one that I think consequentialists especially should take on board. Lewis was inclined to think that good or evil that was beyond our causal control was not worth taking into account in determining what it was moral to do, at least in some respects. For example, this arises when Lewis addresses the concern that his modal realism would produce moral indifference. In response to Robert Adams's question "What is wrong with actualizing evils, since they will occur in some other possible world anyway if they don't occur in this one?" (Adams 1974: 216), Lewis replied:

> If you actualise evils, you will be an evil-doer, a causal source of evil. That is something which, if you are virtuous, you do not want to be. Otherworldly evils are neither here nor there. They aren't your evils. Your virtuous desire to do good and not evil has nothing to do with the sum total of good and evil throughout reality. It has to do with what befalls you and your worldmates, and in particular it has to do with the way in which what befalls yourself and others depends causally on what you do.   (1986a: 127)

You could see this as something he was driven to by modal realism. Instead, I think it is better to see it as allied with the insight in causal decision theory. Just as when you are trying to act according to your beliefs and desires you should take into account the utility of what you expect your action to produce, rather than just what is probable if you perform the action (say, because the action is evidence of something beyond your control), so too, when trying to do good, you should pay attention to what *difference* in good and evil your action may produce, and not what the total of good and evil might be, to the extent that the total is independent of your action. This will make a difference in cases analogous to the ones used to motivate causal decision theory (see Chapter 6 for discussion), but also in cases where, independently of what you do, there is some infinity of good or evil guaranteed. Even if the past contains an infinite amount of goodness, or an infinite amount of evil, or both (or if there is some infinitude of value otherwise outside your control), if there is some amount of goodness or evil under your control, then that should be your concern when deciding what to try to bring about.

Lewis explicitly disavows consequentialism, but there is a puzzle about why he does not think his views delivered consequentialism of at least an attenuated sort. His dispositional theory of value, remember, says that what was a value for a person is what they would desire to desire in appropriate conditions (or perhaps what is valuable is what *we* would desire to desire in ideal conditions, regardless of who the person being considered is). And given his conception of partial beliefs and desires, for an action to be in accord with an agent's desires is for it to maximize expected utility, given the values assigned by those desires to alternative outcomes (in the specific, causal decision theory sense of "utility" discussed in Chapter 6). Those who desire as they should (i.e. those who desire in accord with our values) seek to choose the action that will cause the best outcome according to their desires. So, given that their desires will be in line with what they should be, then presumably their value function will work rather like a consequentialist's good is supposed to: their value function on outcomes will define a quantity that good people will maximize (or perhaps there will be many different quantities that different possible good agents will rightly be maximizing). So it seems Lewis's good agents will at least act how consequentialism, broadly construed, says they should act. Perhaps this means that Lewis should count as a consequentialist in some broad sense (although he would still repudiate it in some more narrow senses). Or perhaps there is some other point that he thought importantly distinguished his views from those of any consequentialist ethic. Unless something new comes to light, it may not be possible to tell.

It would take too long to discuss all of Lewis's contributions to issues in applied ethics and politics, and so I have selected two areas to discuss: some interesting issues Lewis raised about punishment, and Lewis's discussion of how to justify tolerance, both as a consequentialist justification for free speech, and as applied to a puzzle about academic appointments. When deciding what academic appointments to make, why do selection committees often ignore whether the candidates' views are, in fact, true?

Punishment

One of the central parts of the philosophical disputes about punishment concerns the question of what punishment is for: is it for deterrence, protection of others, compensation, retribution, reform or some combination? There are many debates as well, of course, about what sorts of punishment serve what purposes, although these debates are as much empirical debates as philosophical ones. Lewis's contribution, however, is to explore some questions about the morality of our practices of punishment that do not receive as much attention.

One of his papers, "Do We Believe in Penal Substitution?" (1997a) explores some of the tensions in our ideas about penal substitution: the extent to which it is morally permissible for one person to voluntarily suffer another person's punishment in their place. For much of the time, we reject this. We would think it absurd to let an armed robber or murderer go free, provided her innocent best friend agreed to go to prison for those crimes. We would not let a rich criminal hire someone else to have his flogging for him (or not knowingly, at least), if we still had floggings as punishments. Penal substitution, deliberately allowing the innocent to be punished instead of the guilty, often seems to us like an outrage, and it also seems as if it would not excuse the guilty party from the punishment. If someone did somehow substitute themselves, and we later discovered this, we would not think that we should let the criminal get off scot-free just because their friend unjustly took the rap.

Or so we ordinarily think. Lewis points out, though, that one school of thought in contemporary Christianity seems to take the opposite view when discussing the Atonement, when, according to Christians, Jesus "died for our sins" on the cross. One interpretation of this is that Jesus voluntarily took upon himself some or all of the punishment due to us for our sins; he somehow paid our penalty for us. (Or perhaps some portion of our penalty, enough so that justice could be satisfied by God's forgiving the rest at our request.) But this would be penal substitution. How could it be morally permissible for Jesus to be punished for *your* sins? Even if he were, how could that make *you* any less liable to punishment? One problem is that this story about the Atonement seems to be immoral (or just nonsensical) according to our usual views about punishment. Another problem, one that Lewis focuses on more, is that the Christians who believe this do not seem to be consistent. They seem to think that penal substitution is perfectly okay in the Atonement, but are not disposed

David Lewis

to think that it is okay in more everyday cases. It is not even that they have some principled story about why it is proper for Jesus to be put to death for our sins, but it would be a travesty if a prisoner on death row could be forgiven her punishment by having a volunteer give his life in her place. They just seem to have different beliefs about penal substitution at one time and at another. They stand charged with doublethink.

Lewis goes on to point out that some of this doublethink might not be specifically Christian. Ordinary attitudes to punishment also lend themselves to approve of penal substitution in some circumstances. If this is right, then this is not a puzzle peculiar to one theological doctrine, and most of us are in an awkward position on this question. Lewis asks us to consider our attitude towards fines, and not only the small fines that may be more or less like fees or taxes, but the serious fines that are sometimes levelled by our judicial system. These fines can harm a convict quite as much as a prison sentence. Indeed some criminals would rather serve a prison sentence than pay a fine. However, we *do* let people pay fines for other people, and we let others give gifts of money or resources to people who have to pay fines, or have recently paid fines. In such cases, the person who suffers most of the harm is the person who pays the fine, and the effects that punishment might be supposed to have on the convicted person (deterrence, or denial of the means to continue crime, or reform) may well be, to some extent, deflected if someone else pays their fine for them. Not in all cases, perhaps – a criminal might be more chastened by a fine paid for them by their already hard-pressed family – but surely in some the effect of the punishment is deflected, as when a small-time criminal has a fine paid for him by a wealthy crime boss.

Sometimes allowing someone else to pay a criminal's fine might serve some of the purposes of punishment, but so, occasionally, might penal substitution in the case of imprisonment or the death penalty. We think it would be wrong in the latter case, so why do we allow it in the former? Fines might make sense if the punishment is a matter of paying compensation, and when compensation is due it does not matter so much who pays it as long as the injured party is compensated, but since a fine is not handed on to the victim (if there is a victim), compensatory thinking does not seem to be behind fines (unless it is the state or the community that is meant to be compensated, but at most this is presumably only part of the story). It would, of course, be very difficult in practice to try to enforce a rule that everyone must pay their own fines out of their own resources. Secret gifts would be very hard to police, and it would be hard to know how long to keep a ban on gifts to a punished criminal in place. But if this is the problem, then the solution would seem to be to not use fines as an instrument of punishment, rather than allow there to be an instrument that enables penal substitution. If our concern is that the person to be punished suffers the penalty, then imprisonment or flogging or the death penalty or community service would seem to be better remedies than fines ([1997a] 2000a: 135). Our ordinary thinking about punishment seems to be two-faced: on the one hand, we abhor penal substitution; and on the other we think it is not too wrong for someone to have their fine paid for them by someone else, or for this to happen *de facto*, by means of gifts to the condemned criminal. If there is something wrong or absurd about penal substitution, it is not just theorists of the Atonement who need to do some serious revision of their attitudes. And if it is sometimes okay, it would be good to have a better understanding of when it is okay and when it is not.

Another topic in the philosophy of punishment is the question of why we often punish failed attempts less harshly than we punish successful wrongdoing. The assassin whose target ducks while the bullet is already in the air has the same mindset as she would have had if the bullet had struck; she is just as much a menace to society; and we want to deter attempts to kill just as much as we want to deter successful killings. (Indeed, in so far as the attempt is all that is directly under the criminal's control, deterring one seems to be pretty much the same as deterring the other.) It is probably true that the public are more outraged by successful crimes than foiled ones, and the demand for punishment is greater in such cases. But unless the public (or victims, or whoever) are *just* in being more outraged, that does not yet make it right to punish attempts less harshly, Lewis argues (1987); it would merely be to give into unjust demands to treat the cases differently.

Lewis has more sympathy for the thought that we should punish half-hearted attempts more leniently than wholehearted ones. Someone who tepidly attempts a crime, and maybe wavers while they are in the act, may deserve more consideration than one who leaps in without qualms. Success in attempts is some evidence that the attempt was wholehearted; failed attempts are some evidence that the attempt itself was less full-blown. This may all be right, but Lewis argues that it would not explain our practices. Whether an attempt succeeds is too rough an indicator of whether the attempt was full-blooded. Someone who is skilled or well-resourced, for example, might reliably succeed even with a half-hearted attempt, while another may put all their efforts into an attempt but be cheated by a lack of power or by fortune. If we care about "heartedness" of attempts, better to take that into consideration directly in sentencing. (It may be difficult to discover after the fact, but this is true of many features of a crime, including ones we take into account in mitigation such as subsequent remorse or its absence.)

So neither of these considerations justify our general practice of punishing attempts less harshly than successes. In "The Punishment that Leaves Something to Chance" (1987), Lewis suggests that there is a better justification available, although he does not say that this is a justification we in fact rely on, and is uncertain whether in the end it is good enough. This justification begins by discussing the justice of "penal lotteries": cases where the punishment is chancy. An example might be that if you are found guilty, you need to draw straws. Draw a short straw and you are executed, draw a long straw and you go free. Some are *overt*. Lewis cites the practice of punishing mutiny by executing one in ten of a regiment, and perhaps the practice of turning criminals into gladiators in ancient Rome would be another example, since it explicitly involved many of the criminals being killed and some surviving. Other penal lotteries are *covert*, where it is common knowledge that some aspect of the punishment involves taking a risk. Lewis cites the appalling contemporary practice of turning a blind eye to violence in prison. We in effect punish at least some prisoners in part by exposing them to the risk of rape, AIDS and prison violence.

For a lottery to be fair the chance of additional punishment should be correlated with the seriousness of the crime. The actual mechanism may not matter. We could do it by drawing straws, but we could, for instance, run a simulation of the crime, with the same chances of "success" as the original crime, and give additional punishment to someone if the simulation produced a "success". This would make sure that the chance of extra punishment matched the chance that the criminal's intentions would cause harm, which seems a fair thing to punish (it provides more deterrence to competent criminals, for example). What we could even do is let the original events count as the lottery. What better simulation could we have, after all, than what actually occurred? If we do this, then we can see every attempt at crime punished in part by a lottery. Every attempter gets punished by a chance of additional prison time, and the chance is equal to the chance that their attempt would succeed. This has to be right, if we give them more punishment when, and only when, they in fact succeed!

This would be what Lewis called an "impure" lottery, as well as a covert one, impure because some of the punishment is in the form of a penal lottery, and some is not. All of the punishment is due to the attempt, but the punishment comes in two parts. One is some punishment that is not a lottery, and the other is, in effect, a ticket in a penal lottery. The penal lottery gives every attempter a chance of punishment equal to the chance their attempt would lead to a bad outcome, and the determination is by a "simulation" that is just like the attempt itself, because it *is* the attempt itself. Successful attempts automatically count as the equivalent of drawing the short straw.

This would give us the result that we see: some prison time (or whatever) for an unsuccessful attempt, and more for a successful one. What is the chance that an attempt will get extra punishment? Everything else being equal, it is the chance of that attempt being successful. Suppose we did justify ourselves this way. Would it be an appropriate way to proceed? You might think that it was unfair, because it treated cases that should be punished equally with different rates of punishment. This is not obviously right, as Lewis points out: everyone who makes an attempt of a certain sort gets the same chance in a penal lottery, and isn't this equal treatment in some important sense? We might want to consider the case of rewards. Suppose the state decides to reward its firefighters after a particularly dangerous blaze by giving each of them 1000 lottery tickets. In one sense this is an equal reward: each gets the same chance in the next lottery draw. In another sense, it may end up being quite uneven: Smith might win nothing, while Jones wins $500,000. Does that mean that it was an unfair reward? If it does seem like a fair reward in some good sense, then by the same token penal lotteries may well count as fair punishments, even though the *outcomes* of the penal lotteries will be different for different prisoners.

Thinking of the punishment of attempts as, in effect, a penal lottery casts the practice in a different light, and may well be the best we can do to make sense of the practice. If it is not good enough then all of us are left with a problem. What could be a morally defensible reason for our current distinction between the punishment for unsuccessful attempts and the punishment for successful ones?

Tolerance

Today we are inclined to think that tolerance is one of the most important social virtues. We have a society that permits an incred-

David Lewis

ibly wide range of political, religious, social and theoretical opinions. We are cautious about censorship, and the claim that someone's freedom of speech is being violated or ignored is one with a powerful resonance. Of course, our love of freedom of expression and tolerance for others is often not perfect, but even when the views of a minority are persecuted or quashed, people often feel obliged to search for some special reason why that group's freedom of expression can be curtailed, and others are often very wary when such intolerance is advocated.

We do not feel the need to tolerate everyone's *actions*, of course. Even if someone thinks it is okay to treat their children or servants as property, or to use violence to get their way, or pump noxious chemicals into the environment and so on, we believe we are entitled to object when they do so, and in many cases do a lot more than just voice objections. But many of us do think we should tolerate others' speech, and defend their freedom of expression, even when they disagree with us (perhaps especially when they disagree with us). Even more than free speech we value freedom of opinion. Most of us would object to a "witch hunt" where someone was persecuted just for their beliefs, without evidence that they were about to act on them or evidence that they were trying to convince others.

Why should we be tolerant? In particular, why should we be tolerant of people who hold and express views we think are not just false, but dangerous? After all, the wrong policy about education could result in harm to a generation of children; the wrong policy in foreign affairs could lead to unjust and terrible warfare or other disasters; the wrong economic policy could lead to unemployment and poverty for millions. Why should we value tolerance enough to risk this sort of error spreading? There are other questions about tolerance that are hard to answer. Even if we are prepared to tolerate those who tolerate us, why should we tolerate the people who advocate intolerance? Many people advocate political theories according to which speech should be controlled, or they advocate religious doctrines according to which some other beliefs should be restricted or stamped out. Why tolerate the intolerant?

One standard set of justifications offered by John Stuart Mill is discussed by Lewis in "Mill and Milquetoast" (1989c). Lewis lists six justifications that he takes from Mill's discussion. The first is that tolerance has the advantage of not suppressing true views by mistake, in the belief that they are false. The second is that we should not try to prevent falsehoods (or other harmful views) from being discussed because truth and falsehood are sometimes interwoven; suppression of some false or harmful view might accidentally suppress some truth as well. The third and fourth are reasons to welcome continuing challenges, even to true and useful views. These challenges stop the truth from becoming "dead dogma", with even its supporters not understanding the grounds to believe it (the third reason). Even worse, important truths might become empty slogans that eventually lose their meaning, if they are not allowed to be contested (the fourth reason). The fifth and sixth reasons concern the value of people. Autonomy in forming one's beliefs is better than just having beliefs forced down one's throat (even true beliefs), and autonomy does better when people have genuine alternatives presented to them. In addition, Mill (according to Lewis) holds that peoples' characters – both moral and intellectual – are better developed when they have opportunities to think and choose. (Being good at thinking requires practice!) All of these are reasons to tolerate people holding, expressing and promoting views other than the ones we take to be correct.

Lewis suggests some other advantages to go with this list. Along with the point about truth and falsehood sometimes being interwoven, Lewis points out that even a completely false view might be valuable as a source of insight when it is "transformed". It may illuminate new alternatives, or be applicable by analogy somewhere else, even when the original claim is false, or prompt a future discovery in some other way. Lewis also points out that suppression requires paternalism – somebody needs to set themselves up as in effect trying to dictate to others what they shall believe – and such paternalism may well be offensive. Suppression also requires putting a mechanism in place to monitor speech crime and thought crime, and setting up such a mechanism runs the risk of having it perverted in all sorts of harmful ways. Finally, suppression, to be effective, probably needs to put in place a system of disincentives, and disincentives, such as dungeons, gulags, asylums, execution, sackings, fines or whatever, are drawbacks from a utilitarian perspective.

Lewis points out that one advantage of all of these arguments is that they are *neutral*: they offer the same sorts of benefits to all the competing parties, whether those groups are clashing over political goals, religious beliefs, social priorities or whatever. Mill does not have to offer different arguments to different competing groups. Lewis also characterizes Mill's arguments as *utilitarian* defences, not necessarily utilitarian in the narrow sense that they will lead to more happiness than unhappiness, but at least that they are defences that try to show that benefits outweigh costs, when we measure in terms of "utility in the largest sense, grounded on the permanent interests of man as a progressive being", to use Mill's own words (Mill 1956: 14). Despite Lewis's reservations about consequentialism, Lewis seemed to think utilitarian reasoning is appropriate for this sort of issue.

Lewis thinks, however, that these arguments will not be sufficient. The stakes are often too high for the advantages Mill mentions to be worthwhile. At the very least, some of the disputants will believe the stakes are this high. Lewis gives a (hopefully fictional) example of someone who thinks that heresy leads to damnation, and who thinks that the cost of having heretics luring people into damnation is very, very much greater than any of the benefits Mill and Lewis mention. Lewis points out that people might believe the stakes are this high in real life. Here are two examples, which are mine rather than Lewis's. If you believe that a certain social policy would lead to a great deal of child abuse, and you think the best way to stop that policy being implemented is to muzzle the people arguing for it, you might think avoiding that harm was worth the costs Mill points out. After 1945, Germany banned the Nazi party and put restrictions on the sorts of political speech its citizens could engage in: various forms of neo-Nazi propaganda are illegal. Presumably this is because the law-makers thought the benefits of unrestricted free speech and tolerance for different points of view were outweighed by the risk that Nazism could be resurrected in Germany. There are lots of other disputes about very important matters – matters of war and peace, life and death – where tolerance of an opposing view seems to risk something more valuable than the valuable things Mill points to (or that Lewis can find for his tally of neutral reasons for tolerance). It seems that the list is too shaky to support tolerance when the chips are down, or so Lewis suspects.

Lewis does think there is another, more important reason, to have tolerance, and this reason, while it appeals to utilitarian considerations, is not neutral: the same version of it does not work equally well for all the disputing parties. Consider a case that Lewis discusses, of a conscientious but fanatic inquisitor. The inquisitor thinks that the spread of heresy is one of the worst things that can happen because heretics infect innocent people with beliefs that send them to hell. Let us suppose that there are also some heretics around who feel just as strongly about their heresy. In Lewis's example, the heretics believe that it is the inquisitor and his crowd that are damning people to hell.

Let us suppose the inquisitor would rather wipe out the heretics than tolerate them. But, as Lewis points out, there is something worse from the inquisitor's point of view than just tolerating the heretics. Suppose the inquisitor attempted to violently suppress the heretics, and vice versa, but the *heretics won*. That would be worse from the point of view of the inquisitor than if there was tolerance all around because if the heretics won, the inquisitor would be unable to put his case to people who were wavering, and only the heretic would be allowed to speak. The heretics are in the same situation. They'd like to force the inquisitor to shut up and not spread his message, but they'd prefer all-around tolerance to a situation where the inquisitor can impose his will on the heretics.

So tolerance might be a second-best option for the competing factions. The expected benefit of intolerance (a chance of silencing the opposition) needs to be weighed against the risk of harm (a chance the opposition will do the silencing). When the outcomes are uncertain, as they often are in real life (especially when there are a variety of competing groups), a "truce" of toleration may look like a better prospect than an all-out fight to both sides. (It might be that one side or the other is underestimating their chances, but as long as all the sides *think* toleration will probably serve them better than conflict, we have a stable basis for mutual toleration.) This may not be enshrined in anything like a formal agreement – Lewis has long argued that conventions can exist without being backed by explicit agreements – and the custom might exist even if most people were not conscious of the reason.

This reason for tolerance – as a truce called so that different sides can avoid the risk of a violent confrontation going the other side's way – is not quite a neutral reason, because while it offers the same sort of benefit to each party, looked at the other way the benefit it offers is opposite. The inquisitor is being offered deliverance from the risk of heretic victory in return for forgoing his own chance at winning, and the heretic is being offered the opposite; he gets to avoid the risk of inquisitorial victory, at the cost of his chance that heresy will triumph through force. As long as each side thinks he is getting more than he is giving, mutual tolerance will be worthwhile.

Lewis deals with two challenges to this story: how does this explain tolerance of the weak, and tolerance of the intolerant? After all, if one side is significantly inferior to another, the powerful side

David Lewis

may well think the risk of losing is not enough to deter them from using their superiority; and there's no point having a truce with someone who isn't prepared to respect the truce, so you would expect that our tolerance would only extend to people who themselves were prepared to embrace tolerance. But we do tolerate opinions held by people without much power (e.g. small minorities), and we do protect the freedom of speech even of those who advocate its destruction. How could we explain that?

Lewis points out that there are many, many points of disagreement in society, and the make-ups of the groups of believers are always changing: some people are becoming more committed, some less, some are changing their minds, and so on. Trying to have a separate practice of tolerance for each important issue would be unwieldy and unworkable. Imagine trying to keep track of the status of a hundred different controversial topics, and remember who you were allowed to use violence on to silence for each one. Having a myriad of small deals would also be risky. There are too many ways one side or another could miscalculate, either by overestimating their own strength, or being unaware of alliances, or attacking the wrong targets. Far better to have a general, simple agreement: everyone tolerates everyone when it comes to speech. This increases security and certainty all around because once one faction starts throwing their weight around, many others will be nervous that they might be the next target. This general agreement, for simplicity, might protect the speech of weak parties and intolerant parties. An attempt to silence the intolerant could easily lead to the breakdown of the system, especially if intolerant people on both sides have initially tolerant allies. And declaring open season on the weak would have similar problems, problems that are probably even more acute. (Especially since today's weak opinion might become tomorrow's strong opinion. If that happens, the previously strong faction would be in trouble had they been intolerant!)

Of course, it may turn out that some limitations on free speech – legal, but also informal limitations – may be able to be stably implemented. There may even be occasions when particular opinions can be suppressed for a time in an otherwise relatively tolerant society; the case of the suppression of Nazism in postwar West Germany might be an example. But picking and choosing does threaten the fabric of a general practice of tolerance, and Lewis urges us to be careful before we try to institute new exceptions, since the instability caused by a breakdown in tolerance in one area can have unexpected ramifications.

One application of Lewis's utilitarian story about tolerance is an unexpected one. Lewis asks why, in academic hiring decisions, so little weight is put on the question of whether what the candidate believes is *true*, or close to the truth (1989a). Getting to the truth (or close to it) is very important in many academic disciplines (although perhaps not all), and many academics think, and should think, that it is an important goal. Academics often disagree about central questions in their discipline. In philosophy this is endemic, of course, but disagreements about method and about particular hypotheses are widespread throughout academia. Nevertheless, according to Lewis, in hiring decisions the question of whether or not the candidate's opinions are correct is rarely raised, and many would think it inappropriate to raise this question. Related questions, such as how intelligent or diligent or imaginative or widely read a candidate is are appropriate, and that the candidate has what it takes to get things right seems a perfectly fair question for consideration, but why not consider whether the candidate's opinions are in fact correct?

Perhaps Lewis is over-optimistic to say that in many real decisions "the appointing department will typically behave as if the truth or falsehood of the candidate's doctrines are weightless, not a legitimate consideration at all" ([1989a] 2000a: 190). But this certainly captures a strand in academic decision-making: the thought that the level of the candidate's ability might matter, but the mere facts about what the candidate's considered opinion are should not count beyond this. (Of course, ability might not only cover ability to get to the truth, but other things as well, such as teaching and administrative ability, but, nevertheless, the point is that mere correctness can be seen as not mattering.) Academics do not usually seek to justify their decisions about which candidate to support on the basis of whether a candidate has mistaken conclusions (unless the conclusions can be argued to be sloppy or somesuch), and some disapproval is evidenced of places that hire people who toe their party line in preference to hiring the most able applicants. We are inclined to suspect a decision-maker of "bias" if they show preference for people on their side in hiring decisions, where this bias is supposed to be a bad thing, and not just flowing from a worthy desire to advance the truth. Lewis points out that, again, there is a range of "neutral" benefits to diversity of opinion: spreading our bets, avoiding dead dogma, counting on the chance that able thinkers will change their minds when presented with evidence and so will become champions of the truth, and so on. Again, Lewis fears that this neutral list will not be sufficient when the stakes are high, and

David Lewis

suggests that what is a better reason is a tacit convention of tolerance. By tolerating error (by our lights) is worthwhile if it prevents destructive conflict with the holders of error, and avoids the chance that those who are in error (by our lights) will stamp out the truth (as we see it). And the same reasoning, *mutatis mutandis*, will work for our intellectual opposition. They may well also see tolerance as an acceptable compromise rather than trying to build up or destroy theories and opinions through hiring policies. And again, having a general convention of forbearance might also shield unfashionable minorities who have no hope of winning a battle of hiring, and shield some intolerant intellectual opinions that counsel against tolerance. (Some political views do seem to suggest their adherents should try to "stack" departments with fellow travellers, but often proponents of academic tolerance hold that trying to drive these opinions out of the academy would be to sink to their opponent's level, and be doing something that was not the right thing to do.)

One curious, and perhaps worrying thing, about Lewis's defence of tolerance is that it is something that could be undermined by being made explicit. After all, if people thought that tolerance was a "necessary evil", justified primarily because it called for tolerance from the other side, that might increase temptation to do intolerant things while giving the appearance of tolerance. An appointment committee might *say* their reasons are something else, but secretly decide against a candidate just because she's wrong, in the committee's opinion. A government might *say* that it is cracking down on some behaviour – noise pollution, civil disturbances, recreational drug use – and really be aiming to shut down political, social or religious opposition. Of course, these sorts of things already happen from time to time and place to place. But we might worry that they would happen more often if people explicitly thought that it was worth being tolerant only as a conventional "deal" to prevent trouble, than if they unthinkingly held on to tolerance as a valuable ideal without much opinion as to why it is valuable. Lewis points out that there are reasons to be careful about the sort of sneaky intolerance that this might produce. Impressions that this sort of thing is happening can leak out in all sorts of ways and damage other parties' habits of tolerance, but the thought that *my* secret breach of an agreement (for a good cause, of course) is worthwhile given the immediate benefits, even though it may indirectly cause some damage to the convention of tolerance, can seem very tempting. And if enough people become tempted, the convention of toleration itself may collapse.

Chapter 9

Some reflections on Lewis's method

Lewis has had a significant impact in many areas of philosophy. One of his most significant legacies, however, will be in the area of philosophical methodology: how philosophers do philosophy, and how they think about what they are doing. This book is full of examples of Lewis's approach to philosophy, but it is worth explicitly considering some of Lewis's views about how to go about tackling philosophical problems.

Quine and Moore

In Chapter 1, I mentioned some of the ways in which Lewis's philosophy was influenced by Quine's. Lewis is a materialist (at least about this world); the only things we need to believe are found in this world are physical objects, and perhaps sets that have physical objects among their members, if those sets are located here. (If events are sets, for example (see Chapter 3), then sets are among the things we encounter in this world as well.) Lewis is also inclined to think that concrete objects plus mathematical objects such as sets are all we need to explain reality. Aspects of reality such as meaning, morality or necessity are to be explained ultimately in these terms. Unlike Quine, Lewis thinks that we need to distinguish some elite, objectively "natural" properties from the abundant sets.[1] Lewis also thinks that we have to recognize many more concrete objects than Quine does; while Quine is prepared to recognize the existence of objects at other times than the present, he is not prepared to admit the existence of concrete worlds beside the actual.

Still, Lewis's arguments for concrete possible worlds or for natural "sparse" properties have recognizable affinities with Quinean arguments. One sort of argument that Quine is justly famous for is an "indispensability" argument for mathematical objects. Quine argues that we should believe in mathematical objects, such as numbers, sets and functions, because of their importance to our overall theory of the world, and, in particular, because our understanding of the behaviour of physical objects advances through sciences that are completely enmeshed in mathematics, such as physics.[2] According to Quine, we can be justified in believing in the literal truth of mathematics, including the claims about the existence of mathematical objects, even if those claims taken by themselves make very little (or nothing) in the way of specific observational claims that can be tested directly by experiment. By making enough of a contribution to overall theory, mathematics earns its place in our beliefs.

One reason for Quine's confidence here is his "confirmational holism": confirmation or evidence for a theory counts for or against theories as total systems, not in a claim-by-claim way as early logical positivism might have suggested. If this is true of mathematics or the theoretical end of physics and biology, then in principle it may be true of some of the issues discussed by philosophers. (Indeed, some of the issues discussed by philosophers overlap with issues in theoretical physics, theoretical biology and foundational mathematics). In areas that are not immediately referable to experiment, other considerations will play more of a role. Take one example that Quine discusses (1960a): the "molecular doctrine" that everyday objects are made up of molecules. This cannot be tested entirely directly by the unaided senses, but its benefits include "simplicity" of overall theory, and it contributes to the "scope" and "fecundity" of our overall theory, allowing for new testable consequences about the things we can test directly that we would not have expected (and those new tests have so far gone well). The molecular doctrine is more testable and closer to experiment than mathematics, but for Quine some of the justifications for each are the same.

Lewis explicitly compares his style of argument for possible worlds to an argument for accepting set theory (1986a: 3–5). Set theory is a "paradise for mathematicians", as the mathematician David Hilbert put it; it provides "great economy" in organizing and understanding mathematics. As Lewis says, "Their thesis of the plurality of sets is fruitful; that gives them good reason to believe that it is true" (*ibid.*: 4). As well as benefits in the simplicity of the basic postulates, and the fruitfulness of the unification of the basic concepts of mathematics that set theory can provide, set theory also has the advantage of explaining many different concepts in mathematics in terms of a handful of concepts. For example, we can explain all arithmetical operations, functions, and much else ultimately in terms of set-membership, and Lewis argues that we may be able to understand the set-membership relation itself in non-mathematical terms (see Lewis 1990, 1993c).

Lewis outlines his strategy for arguing for the existence of possible worlds in a deliberate parallel.

> As the realm of sets is for mathematicians, so logical space is a paradise for philosophers. We have only to believe in the vast realm of *possibilia* [possible objects], and there we find what we need to advance our endeavours. We find the wherewithal to reduce the diversity of notions we must accept as primitive, and thereby to improve the unity and economy of the theory that is our professional concern – total theory, the whole of what we take to be true. What price paradise? If we want the theoretical benefits that talk of *possibilia* brings, the most straightforward way to gain honest title to them is to accept such talk as the literal truth. It is my view that the price is right, if less spectacularly so than in the mathematical parallel. The benefits are worth the ontological cost. Modal realism is fruitful; that gives us good reason to believe that it is true. (1990: 4)

When Lewis talks of reducing "the diversity of notions we must accept as primitive", he is talking about reducing the number of notions that we accept as basic and not further explained. The "unity and economy" of total theory is improved by taking a diverse class of phenomena, such as causation and belief and value and properties and others, and making sense of them in a unified framework. There are many specific debates that can be had about the best way to make a unified and economical framework that accommodates all of these things, and provides accounts of the different "notions" we have in different parts of everyday life and the sciences. But beyond this, Lewis has a commitment to a certain way of doing philosophy. It supposes that we have standards of economy and unity, and that we can somehow assess the theoretical benefits of a theory and set them against the costs. There are many dimensions of economy, and presumably a theory may be unified in some ways but not in others. There are other sorts of costs too; as we shall see below, going against common sense is another cost that Lewis thinks we should take into account when producing philosophical theories.

Lewis's argument for natural properties (see Chapter 1) is similar in some ways to his argument for possible worlds. In "New Work for a Theory of Universals" (1983c), for example, a commitment to natural properties is justified in terms of the philosophical work they do: in explaining similarity of type, and in the work they do in theories of laws of nature and causation (see Chapter 4); in providing the materials for understanding "eligibility" of content (see Chapter 6). Again, a philosophical thesis can be justified by showing how it helps provide accounts of aspects of our world. Lewis's views about what the best trade-offs are no doubt differ from Quine's, but his more general conception that this is an important part of philosophical theorizing has affinities with Quine's methodological views.

In some important respects, Lewis's attitudes to the world differ from Quine's. One example is Lewis's approach to language, meaning and mental content. Quine tends to be suspicious of these things as "murky" or unscientific, and, famously, Quine describes talk about propositional attitudes such as beliefs and desires as "second-grade" discourse (Quine 1969: 146), a way of talking that does not properly match anything in the "true and ultimate structure of reality" (1960b: 221). Another example is modality, especially the *de re* part of modal discourse, which involves ascribing possibilities or necessities (essences) to objects. Despite this being a pervasive feature of our talk about the world and understanding of the world, Quine is inclined to be very suspicious of it (1953b, 1953c).

There is no doubt a wide range of factors that are relevant to these differences; apart from everything else, the philosophical climate when Quine was forming his opinions in the 1940s and 1950s was more behaviouristic and positivistic than the philosophical climate in the 1960s and 1970s. But one difference may be that Lewis thinks it is important to take common opinion seriously: that we have to have good reason to disagree with what we usually believe, and that our philosophical theories cannot stray too far from common sense. As he writes:

> In trying to improve the unity and economy of our total theory by providing resources that will afford analyses ... I am trying to accomplish two things that somewhat conflict. I am trying to *improve* that theory, that is to change it. But I am trying to improve *that* theory, that is to leave it recognisably the same theory we had before. For it is pointless to build a theory, however nicely systematised it might be, that it would be unreasonable to believe. And a theory cannot earn its credence just by

its unity and economy. What credence it cannot earn, it must in-
herit. It is far beyond our power to weave a brand new fabric of
adequate theory *ex nihilo*, so we must perforce conserve the one
we've got. A worthwhile theory must be credible, and a credible
theory must be conservative. It cannot gain, and it cannot
deserve, credence if it disagrees with too much of what we
thought before. And much of what we thought before was just
common sense. Common sense is a settled body of theory –
unsystematic folk theory – which at any rate we *do* believe; and I
presume that we are reasonable to believe it. (*Most* of it.)

(1986a: 134)

Our starting opinions must be our starting-point (where else?),
and so when we are trying to evaluate changes to our theories, we
shall need to evaluate the plausibility of those changes from where
we began. This need not lead to unbridled dogmatism, of course.
Apart from anything else, our common-sense opinions tell us that
sometimes evidence can come in that shows that we were wrong, or
new theories can be developed that do a better job than old ones.
When Lewis appealed to common sense, it was not because he
thought his theories just *are* common sense, or somehow contained in
it, they were often offered as improvements on the views that we previously held, or as one of the rival views that we might come up with
when trying to solve a philosophical problem. In fact, the quoted passage above comes from a section where Lewis is responding to the
challenge that his belief in concrete possible worlds departs too far
from our ordinary opinions to be credible. Lewis admits that it was a
departure, and it is only because he is satisfied that the departure is
not too extreme to outweigh its benefits that he is prepared to believe
it. (Other philosophers, of course, have thought it was too extreme.
The point here is to illuminate the standards that Lewis took himself
to be accountable to.)

As well as thinking that common sense in general is an important
guide, Lewis also seems to think that some pieces of common sense
are so central that they are not up for grabs, and that a theory that
rejects them ought to be rejected, whatever its other appeal, just on
the grounds that it rejects them. One example is the law of non-
contradiction (that no truth has a true negation). Any proposal to
abandon this principle of logic "should be dismissed just because the
hypothesis it invites us to entertain is inconsistent" ([1982] 1998:
434). One category of common-sensical claims that ought not be
rejected by philosophical theories are those that Lewis characterizes

as "Moorean facts". In doing so, he is making reference to G. E. Moore, who famously argued against the view that, for instance, existence consists of a single, unified "Absolute" and nothing else by saying "Here is one hand . . . and here is another".[3]

Lewis seems to derive the terminology of "Moorean facts" from Armstrong (see Armstrong (1980), cited in Lewis ([1983c] 1999a: 20)). Lewis does not offer a canonical definition for what he means by a Moorean fact. He quotes Armstrong approvingly as saying that a Moorean fact is "one of the many facts that even philosophers should not deny, whatever philosophical analysis they give of such facts" (quoted from Armstrong (1980) in Lewis ([1983c] 1999a: 20)). There is more to it than this, presumably; *any* truth has some claim to be something that "even philosophers should not deny". Closer to Lewis's use is the characterization of a Moorean fact in "Elusive Knowledge": "one of those things that we know better than we know the premises of any philosophical argument to the contrary" ([1996b] 1999a: 418). Perhaps we should talk about what we have "rational confidence" in, or "rational certainty". Talk of knowing one thing better than another is not entirely clear; nor is it clear that we could know a proposition and also know all of the premises of a good argument to the contrary (even if the former is known "better" than the latter). In another place, Lewis says that if you deny a Moorean fact, "the most credible explanation of your denial is that you are in the grip of some philosophical (or scientific) error" ([1997c] 1999a: 333), although, again, this is true of almost any truth. The denial of it is the result of *some* error.

The idea, I take it, is that there are some things that are so certain, or so obvious, that they are, and should be, more certain or obvious than the premises of any reasoning that would lead us to deny them. If common sense does provide us with such certainties, we had better not give them up in our philosophical theorizing! Lewis declares various things "Moorean" at different points. In "New Work for a Theory of Universals" it is facts of "apparent sameness of type" ([1983c] 1999a: 20), that some things have the same shape as other things, for example. It is also Moorean that "our language does have a fairly determinate interpretation" (*ibid.*: 47). Putnam's argument to the contrary (see Chapter 1) is to be rejected in part because it conflicts with this Moorean fact. Other Moorean facts include the claim that "the folk psychophysics of colour is close to true" ([1997c] 1999a: 333). This includes a bundle of claims, such as the claim that objects have colours, they have colours even when nobody is looking at them, that we are able to detect colours by looking at objects, and so on. Another is that "we know a lot": "We have all sorts of everyday knowledge, and we have it in abundance" ([1996b] 1999a: 418). To be led by considerations of philosophy of mind, or the theory of relativity, or the metaphysics of value, to "deny that there existed any such things as sensations, simultaneity, and values" would be to "lose our Moorings" ([1994a] 1999a: 246). Sensations, or simultaneity, or values may not turn out quite as we thought, but it would be a serious mistake to deny that they exist on the basis of a philosophical argument that nothing in the world quite fits the original bill.

So one reason why Lewis may have been more inclined to think that there were philosophically respectable truths about modality, or about the contents of beliefs and desires, may have been his conviction that our certainty that there are modal facts, or facts about what people believe or desire, is stronger than any beliefs we might have that could furnish the premises of an argument that there are no such things.

It is hard to see how to argue conclusively that some things are more certain than any premises that would furnish an argument against them. But it may well be plausible that there are such things. Consider, for example, the claim that at least one of the things I currently accept is true. It is hard to see how you could provide me with premises that I accept that would rationally undermine that claim. We might be more suspicious that anything very specific and interesting has this status, even the claim that some objects have colours, or that people have hands. However, for many of the purposes that Lewis employs "Moorean facts", something weaker would probably serve. Even if some possible series of scientific and philosophical discoveries should convince us that there are no colours after all (perhaps there is some kind of biologically useful systematic illusion instead), we should nevertheless be very *reluctant* to assume that we have discovered that nothing is coloured. Some other theory, which tells us that there are colours but they are not quite as we thought they were, or that they are not very unified or theoretically explanatory, might be preferable. Or if you doubt that colour even has this status, we could select some other example. We might be entitled to be reluctant to give up the claim that 2 + 2 = 4, or that some people believe they have hands, or that cars have parts and so on. For many of these common-sense claims, Lewis suggests we should at least be very reluctant to give them up on the basis of philosophical argument (and he probably should be read as saying that it is always irrational to give up these claims, if they are "Moorean").

Lewis appears to claim that certain common-sense claims are non-negotiable. Interestingly, this is not because he thinks common sense is infallible on these matters. It is more that we could not have a good enough reason to believe anything else. Given our powers of discovery, we are just not in a position to do anything better than try to improve our theories piecemeal.

> Common sense has no absolute authority in philosophy. It's not that the folk know in their blood what highfalutin' philosophers may forget. And it's not that common sense speaks with the voice of some infallible faculty of "intuition". It's just that theoretical conservatism is the only sensible policy for theorists of limited powers, who are duly modest about what they can accomplish after a fresh start. Part of this conservatism is reluctance to accept theories that fly in the face of common sense. But it's a matter of balance and judgement. Some common sense opinions are firmer than others, so the cost of denying common sense opinion differs from one case to the next. And the costs must be set against the gains. Sometimes common sense may properly be corrected, when the earned credence that is gained by making theory more systematic more than makes up for the inherited credence that is lost.
>
> (1986a: 134)

Working from a background of common sense and our other theories, making improvements only when we judge that the theoretical benefits outweigh the costs, we have no better option than to improve what we have; there is no option of just starting completely afresh. This is by no means a view peculiar to Lewis. Many contemporary philosophers would agree with Otto Neurath's metaphor of enquiry as a ship already at sea, whose crew must race around keeping it going and modifying what they have, rather than having the luxury of somehow rebuilding the entire edifice from scratch. However, Lewis is more explicit than many about the need to respect common sense and the boundaries of this respect.

Given Lewis's view about Moorean facts, his view of knowledge claims is odd. He starts his paper "Elusive Knowledge" by saying that we have an abundance of everyday knowledge, and that this is a Moorean fact ([1996b] 1999a: 418); that is, given his account of Moorean facts, we should prefer to reject the premises of any philosophical argument that contradicted it, on the basis that the premises of that argument are less secure than our rational confidence that we have a lot of everyday knowledge. But within a few pages he is telling us that in the epistemology classroom we should agree with the sceptic that we know very little at all. (See Chapter 7, p. 176). What Lewis claims is going on here is a context shift. Although we may agree with the sceptic that we know very little, in one context, this does not conflict with its being true that we know a lot, when we consider the claim that sentence makes in a more ordinary context. Since we never reject the claim we might make ordinarily with the sentence "We know a lot", we do not reject the Moorean fact, even though we do reject that sentence in a specific context.

The story is not self-refuting (see *ibid.*: 444–5). But it is still strange that we should allow the sceptic to convince us that "We know a lot" is false, even if our explanation of how the sceptic could do this is by changing the context to one where that sentence expressed something unusual. Why should we grant the sceptic even this much? The sceptic's arguments rely on premises, different premises in different arguments, but often premises that take the form of theoretical claims about knowledge that are not at all Moorean. Why not just reject those premises, instead of allowing that there is a context in which some such argument is correct, a context we may not have independently suspected, apart from the arguments that threaten scepticism? This device of context shifting, so that we can allow sentences that seem obviously true to become false in a context created by philosophical argument, poses a risk that we can accept all sorts of claims that apparently run against common sense, provided we are allowed to say that there is some context where the common-sensical sayings are correct. This might undermine the usefulness of Moorean facts, or it may just be an illustration that there are few shortcuts in philosophy, and even the question of what it takes to not depart from common sense is itself a contestable philosophical question.

So the goal (or one important goal) in philosophical theorising is to produce an account that does the best when one weighs up the theoretical costs and benefits. The benefits could include the reduction of unexplained notions in the theory and simplicity or economy (although economy in fundamental postulations and axioms often seems to be more important than keeping the number of kinds of entities postulated low). The unity of different areas of theory is also a benefit. Another important area of benefits or costs is how well theories could line up with the "inherited credence" of common sense and our starting theories. No doubt the question of what general sorts of costs and benefits there are, and how they are to be weighed up, is a philosophically difficult one, and one that Lewis tends to

David Lewis

address only in passing. Assessment of theoretical benefits and costs remains more of an art than a science, and it may sometimes not be able to be resolved:

> But when all is said and done, and all the tricky arguments and distinctions and counterexamples have been discovered, presumably we will still face the question which prices are worth paying, which theories are on balance credible, which are the unacceptably counterintuitive consequences and which are the acceptable counterintuitive ones. On this question we may still differ. And if all is indeed said and done, there will be no hope of discovering still further arguments to settle our differences.   (1983a: x)

Some might find this limited conception of what philosophy can achieve a pessimistic one. And it would be more comforting, perhaps, if there were some sure-fire method that would sweep everyone to the same conclusions, with a guarantee of truth. Unfortunately, it does not seem to be like that. Intelligent people of good will who try very hard do end up continuing to disagree on fundamental issues, and the best we can do may still leave us in disagreement about some things, or perhaps many important fundamentals.

While Lewis thinks that philosophers have no guarantee of coming up with the truth, or even of coming up with an uncontroversial yardstick for how to select the best theory where there is disagreement, it is not because he thinks the truth is somehow relative, or that somehow there are not genuine issues where there is persistent disagreement:

> Once the menu of well-worked-out theories is before us, philosophy is a matter of opinion. Is that to say that there is no truth to be had? Or that the truth is of our own making, and different ones of us can make it differently? Not at all! If you say flatly that there is no god, and I say that there are countless gods but none of them are our worldmates, then it may be that neither of us is making any mistake of method. We may each be bringing our opinions to equilibrium in the most careful possible way, taking account of all the arguments, distinctions, and counterexamples. But one of us, at least, is making a mistake of fact. Which one is wrong depends on what there is.   (*ibid*.: xi)

It is not that anything goes. It is not even that the only standards for correctness are subjective ones: there *is* usually an independent fact of the matter. Sometimes the stakes are high: an understanding

212

of our minds, or of the working of the physical world, or of value. None of that means that we are guaranteed to end up agreeing with each other, even if we are intelligent and conscientious. In philosophy, as in life, there are no guarantees.

Philosophical analysis

Often when Lewis tackles a philosophical puzzle, it is, in whole or in part, by providing a philosophical analysis. This is true of his first book, *Convention* (1969), which has as its centerpiece an analysis of conventions, and the application of that analysis to an explanation of language use as a kind of conventional activity. His theories of mind and language, of morality, and of metaphysics, all importantly involve providing "analyses", for example, of sensations, or of causation, or of value. Often Lewis just goes ahead and produces an analysis, without telling readers exactly what he thinks he is doing, and this is often fair enough, since producing a theory of something is often more straightforward than producing a theory *of* producing a theory of that thing, and constantly trying to look over your own shoulder to explain what is happening can be disruptive. Nevertheless, from different things Lewis writes at different times, a picture of the method of Lewis's "philosophical analysis" can be built up.

Part of the analysis is the "Ramsey–Carnap–Lewis" analysis of theoretical terms (see especially "How to Define Theoretical Terms" (1970b) and "Psychosocial and Theoretical Identifications" (1972)). When we have a theory of some phenomenon, we can put together all the claims of the theory, and turn them into a generalization that serves the same purpose as the original theory, but contains none of the problematic expressions to be analysed. This generalization, in turn, is a way to grasp the contribution of the expressions in the theory. This allows us to capture the meaning of any problematic expressions in previously understood terms.

Let me illustrate with an example. Suppose I am given some very basic lessons in atomic chemistry. I am told that there are three sorts of fundamental particles: electrons, protons and neutrons. I am told that electrons are much smaller than protons and neutrons, and that in atoms, protons and neutrons are clumped together in the centre in a nucleus, while electrons whiz around at some distance from the nucleus. I am told that atoms make up all matter, and macroscopic matter comes in two varieties: elements and compounds. Elements

213

are made up of only one sort of atom, while compounds are made up of more than one sort. Finally, I am told that different atoms differ because of the numbers of protons and electrons in them. An atom normally has the same number of protons and electrons, and different kinds of atoms have different numbers of protons. Each kind of element is made up of a different kind of atom.

If I am told all that (and suppose I had never heard anything about chemistry before), I would learn some things about atoms, electrons and so on. (And some of the things I learn are not entirely true, but no matter.) I would also gain some mastery of the expressions "proton", "atom", "element", and the rest. It would be a partial understanding, both of atomic chemistry and the meanings of those expressions. In particular, notice that with that piece of theory alone I would not be able to make much in the way of specific predictions. I would need to be told in addition what some of the elements and compounds were, and some of the ways one could be turned into another, before I could answer questions about whether gold could be decomposed into other substances, or how many elements you would need to create some water.

Lewis, following Rudolf Carnap, argues that the information contained in the little theory above could be divided into two parts. Carnap treats the division as dividing the theory into two parts: its "factual content" and a claim about the meanings of some of the expressions (a "meaning postulate"). Lewis does not put things this way, but does think it is worthwhile to separate the theory into two parts in order to understand what information about the meanings of terms it conveyed.

Let us suppose that I already knew many of the ordinary words in the lesson above. I knew "make up" and "smaller" and "whiz" and even a couple of the terms such as "macroscopic" and "matter" and "particle". Following Lewis, call these the *old* terms, or *O* terms for short. And let us suppose that I had not previously encountered many of the terms of the theory: "proton", "neutron", "electron", "atom", "nucleus", "element" and "compound". Call these the *theory* terms since they are introduced by the new theory (*T* terms for short). We are supposing that before being told about all of these new things, I had never heard of them. Even so, I can state much of what I discovered in terms I already knew. For example, I learned

> There are some things, Vs, Ws, Xs, Ys, and Zs, and the Xs, Ys and Zs are three sorts of fundamental particles, and the Xs are much smaller than the Ys, and in the Ws, the Ys and Zs are clumped

together in the centre in a *V*, while the *X*s whiz around at some distance from the *V*.

That sentence is a bit less easy to scan than the sentence with the terms "electron", "nucleus" and so on put in, and if I tried to put it in more ordinary English by talking about "things of the first sort", "things of the second sort" and so on, it would be more awkward still. But someone can understand the sentence with the *V*s, *W*s, and so on in it, even if they never come across the *T* terms. If I had a comprehensive enough theory of atomic particles, and replaced it with the above sort of generalization, with a variable (*X*, *Y*, etc.) for each of the *T* terms, I would capture the same information as the comprehensive theory without all the new jargon. Or so Lewis claims. A sentence with new terms replaced instead with variables is what Carnap and Lewis call a "Ramsey" sentence. Lewis sometimes talks about the "Ramsification" of a theory; when you Ramsify a theory, you turn it into a corresponding Ramsey sentence, by taking out some of the terms of that theory and replacing them with variables, together with some quantifiers at the start: "There are some *X*s, there are some *Y*s ..." and so on.

One other thing that Lewis does when producing a Ramsey sentence is he introduces a device for generalizing predicates by talking about the corresponding properties. So, for example, suppose I was presented with the theory "Some shirts are coloured grue, and grue shirts are prettier than burple pants, but not as attractive as puce hats", but wanted a Ramsey sentence without "grue", "burple" or "puce" in it. Instead of those predicates, I could take the sentence about the corresponding properties: "Some shirts have the colour property grueness, and shirts with the property grueness are prettier than pants with the property of burpleness, but are not as attractive as hats with the property of puceness". Then I could generalize over those properties with ordinary first-order quantifiers and variables: "There is an *X* and there is a *Y* and there is a *Z* such that some shirts have the colour property *X*, and shirts with *X* are prettier than pants with *Y*, but are not as attractive as hats with the property *Z*". Logicians are used to generalizing about objects more than generalizing through predicates, but the technical details here are not of central importance. What is of importance is that these generalizations can be given without using any of the *T* terms, but can be stated and understood entirely with *O* terms.

So we can extract the information from a theory without needing to understand very much about the new vocabulary it brings. The

other half of the story is how we can learn new vocabulary, just by
seeing it used in a theory. (Perhaps our understanding is only partial,
especially when we are given small bits of theory, but it is plausible
that my understanding of "electron", "atom", "element" and so on
would be somewhat better if I was given the little theory above than
if I had never come across the words at all, or only seen them in a list.)
We may not get very much information about how to use the words in
a variety of situations. But one thing we do learn from the theory, if
the theory is authoritative, is something about how the words are to
be used in a particular case. If the world is as the theory says it is,
then the words apply to the things that they would need to apply to
for the theory to be correct. That might sound obvious, but it gives us
a partial handle on the meaning of the unfamiliar vocabulary. Call a
theory that we want to analyse T. Call the Ramsey sentence we get
from that theory by replacing some of the new vocabulary with quantifiers and variables R_T. Then the following claim is true:

$$R_T \supset T$$

where $\supset$ symbolizes that either the first claim is false or the second
claim is true. It is often a useful substitute for "if ... then ..."; see
Chapter 3.

A sentence of that form – one that states that either a theory's
Ramsey sentence is false or the theory itself is true – is called a
"Carnap sentence" by Lewis. The interesting thing about the Carnap
sentence is that it does not say anything about the world. It could
well be true whether or not the Ramsey sentence is true. (Indeed, it
will automatically be true if the Ramsey sentence is false.) Carnap
claimed that the Carnap sentence of a theory was entirely *analytic*:
true solely in virtue of the meanings of the words. Carnap offered this
scheme as a way of dividing a theory into the claims it made about
the world, and the claims it made about meaning: the Ramsey
sentence told the full story about the world that came with a theory,
and the Carnap sentence told you what you needed to know to interpret the new vocabulary, and was true by definition (see Carnap
1963). Carnap told this story about all the theoretical terms of a
theory. The only terms left that were not to be Ramsified out were
logical vocabulary and observational vocabulary.

Lewis thinks the Carnap sentence is not quite what is needed to
capture the analytic component of a theory. One problem is a problem
of *multiple realizers*. Suppose more than one group of objects fit the
Ramsey sentence of a theory. Then there might be some further ques-

tion of which of the different sets of candidates the theory was *really* about, or, if there were too many groups of objects and properties that fit the bill, we might decide that the theory did not refer to any in particular. Whether this means that the theory would be true but have "ambiguous reference", or whether it means the theory would be false, or whether it would mean something else, is something we need not settle here – Lewis changed his mind about what to say about that sort of case (compare [1970b] 1983a: 83 and [1972] 1999a: 242 with [1984b] 1999a: 59 and [1994b] 1999a: 310).

The theory at least seems to imply this much about the meanings of the terms: *if* there happens to be only one set of candidates that does the job, then the terms in the theory apply to those objects. If we employ a modified Ramsey sentence that says that the different theoretical roles are filled uniquely, then the associated modified Carnap sentence seems acceptable. The little theory about atoms given above tells us that *if* there is exactly one X, exactly one Y ... such that ... *then* the property of being an electron, the property of being a proton ... are such that ....

Lewis thinks that we can extract another useful piece of analytic information from a theory. To a first approximation, this is the information that if the Ramsey sentence is *false*, then the terms do not refer. If the Ramsey sentence associated with atomic physics is sufficiently false, then there are no such things as electrons, protons, elements, atoms and so on. It is not as if those terms could turn out to refer to completely different things; that electrons could turn out to be a type of sofa, for example, or that protons turn out to be golf-ball-sized particles found only on Alpha Centauri.

This is only "to a first approximation", since Lewis does allow that the Ramsey sentence can be somewhat false, and yet objects that do a good enough job of playing the theoretical roles still count as being the referents of the terms. Many of our theories turn out to be wrong in some detail or other, and we do not declare that all of the terms in them therefore fail to refer to anything. In fact, the sketch of an atomic theory I gave above is probably not strictly speaking correct. It's not clear whether electrons and so on are *particles*, at least in anything like the everyday sense, and while electrons are somehow located in a region around the nucleus of atoms, it's not at all clear that there is any sense in which they "whiz" around like a swarm of flies or orbiting satellites. But when physicists discovered that the old models, according to which sub-atomic particles were particles in the usual sense and electrons did orbit nuclei, were inaccurate, they decided that they had discovered new and unexpected facts about electrons, nuclei and so on, and not that there were no such things after all.

So what a theory tells us about the meanings of its T terms, its theoretical vocabulary, is that *if* the theory's Ramsey sentence has a set of objects and properties that uniquely satisfy it,[4] or that uniquely come close to satisfying it, *then* the T terms apply to those objects and properties. The other component of the meaning of the T terms is about what happens if the Ramsey sentence is false, and in addition no group of objects come close to satisfying it. If that happens, then the T terms do *not* refer.

In his famous paper "Two Dogmas of Empiricism" (1951), Quine argues that an analytic–synthetic distinction cannot be drawn; we cannot divide our theories into a component that is about the world, and a component that is true solely in virtue of the meanings of our expressions. Carnap's division between the Ramsey sentence of a theory and what Lewis calls the Carnap sentence of a theory offers a response to this challenge. (Carnap had additional beliefs that Lewis did not endorse: that language can be divided into "observational" terms and "theoretical" terms, and that all theoretical terms gain their meaning only through their relationships to observational terms. But these do not seem essential for the proposal that Lewis adopts and defends.) For some terms, the T terms, understood against a background of already meaningful O terms and logical vocabulary, a theory that uses those terms can provide us with information (couched in the language we already understand) about the conditions under which those terms refer, and to what, and the conditions under which those terms do not refer. The Carnap sentence (or its modification to ensure uniqueness and to allow for near-enough deservers) does not tell us anything about how the world really is. If it is true at all, it is true in virtue of the meanings of the T expressions.

If this is right, then we have a general recipe for understanding the meaning of terms in a presented theory. This recipe can be useful, for example, in determining when objects described by one vocabulary are objects described by another. If a certain movement of electrons looks like lightning, for example, occurs when lightning occurs, and has the effects that lightning has, then it *is* lightning. Or, to take a historical example, chemistry defined "covalent bonding" between atoms, and atomic physics defined "electron sharing". It turned out that a certain sort of electron sharing did exactly what covalent bonding was supposed to do, and plausibly occurred whenever covalent bonding did. So it could be established that covalent bonding was a particular sort of electron sharing, and an identity between a physical state and a chemical state was established. (It is not that anyone explicitly applied anything like Lewis's method to establish this; rather, that Lewis's conception of the meaning of expressions as being defined by their theoretical roles explains how this identity can be justified).

One question that needs to be answered when applying this method is: when does a theory count as authoritative enough to be effectively defining its T terms? Not any theory using puzzling expressions should count for as much as any other. Suppose I open a book in a New Age shop and find the following:

> Electrons carry life-energy through the universe. Living creatures contain many more electrons than non-living creatures, and it is these electrons that give them the power to move, to breathe, and to think. Too much life energy can of course be dangerous – the current in electrical wires is a surge of life energy (electrons), and too much of that can kill you! But it is also true that too few electrons are equally harmful. Concrete, saturated fat, and negative feelings all absorb electrons, so a life without nature, or with the wrong diet or mental attitude, can be harmful.

I should be making a terrible mistake if I thought that this theory implicitly defined the meaning of the word "electron" (along with the expression "life energy", perhaps). I should come to think that there were electrons only if there were some things that behaved the way that the above paragraph says electrons do, or near enough, and that otherwise there were no such things as electrons. Not only should I be likely to make a factual error, but I should also misunderstand the word "electron".

Sometimes the problem of finding the right theory to use in understanding the term – call it the "canonical theory" – will be easy enough to solve. Sometimes a novel word will only appear in one theory; presumably we can then accept that the theory is authoritative. Sometimes we shall know enough about patterns of linguistic authority to know "who gets to decide" what a word means. In the case of "electron", the relevant theories might be found in orthodox textbooks, or the widely recognized journals in physics, or something like that. If different sources of authority all agree, or near enough, then we may not need to find some procedure to choose between

David Lewis

them. Sometimes we may be happy with something less than information about what a word really means. We might engage in the simplifying fiction that some theory we have in front of us is the canonical theory, confident that this assumption will serve well enough for our particular purpose (for example, working out which theoretical identifications are defensible if the theory is true).

Lewis does worry about this problem in "How to Define Theoretical Terms" ([1970b] 1983a: 94–5). He considers several suggestions. One is that we should take as canonical the first theory that introduces a term, although this would mean that many contemporary users would only have hazy access to the meaning of the term, compared to the historian of science. Another is that we use the "currently accepted" version of the theory, although he points out that this will have the problems that there are disagreements: there may be cases where we have suspended judgement between versions of a theory; and there may be cases where a theory is not accepted any more. How can we then tell what the referents of its vocabulary are, if any? Lewis hopes that there is some "intermediate" theory more satisfactory than either of these. No doubt there is more to be said about this question, and more should be said by those who are sympathetic to Lewis's picture of the meaning of theoretical terms.

Another challenge Lewis's story faces is from those in the philosophy of language who argue that many of the expressions in theories, including names and "natural kind terms" such as "water", "gold" or "electron", have little or no descriptive content associated with them. (This view is associated with Kripke (1980) and Putnam (1975c), among many others.) Lewis's view of the meaning of such terms is a version of "descriptivism", and he responds in various places to the standard arguments against descriptivism for natural kind terms, although usually in passing ([1970b] 1983a: 86–7; [1984b] 1999a: 59–60; [1997c] 1999a: 353 n. 22). A full discussion of the argument between descriptivists and their opponents would take us too far afield, but readers interested in this debate may find Lewis's suggestions interesting.

The procedure outlined for theories introducing new vocabulary can do the same for concepts that are not parts of a canonical scientific theory, by treating them as expressions in a *folk theory*. A particular philosophically controversial application of using this understanding of theories to establish an identity is discussed in Chapter 5: using the roles defined by our theory of the mind to provide causal criteria for what it is to be a mental state, which shows how mental states are to be identified with brain states. (In such a case, the *O* terms will be non-mental vocabulary, and the *T* terms mental vocabulary, although neither will necessarily be "older" than the other.) In order to establish such an identity, we need to be able to find a theory of the mind to use. Many psychologists, psychoanalysts, cognitive scientists, self-help book writers, and others have opinions about the mind and mental states, and our culture has been awash with more or less articulated theories for thousands of years (and human beings have had implicit understandings of mental states for as long as our species has existed). Which sentences, out of all the opinions people have produced about the workings of the mind, and all the opinions people would produce with a bit of prompting, should we pick when we want to find our canonical theory?

Lewis's suggestion is that "folk psychology" is "common knowledge" among us ([1994b] 1999a: 298). There is a set of views about the mind that are not only believed by all of us, but all of us realise that all of us believe them, and all of us realize that we take this recognition to be mutual, and so on. Perhaps folk psychology is just the maximum of our common belief about the mind. Lewis says that this common knowledge is tacit, and it might be hard to make explicit: "eliciting the general principles of folk psychology is no mere matter of gathering platitudes" (*ibid.* 298 n. 10). He compares it to our implicit knowledge of grammar (*ibid.*: 298). We might wonder whether our implicit knowledge of grammar is enough to capture the full range of English grammar. Perhaps we are a mass of overlapping groups each of which knows much of English grammar, but very little of it is entirely common knowledge.[5] This might be even more so for human psychology. I assume virtually all of us have some grasp of it, and my understanding of the mind is rather similar to that of many other people in my social circles. All of humanity (or the vast majority) have a fair amount of genuine knowledge of the mind, but is there a significant body of beliefs about the mind that is known by us all, and known to be known by us all? Lewis assumes that there is, and that this theory serves as the canonical theory for defining our mental vocabulary. (Perhaps instead of all of humanity, our focus should be on all English speakers, if our target is the meaning of the words "belief", "pain" and so on, since someone who had a good grasp of folk psychology but no grasp of English could hardly be particularly expert about the meanings of those words.)

Again, it may not matter, within limits, which claims about the mental we take to be canonical, and for some purposes we may be able to bracket the question. For instance, we could fill a few pages with relatively uncontroversial claims about sensations, beliefs, intentions, actions and so on, and ask whether there is any group of states and properties of people that fits *that* theoretical bill, and not worry about how well we had captured the meaning (or meanings) in English of the expressions "sensation", "belief", "intention" and so on. Once we have a canonical statement of folk psychology (or some acceptable substitute), we can produce a Ramsified version that strips out the mental vocabulary. We can use that to specify a role for a range of states and properties, and then see whether indeed something close enough to that role is filled. Lewis thinks that we shall find the roles for much of our mental vocabulary filled by our brain states (see Chapter 5).

A crucial aspect of the task of doing this sort of linguistic analysis is to have methods for making such a folk theory explicit. Lewis's analogy with our knowledge of grammar points to one way of doing this. All competent English speakers have an implicit grasp of which English sentences are grammatical and which are not. Some of us may be better at detecting grammaticality than others, but all of us can tell that "Mary went to the supermarket" is grammatical, but "In Susan up hit fish Tuesday bathtub" is not. One way philosophers often grapple with conceptual analysis is to produce claims about a subject matter that seem obvious, or hard to deny, which they guess are the sorts of claims that linguistically competent people would not deny. We may test whether such a claim has this status by thinking about how we would diagnose someone who rejected it. Do they just have an odd view of the world, or are they linguistically incompetent? Proposed linguistic analyses are often met with counter-examples; thought-experiments outline apparently possible scenarios where it would seem reasonable to deny the supposed conceptual truths. These counter-examples can also be seen as relying on our implicit knowledge of the meaning of the expression for their force. We see that some analysis is wrong (or at least has a theoretical cost to bear) by making explicit some piece of our grasp of the word that conflicts with it.[6] Perhaps no very explicit method for articulating such implicit theories can be offered, and Lewis does not offer one (unless the method of "assembling the platitudes" counts, but he explicitly disowned that later).[7] Philosophers tend to treat this as an art rather than a science, and with few exceptions tend to rely on informal tests rather than, for example, the sorts of surveys that are conducted when linguists test hypotheses about linguistic behaviour. Whether this is a good way to carry out Lewis's method is no doubt controversial.

The method Lewis applies can be generalized. Lewis also applies it to colour (1997c) and in his work on the foundations of mathematics (1990), and I suspect he would have understood much of his other work in philosophical analysis as employing this method, at least implicitly. Others have adopted this conception of philosophical analysis as well. Lewis refers to the project of doing this the "Canberra Plan" (2000b), since a group of theorists who were working in, or associated with, Canberra are prominent among its practitioners.[8] One assembles pieces of relatively uncontroversial theory (whether from a "canonical" source or, more often, by articulating a "folk" theory), and then Ramsifies out the target vocabulary. Then, armed with the "theoretical roles" assigned to each of the terms, one investigates the world to see what sorts of things do those jobs. Often there will not be anything that does it perfectly, but if there is something that does the jobs well enough, and better than the other candidates, it is proposed as being a "best deserver" for what the original talk was about. It might be alleged that brain states are mental states, or certain physical properties of surfaces are colours, or certain relations in the world are relations of causation, or certain relations across time are the relations that unify person stages into persons, or it might be that certain stretches of DNA count as what we meant by genes, or certain connections to reasons for action or preferences count as what it is to be morally valuable, or whatever. Provided the materials that go into the analysis are uncontroversial enough, and a demonstration is possible that the proposed "deserver" does the job it is supposed to, such an argument can be compelling, or at least as compelling as philosophical arguments ever are.

The first step in these analyses yields claims that are meant to be *analytic*, in the sense that they are supposed to be true simply in virtue of the meanings of the words involved, or the content of the concepts employed. (Lewis has little to say about concepts, so let me focus on the words, although it should be understood that these "analyses" will typically be ones that would survive translation into other languages.) But Lewis allowed that this can be *unsharp* analyticity ([1974a] 1983a: 118), or "equivocal analyticity" ([1989b] 2000a: 86–7). There are several different ways analyticity can fail to be sharp. There can be "semantic indecision". When the conventions of language have left some details of meaning unsettled, there may be no fact of the matter about some questions, so a clear and precise analysis might take stands on things that meaning left undetermined. Then an "analysis" might not quite match our messy practice, but if it is more determinate than the previous state of play, in a way left open by the previous state of play, that is not such a problem. Another way there can be equivocal analyticity is if there is "semantic variation" (*ibid.*: 86). Maybe some expressions get used differently by different people, with enough overlap so that communication is possible, but enough difference so that meanings conflict when we come to some interesting issues. Lewis mentions this in his analysis of value, for example (*ibid.*: 85, 92). He raises the possibility, for example, that the meaning associated with some people's use might permit more relativity in value than others. For example, some might use the word in such a way that if some people value some things in ideal circumstances, and others value others, then there are no values, properly speaking, while other people might much more readily allow that something can be valuable-for-one-person, and not valuable-for-another. Lewis claims for his analysis of value that it "lands somewhere near the middle of the range of variation and indecision" (*ibid.*: 87). This might be because he is particularly dubious about our value talk (or particularly dubious about his analysis). But I suspect he would be prepared to say the same for various of his other analyses; they land somewhere in an acceptable range, or make precise some things that ordinary usage leaves unsettled or allows to vary.

Yet another way in which Lewis allows issues of meaning to be indeterminate is in allowing that imperfect deservers can be good enough. An analysis that selects one imperfect deserver rather than another may go beyond what is determinate about the original meaning, for the original meaning may not have specified very precisely what sort of imperfect deserver would be better than another (*ibid.*: 92). In such a case, Lewis seems to speak as if the account, including the specification of which thing deserves the name, is analytic. I suspect he would be better off saying that the analytic component of such an account is the story about what is needed to be an ideal deserver of the name, and which conceivable imperfect deservers would be better than others. Which thing is in fact the best deserver depends not only on the words we use, but also on which sorts of things exist (or are actual). And presumably this is not an analytic matter. (If there had been truly indivisible smallest units of chemicals, then presumably they would have been the chemical "atoms", but as it is, we allow that the chemical atom itself has parts and can be "split", despite the fact that "atoms" (from the Greek for "uncuttable") were originally supposed to be indivisible.

It will often be true that our theories of the world will not be perfect, particularly when it comes to philosophical theories, which often address particularly difficult questions (such as the nature of consciousness, free will, properties, knowledge, etc.). When this is so, our theory of what the world contains will often not contain a perfect candidate for the role. We may even have a guarantee that there will be no perfect deserver, if the folk theory or philosophical development of that folk theory is inconsistent, or has different strands in it that conflict with each other. If a free decision is supposed to be *both* undetermined by anything else, *and* determined by an agent's character, then nothing in the world will perfectly satisfy these two demands. So the usefulness of Lewis's method will often hinge on what tools we have to decide which of a range of imperfect candidates is good enough, if any. This decision hinges on at least two things: what the various deservers available *are*, and what principles can be relied upon to work out when to prefer one deserver to another.

Lewis's materialism means that he can restrict what sorts of deservers might be found in our world. For a reductive materialist, mental states are not going to turn out to be states of special mental substance or involve a special set of fundamental mental properties; they are going to turn out to be physical states of some sort, or nothing. Free choice is going to be something that complicated physical systems governed by physical laws can have, or it is going to not exist. What makes a person-stage at two different times count as being parts of the same person is going to be matters of physical fact (presumably complicated ones); there is not going to be a special "further fact" unifying people over time. That still leaves plenty of leeway. Which brain states are mental states? Which features of a decision make it free? Perhaps there is not much to say in general about working out what is out there to answer to our concepts. Maybe much of this has to be done on a case-by-case basis, and may require plenty of information from other disciplines about how the world works. Philosophical analysis may not answer these questions by itself, but at least the Ramsey–Carnap–Lewis method has something to say about how investigation of the world can be integrated so as to provide answers about, for example, what consciousness really is, or the nature of free will, or of knowledge. It does not assume either that philosophers can answer these questions in isolation, or that these questions can be answered without any philosophical analysis, as if neurobiologists or psychologists could discover consciousness in the head without having any philosophical analysis to tell them what they are supposed to be looking for.

Lewis says very little about how to select among less-than-ideal deservers, that is, among objects or properties that filled some of a theoretical role, but not all of it. In extreme cases, perhaps no deservers are good enough and we should be "eliminativists", holding that the terms do not refer. This is what we did with words such as "phlogiston" and "luminiferous ether",[9] and it is what we may do with words like "the soul". Often, though, different deservers will be in competition. There are many competing "naturalistic" accounts of moral value, all of which can point to some feature their candidate has that moral value is supposed to have. There are many different philosophies of colour, each identifying colour with some natural feature of the surfaces of objects, or in the holding of some relation between the surfaces of objects and our eyes, or our minds. When deservers do equally well, or nearly as well, in playing a theoretical role, there can be indeterminacy about which deserver should count as the one that is referred to. But how do we compare deservers that are imperfect but play some of the relevant theoretical role in the first place?

Sometimes it may be clear. Sometimes deserver A will do everything that deserver B does, and then some. Sometimes the *naturalness* of the deserver will come into play. If deserver A is significantly more natural than deserver B, in the sense that A is a more natural property than B, or has more natural characteristics than B, then, according to Lewis, it is more semantically eligible and more fit to be referred to. (See Chapter 6 for eligibility for content. Eligibility for reference by expressions in language should have a similar constraint, according to Lewis (1984b, 1992).) Perhaps there are other constraints as well, although Lewis left these vague. (Of the relevant notion of "near-realization" he said that it is "hard to analyze, but easy to understand" ([1972] 1999a: 253).) Perhaps some of the claims theories make are more "central" or more meaning-connected than others. Perhaps some are ones that we are more confident of, and so less inclined to revise. Outside clear-cut cases, principles to choose between near-deservers would be useful, and are perhaps to be found implicitly when philosophers engage in linguistic analysis or conceptual analysis; not every belief they have is treated as equally definitional. But this is a development that is yet to be carried out systematically.

It is ironic that one of Quine's students should reinvigorate upfront linguistic analysis: providing meaning-claims about important philosophical terms that could be put with the synthetic, non-analytic truths about the world to yield the whole truth about a subject matter. Those who remain suspicious of the analytic–synthetic distinction will also be suspicious of this method, as will those who doubt that there are bodies of implicit doctrine ("folk theories" or other canonical theories) that we can appeal to in order to improve our understanding of contested philosophical expressions. Those who reject the idea that the meaning of theoretical expressions is given by their role in a theory will also be suspicious of Lewis's method of analysis, even if they do think that there are analytic truths involving philosophically interesting terms, and even if they think we can somehow articulate them.

Whether Lewis's proposal about philosophical analysis could remain useful without the underpinning doctrines about meaning is an interesting question. After all, for a theory that a particular investigator accepts, she should also accept the corresponding Ramsey sentence: if A, B and C stand in such-and-such relations to each other, then *some X*, *some Y* and *some Z* stand in those relations to each other. And, conversely, if some entities identified in quite different vocabulary do what A, B and C do, there is a case to be made that those entities are A, B and C, especially if the theory the investigator holds tells her that there is only one thing that does each of A, B and C's jobs. So such an identification could seem compelling to such a theorist, regardless of her theory of how the names A, B and C got their meaning, or even if she has no theory of the meaning of theoretical expressions.[10] I expect that whether or not Lewis's views about meaning are widely shared, the method of assembling the doctrines of folk opinion ("assembling the platitudes"), Ramsifying over them to produce the specification of a range of interdefined theoretical roles, and the hunt for "deservers", along with disputes about which deservers are better than others, will remain one way of doing philosophical analysis for some time to come.

Conclusion

In this chapter I have attempted to distil some philosophical methods from Lewis's works, from both the way he did philosophy, and the things he had to say about what he was trying to do and how he was trying to do it. I expect much of the importance of Lewis's specific contributions to philosophical debates does not rely entirely on the general philosophical method, and the usefulness of the methods could survive trouble with Lewis's particular applications. Lewis expressed his hope that "the sceptical reader will consider breaking up the package and taking the parts that suit him" (1983a: x). Although Lewis has a philosophical system, with some parts supporting others, it is not a monolith that must be taken or left as a whole.

I look forward to seeing what Lewis's influence will be on philosophy as it is practised by professionals and on the philosophical views of other people, both inside and outside the academy, over the next few decades. My guess, for what it is worth, is that his work will be considered more influential in 20 years' time than it is today. What is even harder to predict is which parts of his work will be the most influential. I hope I have provided an outline and guide to many of Lewis's philosophical concerns. In some ways it is a very poor substitute for reading Lewis's own works, but in other ways a map can be more helpful than the landscape itself. If this book has served as a useful map and introduction to Lewis's work, and at least as importantly as a window into some of the philosophical questions that Lewis grappled with, it will have served its purpose well.

Notes

Chapter 1: Metaphysical and scientific realism

1. The list of "discoveries" Lewis talks about are not things he thinks that philosophy has actually discovered, but a list of things that prominent philosophers claim to have discovered. Some are from the history of philosophy, but some are defended by contemporary philosophers. The reader may want to try to work out which philosophical views Lewis had in mind.

2. There are two other conditions that need to be met for Putnam: there need to be enough objects in the world, and the ideal theory needs to be consistent (although since consistency is one of the theoretical standards, perhaps an ideal theory is by definition consistent). These are relatively insignificant in the dispute between Putnam and his opponents.

3. I apologise for the proliferation of senses of "realism". This happens to terms in metaphysics when they are around too long!

4. He attributes his change of mind to being convinced by D. M. Armstrong. Armstrong has waged a long campaign in favour of believing in universals that correspond to the fundamental properties and relations of our world (which Armstrong believes are the fundamental properties and relations discussed by physics): see Armstrong (1978a).

5. This argument goes back at least to Pap (1959) and Jackson (1977), and is discussed in Armstrong (1978a). Cases of property talk in science are also discussed in Putnam (1970). We might easily think sentences such as "There are still undiscovered fundamental properties" are true in the context of a discussion of physics. This sentence is probably true today, and seems to have been definitely true 100 years ago when electron spin and quark flavour had not been discovered, but it is very hard to see how to paraphrase such sentences so they don't talk about properties!

6. This style of paraphrase seems even less tempting when we remember that the nominalist will want to paraphrase apparent talk of "red", "magenta" and other such colours. Can we restate the claim in terms of preferences for coloured objects of different sorts?

Chapter 2: The Humean mosaic

1. Here and elsewhere I talk about spacetime or spatiotemporal relations, rather than space and time, or spatial relations and temporal relations,

because of the theory of relativity, which suggests that space and time are not ultimately that dissimilar from each other, and ultimately form a four-dimensional system. In Lewis's metaphysics, space and time are treated very similarly, and he often talks about spacetime, rather than space and time separately.

2. Such a "vital force" would be like some conceptions of "substantial forms" for animals postulated in medieval biology. While that biological doctrine today strikes us as strange, it should not strike us as inconsistent.

3. There may need to be some other minor qualifications as well: see Lewis ([1994a] 1999a: 226–7).

4. We need an extra assumption here. We need to suppose that there are not any fundamental parts besides the point-sized parts. If there could be indivisible parts that filled larger-than-point-sized regions, for example, then fixing what point-sized things there are would not yet fix what wholes there are (since there could be a difference in the wholes because of a difference in what larger-than-point-sized fundamental parts there are). Presumably these region-sized fundamental parts would be "alien" to a Humean supervenience world, in the sense mentioned on p. 29.

5. Some readers might find it strange that there is a study of parts and wholes, and wonder what it could consist in. Mereology is somewhat like set theory. Axioms for the part–whole relation are proposed, and people study these axiom systems to see what follows from them, how they relate to each other, and so on. Unlike set theory, there is a lot more debate over what the correct axiom system is (or whether there might be more than one). Although this sort of debate about sets does go on in mathematics and the philosophy of mathematics, the proportion is much smaller. This probably explains why set theory is mostly done by mathematicians, while mereology is more the preserve of philosophers and logicians. Mereologists debate questions about when things have fusions, whether there are any indivisible objects (mereological "atoms") or whether everything has multiple parts, which themselves have multiple parts *ad infinitum*, and so on.

6. Lewis's "argument from vagueness" for unrestricted composition is receiving considerable scrutiny in the literature, with people paying careful attention to the details of the argument, or the best way of trying to construct a formal argument from Lewis's remarks. See, for example, Markosian (1992), Sider (2001: 120–34) and Noonan (2001). I have tried to give the flavour of the argument here, trying to avoid the technical details, but someone interested in a close scrutiny of the argument would do well to look at Lewis (1986a: 212–13) and some of the secondary literature mentioned.

7. Strictly, Lewis discusses several versions of the view that the future branches, and this is only a discussion of the one he spends the most time on. Those interested in Lewis's remarks here can find them in Lewis (1986a: §4.2).

8. Of course there are puzzles about how it could be possible to change the past. One is the apparent possibility of closed causal loops (e.g. where a time traveller travels back to tell their young self the secret of time travel, which is the only reason the traveller was able to build a time machine in the first place). Another is the "grandfather paradox". Suppose a time traveller goes back and tries to kill his grandfather before the time traveller's parents are conceived. What consistent story could be told about that possibility? Lewis discusses these and other puzzles in one of his most readable papers: "The Paradoxes of Time Travel" (1976c).

9. There is another reason you might think that hot and cold are relational that is not relevant in the present context. You might think "hot" really turns out to mean "significantly hotter than average around here" and cold to mean "significantly colder than average". Then hot and cold will be relational, because they will depend on what else is around. Water about to boil might count as hot in a lot of contexts, but might be comparatively very cold near the surface of the sun or in a furnace. If this bothers you, instead of "hot" and "cold" consider properties like "being 200 °C" and "being –5 °C".
10. This seems to be Mark Johnston's proposal (1987).

Chapter 3: The plenitude of possibilities

1. Here and elsewhere I am a little reluctant to use the word "universe", since some people think the "universe" by definition includes everything that exists, including all disconnected spacetimes, if there are any. I suspect, though, that only pedants are so wedded to this definition that they cannot understand what people are talking about when they talk about "multiple universes".
2. Here I will only attempt to give the outlines of the objections. For the details see Lewis (1986a: 150–65).
3. Presumably pictures can represent by means other than resemblance (or other isomorphisms). There can be symbolism, genre conventions and causal factors (a painting may represent one identical twin rather than the other because of which one sat for it). But these abstract pictorial structures are meant to do their representing by isomorphism. This raises the option of thinking that worlds represent partly through isomorphisms and partly through language-like conventions, but I expect Lewis would think that such an approach would have some of the problems of each of linguistic and pictorial ersatzism.
4. Wasn't the linguistic ersatzer talking about propositions when she was talking about abstract sentence-like representations? The difference is that the linguistic ersatzer had a story about how her entities represent that is like the story about how sentences represent: interpretations assigned to them because of their structure. The magical ersatzer's "propositions", on the other hand, are "self-interpreting". They are true or false just in virtue of how the concrete cosmos is. They also lack relevant structure, since they are simple.
5. I am ignoring objects that are mereological fusions of things from different worlds. Lewis thinks there are wholes made up from these parts, but they play no important role in his system.
6. The paradox to be discussed is a version of a puzzle discussed by Chisholm (1967). It has also been discussed by Salmon (1981) and Chandler (1976), among others. (Chandler uses a bicycle in his example.)
7. There is more that could be said about Lewis's counterpart theory, how it deals with other paradoxes of transworld identity, and how it compares to other versions of counterpart theory that have been proposed. But this is not the place for further discussion. Interested readers could start by looking at Lewis (1986a) and his "Counterpart Theory and Quantified Modal Logic" (1968) and its postscripts (1983a: 39–46).
8. If you are not convinced, consider some more extreme hypothetical example. Even if all and only spheres were negatively charged, that would not make "being a sphere" and "being negatively charged" the same property.
9. Assuming "one of the hundred best cricket players" means the hundred best

in their own world. I doubt there would be any such thing as the hundred best possible cricket players (either there is no best, since you can always do better, or if there is a best level of cricket, there are likely to be infinitely many possible players with that level of ability).

10. Strictly speaking, of course, for Lewis they are worlds where a counterpart of America tries to invade a counterpart of Sweden. But I will leave out this qualification about counterparts in the discussion. It should be easy enough to see how the counterpart version of the discussion will go.

11. See Montague (1974) and Stalnaker (1999) for examples of their contributions.

Chapter 4: Laws, causes, dispositions and chance

1. "Nomic" is an adjective applied to these cluster of notions on the assumption that they have something distinctive to do with laws of nature.

2. Some people argue about whether laws of nature might have some exceptions, for example, "miracles" that are a result of supernatural agency. Perhaps our concept of laws of nature does not rule this out, but at any rate laws of nature are typically generalizations that describe how the world is, not just how it should be. For an alternative view, though, see Cartwright (1983).

3. He says this about Armstrong's view, for example ([1983c] 1999a: 40).

4. Lewis (1986c). Despite the short space given to the paper here, it is both accessible and engaging. I recommend it to people interested in what is going on when something is being explained.

5. Many call this phenomena "overdetermination", but Lewis reserves "overdetermination" for a specific kind of redundant causation. See "Causation as Influence" (Lewis 2004a) and note 11 below.

6. Of course, there might have been a new sort of overdetermination if the traffic on the bridge was busy enough, since then it might be that if the truck had missed the mines, the bridge would have collapsed anyway when other traffic came along. But for the sake of a simple example, let us suppose the truck was the only piece of traffic to come along.

7. There are other types of late pre-emption (1986b: 202–3), but these are more esoteric.

8. This disadvantage is one of the reasons Lewis abandons his "middle period" counterfactual theory of causation, one in terms of "quasi-dependence". See Lewis (1986b: 205–7) for quasi-dependence, and Lewis (2000b: 184–5; 2004b: §IV) for its repudiation. Absences are one of the reasons Lewis offers to reject quasi-dependence.

9. Starting-points in Lewis are in the postscripts to "Causation" ([1973b] 1986b: 172–213) and "Causation as Influence" (2000b, 2004b).

10. C. B. Martin is responsible for the "finkish" label. The point that some dispositions are finkish was circulating at least since the early 1970s because of Martin's unpublished works, but Martin's presentation of the point is in Martin (1994).

11. In particular, I am ignoring the clause about being a "complete-x cause", which is a wrinkle included to handle situations where a disposition is partially finkish.

12. Lewis responds to a point like this in his discussion of the "Hater of Styrofoam" ([1997b] 1999a: 145). But the point does not seem to just be about stock dispositional expressions, such as "fragile", or, in the tree case, "explosive". It also seems to apply to whether we should say the thing "has a

disposition to ...". In Lewis's example, it seems wrong to say that styrofoam plates have the disposition to be destroyed when struck, even if their being struck makes someone come and tear them up, and that this is so is because of their intrinsic nature.

13. These include Lewis's "triviality results", showing that the probability of a conditional cannot be the associated conditional probability (1976b, 1986e), and some of the details of Lewis (1980c, 1981a, 1994a, 1999b), and papers in decision theory like Lewis (1988a, 1996a),

14. Lewis occasionally talks as if "credence" is itself given by a person's *rational* partial belief (see some of the remarks in Lewis ([1980c] 1986b: 83–4)), but most of his usages seem to suggest that by "credence" he usually means what I say he means in the text.

15. One of the classic introductions to decision theory is Jeffrey (1983).

16. Some people prefer to ascribe probabilities to possible events, rather than to propositions. Whether or not this makes any difference usually depends on the theories of events and propositions that people hold.

17. Lewis takes physics to strongly suggest that the world is indeterministic: that there are events with chances of other than 1 or 0. If determinism (in one of the many senses of that word) were true instead, things would happen or not happen either with chance 1 (if they happened) or chance 0 (if they did not). In the text I talk about this as there being "no objective chances" but, strictly speaking, perhaps I should say "no objective chances other than 1 and 0".

18. How Lewis squares this with his belief in the possibility of time travel is interesting. When a time traveller sets off to change something in the past, aren't we inclined to think she has some chance of succeeding and some chance of failing?

19. Lewis ([1994a] 1999a: 238). They are also defined in Lewis (1980c). The definition is worded differently there, but is intended to come to the same thing.

20. Strictly speaking, the ordinary cases should be characterized not as the ones where there is no information flow from the future to the past, but the ones where there is *no good evidence* of information flow from the future to the past. Since we are talking about what it is rational to believe, I may be rational to believe there is an information flow from the future to the past even if there is not one (say because I am hoaxed by a pretend time traveller with a big budget, who leads me to believe she is a time traveller by giving me a complex internally coherent story, successfully predicts things I assumed she would have no way of knowing, etc.). Likewise, even if there are people who directly precognize the future around, if I have no reason to think their rantings are correlated with what really will happen, they will not give me any reason to have a credence in a future outcome other than the credence equal to the objective chance.

21. This can be found in Lewis ([1994a] 1999a: 242–5).

Chapter 5: Realism and reductive materialism about the mind

1. Not all self-styled anti-realists would see themselves as idealists, however. "Anti-realist" is a rather general term, and which positions it should be applied to, and what, if anything, anti-realist philosophical positions have in common are very controversial.

2. Like most broad-brush philosophical terms, exactly which views are "dualist" in this sense is contested. Some people who claim to be materialists (e.g.

some "non-reductive materialists") seem to fall under this characterization of dualism. And there are "pluralists" who think there are many fundamental aspects of reality, as well as the physical and the mental, and they may well object to being lumped together with dualists. Finally, the word "dualist" gets used in contexts other than the relation between the mental and the physical. Still, something like the use specified is the most common in contemporary Anglo-American philosophy of mind.

3. We can, if we like, draw finer distinctions. In particular, there are some philosophers who want to be materialist about some aspects of the mind, but dualist about others. David Chalmers (1996), for example, is a materialist about beliefs and desires, but a dualist about some aspects of experience.

4. More of the details became apparent in Lewis's "Psychophysical and Theoretical Identifications" (1972).

5. Lewis discusses this in many places, but for the most focused discussion see *ibid.*

6. One of the earliest statements of this form of functionalism is by Putnam (1967).

7. Which I take it Lewis offers ([1994b] 1999a: 307–8).

8. This sort of objection might be one that behaviourists would endorse since they think that exactly what goes on inside is basically irrelevant if the behavioural dispositions are right. Some "analytic functionalists" who are less sympathetic to the identity theory might also endorse this objection. See Braddon-Mitchell and Jackson (1996).

9. "... it's not really credible that there might turn out to be no beliefs, no desires, no pains ..." ([1989b] 2000a: 91), and see, for example, Lewis (1990: 58).

10. What Lewis takes to be the distinction between analytic truths and synthetic truths, exactly, is not an easy question, and will come up again in the discussion of his method in Chapter 9.

11. See "How to Define Theoretical Terms" (1970b) and "Psychophysical and Theoretical Identifications" (1972) for two canonical presentations of this idea.

12. What to say about the actual investigation of whales might be more complicated than the example. Did they mean by "fish" what we mean? Is it right that our word "whale" means what theirs does? How long had people known whales were hairy, gave birth to live young, and all the rest? The historical details do not matter for my illustrative purposes, although they might be interesting in their own right.

13. Lewis cites Adams (1987) as an example.

14. Lewis suggests that Kripke is relying on this in Kripke (1980: 152).

15. Who are sometimes called, and sometimes call themselves, "qualia freaks".

16. Lewis discusses the Mary argument in several places (1983a: 130–32; 1988c; [1994b] 1999a: 293–4).

17. See Nemirow (1980, 1990). Nemirow's views were first argued in his unpublished 1979 dissertation (1979).

Chapter 6: Representation and mental content

1. Perhaps it sounds a little funny to say that a feeling of heat is "about" heat. It sounds less funny to say that it represents heat, though, and so it seems to be a representational state like the others (although there may, of course, be significant disanalogies between the cases too).

2. For a book-length defence of this way of thinking about content, see Stalnaker (1984).

3. As far as I can tell. See his discussion ([1994b] 1999a: 310–24, esp. 311).
4. The example is basically from Lewis ([1983b] 1999a: 399).
5. Some of the challenges discussed in this section are also addressed by Stalnaker (1984). Stalnaker does not agree with Lewis on all the details, but he is also concerned to explain and defend a sets-of-worlds conception of mental content.
6. See "Logic for Equivocators" (1982). For an extended presentation of a non-adjunctive logic to handle inconsistency see Rescher and Brandom (1980).
7. One vigorous development of this idea can be found in Priest (1987).
8. "Causal Decision Theory" (1981a) and its postscripts in *Philosophical Papers, Volume II* (1986b), "Desire as Belief" (1988a), "Desire as Belief II" (1996a), "Why Ain'cha Rich?" (1981c), "Devil's Bargains and the Real World" (1984a) and mentions in other papers.
9. This is because the probability (rational credence) that he is the nocturnal window-breaker, conditional on him using his right hand, is higher than the probability that he is the nocturnal window-breaker, conditional on him using his left hand.
10. For more on Newcomb's paradox and the prisoner's dilemma, see Lewis (1979c, 1981a).
11. See, for example, Lewis (1986a: 30).
12. Using supervaluations to represent indeterminacy is a technique pioneered by Bas van Fraassen (1966).
13. The best source for Davidson's views on this are the papers collected in Davidson (1984).
14. See the discussion of Lewis's disagreement with Putnam in Chapter 1. See also Lewis ([1983c] 1999a: 45–55; 1984b) and for Putnam's "model theoretic argument", which is one of the main things Lewis is responding to, see Putnam (1977, 1980, 1981: Ch. 2). Lewis also thinks that an appeal to natural properties here can solve Kripke's version of the "rule-following problem"; see Lewis ([1983c] 1999a: 53) and Kripke (1982).

Chapter 7: Language, use and convention

1. If you are the reader who engages in fearless public nudity, please think up another example.
2. In Chapter 6, we saw that Lewis thought that sets of individuals rather than sets of worlds were the best candidates to be mental contents. Should Lewis do the same thing here, and instead of "truth-conditions" have "truth-of-conditions", which specify which possible individuals a sentence is true-of? Presumably a variant like this could work technically, but I suspect it would not have any particular advantages.
3. One of the classic treatments of these terms is Kaplan (1989).
4. There is another sort of view, sometimes also called contextualism about knowledge, according to which a claim about knowledge depends for its truth partly on the "context" of the supposed knower. So on this version of "contextualism", when I say that Bill knows that planets move in ellipses, whether or not I am correct depends on the "epistemic context" of Bill. Such a view does not really deserve to be called "contextualism". Everyone agrees that whether or not Bill knows something has something to do with how Bill is, and most agree it depends on how Bill is with respect to other things (e.g. how the world is).

David Lewis

Chapter 8: Values and morality

1. I am not suggesting that fashion-followers typically have these sorts of desires to fit in. Indeed, it might even be that people's non-instrumental desires are shaped by prevailing fashions. But it certainly happens that people want to be a certain way (including their wanting to have certain desires and preferences) in order to fit in with a group.
2. Personally, I should not be too confident. This makes it sound like evil people have some sort of *medical* defect: that self-aware sadism and disregard for others is the result of some kind of fault in one's imagination. There certainly are some people who do horrendous things because of mental illness or impairment of some sort or other, but that this is always what is going on seems a bit hard to swallow.
3. See not only Lewis ([1989b] 2000a: 88), but also Lewis ([1993a] 2000a: 105).
4. This is suggested most strongly in "Illusory Innocence" (1996c). Note that this point does not just apply to consequentialist theorizing that insists we ought to act to maximize everyone's good (or even that we ought to act when we can greatly improve someone's situation with little effort). It applies, for example, to Unger's view (1985), that it is immoral to ignore the suffering of strangers in the way we apparently do, but Unger does not base his argument on consequentialist principles. (Unger's book is the primary subject of "Illusory Innocence".)

Chapter 9: Some reflections on Lewis's method

1. Quine himself eventually thought that we needed to distinguish "natural kinds" from other classifications of objects (1969: 114–38), but Quine was inclined to give an anthropocentric account of the "naturalness" of these kinds, rather than take it as a basic metaphysical fact.
2. Quine (1960b: 262–70). This sort of argument is also advanced by Putnam (see especially Putnam 1971). For a recent book-length discussion and defence of such indispensability arguments, see Colyvan (2001).
3. Moore (1939: 146). The best places to find Moore's "Moorean" defence of common sense are Moore (1925, 1959).
4. I am being somewhat lax here, swapping from talking about the Ramsey sentence, a quantified sentence, and a set of objects satisfying a condition. The condition would be the open sentence we get by removing the initial quantifiers from a Ramsey sentence. Those who want to be careful about the technical details can probably see how they would go themselves, or can consult Lewis (1970b, 1972).
5. I assume Lewis is drawing an analogy with knowledge of a specific grammar, such as that of English. He may instead be comparing it to our supposed knowledge of an innate universal grammar (as postulated by Chomsky). Some theorists do indeed think that our brains come equipped with a "folk psychology" module for predicting other human beings' behaviour, which is analogous to a "language module" that contains a good deal of information about universal features of grammar. I suspect this is not the analogy Lewis has in mind here. He refrains from invoking such "grammars" when saying what the grammar of a language is, and I suspect he would think that we had little common knowledge about what such grammars contain, as opposed to information we might get from testing hypotheses in linguistics. (See his discussion ([1975] 1983a: 178).)
6. Jackson (1998) argues that these philosophical practices of articulating analysis and challenging them with thought-experiments is to be under-

stood as something like Lewis's project of articulating folk theories.

7. My impression is that "platitudes" has entered philosophical vocabulary with a slightly different meaning from Lewis's use in "Psychophysical and Theoretical Identifications" (1972), or rather with a sometimes confusing range of meanings. This does not matter for the current discussion, but is a caution to readers who come across talk of "the platitudes" elsewhere in discussions of philosophical analysis.

8. The term was originally employed by Huw Price and John O'Leary-Hawthorne (1996). Canberra, the capital of Australia, is a planned city, and, according to its detractors, is organized in such a way as to be rather bland. Price and O'Leary-Hawthorne's suggestion was that this method of philosophical analysis was also insensitive to the "rich diversity" of linguistic usage. Despite that, the term has been "reclaimed". Lewis mentions Michael Tooley and Peter Menzies as applying the "Canberra plan" to causation (Tooley 1987; Menzies 1996). Both worked at the Australian National University during the 1990s. Other prominent Canberra planners include Frank Jackson (see Jackson (1998) for, in effect, a book-length defence of the approach) and Philip Pettit. There are many others who can be described as Canberra planners with some degree of accuracy.

9. "Phlogiston", according to an outdated chemical theory, was a substance that was always given off by substances when they were burnt. "Luminiferous ether" was a substance postulated in nineteenth-century physics that was supposed to be located everywhere and was the medium through which light waves were propagated.

10. Note that both the Ramsey sentence and the Carnap sentence of a theory will be uncontroversially implied by the theory, whatever someone's views of meaning, and that the outline of the method seems to rely primarily on manipulating the Ramsey and Carnap sentences (or slightly modified variants). Rejecting Lewis's method because of a disagreement about meaning risks missing the meat of the position, although if one keeps Lewis's method while rejecting its theoretical underpinning, it might be right to stop calling it "linguistic analysis" or "conceptual analysis".

Bibliography

Selected works by David Lewis

1966. "An Argument for the Identity Theory", *Journal of Philosophy* **63**, 17–25. Reprinted in Lewis (1986b), 99–107.

1968. "Counterpart Theory and Quantified Modal Logic", *Journal of Philosophy* **65**, 113–26. Reprinted with postscript in Lewis (1983a), 26–46.

1969. *Convention: A Philosophical Study*. Cambridge, MA: Harvard University Press.

1970a. "General Semantics", *Synthese* **22**, 18–67. Reprinted with postscript in Lewis (1983a), 189–232.

1970b. "How to Define Theoretical Terms", *Journal of Philosophy* **67**, 427–46. Reprinted in Lewis (1983a), 78–95.

1972. "Psychophysical and Theoretical Identifications", *Australasian Journal of Philosophy* **50**, 249–58. Reprinted in Lewis (1999a), 248–61.

1973a . *Counterfactuals*. Oxford: Basil Blackwell.

1973b. "Causation", *Journal of Philosophy* **70**, 556–67. Reprinted with postscripts in Lewis (1986b), 159–214.

1974a. "Radical Interpretation", *Synthese* **23**, 331–44. Reprinted in Lewis (1983a), 108–21.

1974b. "Semantic Analyses for Dyadic Deontic Logic". In *Logical Theory and Semantic Analysis: Essays Dedicated to Stig Kanger on his Fiftieth Birthday*, S. Stenlund (ed.). Dordrecht: Reidel. Reprinted in Lewis (2000a), 5–19.

1975. "Language and Languages", *Minnesota Studies in the Philosophy of Science* **7**, 3–35. Reprinted in Lewis (1983a), 163–88.

1976a. "Convention: Reply to Jamieson", *Canadian Journal of Philosophy* **6**, 113–20. Reprinted in Lewis (2000a), 136–44.

1976b. "Probabilities of Conditionals and Conditional Probabilities", *Philosophical Review* **85**, 297–315. Reprinted with postscripts in Lewis (1986b), 133–56.

1976c. "The Paradoxes of Time Travel", *American Philosophical Quarterly* **13**, 145–52. Reprinted in Lewis (1986b), 67–80.

1976d. "Survival and Identity". In *The Identities of Persons*, A. O. Rorty (ed.), 17–40. Berkeley, CA: University of California Press. Reprinted in Lewis (1983a), 55–72.

1978. "Reply to McMichael", *Analysis* **38**, 85–6. Reprinted in Lewis (2000a), 34–6.

1979a. "Attitudes *De Dicto* and *De Se*", *The Philosophical Review* **88**, 513–43. Reprinted with postscript in Lewis (1983a), 133–60.

1979b. "Counterfactual Dependence and Time's Arrow", *Noûs* **13**, 455–76. Reprinted in Lewis (1986b), 32–66.

1979c. "Prisoner's Dilemma is a Newcomb Problem", *Philosophy and Public Affairs* **8**, 235–40. Reprinted with postscript in Lewis (1986b), 299–304.

1979d. "Scorekeeping in a Language Game", *Journal of Philosophical Logic* **8**, 339–59. Reprinted in Lewis (1983a), 233–49.

Bibliography

1980a. "Index, Context and Content". In *Philosophy and Grammar*, S. Kanger & S. Öhma (eds), 79–100. Dordrecht: Reidel. Reprinted in Lewis (1998), 21–44.
1980b. "Mad Pain and Martian Pain". In *Readings in the Philosophy of Psychology*, vol. I, 216–32. Cambridge, MA: Harvard University Press. Reprinted with postscript in Lewis (1983a), 122–33.
1980c. "A Subjectivist's Guide to Objective Chance". In *Studies in Inductive Logic and Probability*, vol. II, R. Jeffrey (ed.), 263–93. Berkeley, CA: University of California Press. Reprinted with postscript in Lewis (1986b), 83–133.
1981a. "Causal Decision Theory", *Australasian Journal of Philosophy* **59**, 5–30. Reprinted with postscript in Lewis (1986b), 305–39.
1981b. "What Puzzling Pierre Does Not Believe", *Australasian Journal of Philosophy* **59**, 283–89. Reprinted in Lewis (1999a), 408–36.
1981c. "Why Ain'cha Rich?", *Noûs* **15**, 377–80. Reprinted in Lewis (2000a), 37–41.
1982. "Logic for Equivocators", *Noûs* **16**, 431–41. Reprinted in Lewis (1998), 97–110.
1983a. *Philosophical Papers, Volume I*. Oxford: Oxford University Press.
1983b. "Individuation by Aquaintance and by Stipulation", *Philosophical Review* **92**, 3–32. Reprinted in Lewis (1999a), 373–402.
1983c. "New Work for a Theory of Universals", *Australasian Journal of Philosophy* **61**, 343–77. Reprinted in Lewis (1999a), 8–55.
1984a. "Devil's Bargains and the Real World". In *The Security Gamble: Deterrence in the Nuclear Age*, D. MacLean (ed.), 141–54. Totowa, NJ: Rowman & Allanheld. Reprinted in Lewis (2000a), 201–18.
1984b. "Putnam's Paradox", *Australasian Journal of Philosophy* **62**(3), 221–36. Reprinted in Lewis (1999a), 56–77.
1986a. *On the Plurality of Worlds*. Oxford: Blackwell.
1986b. *Philosophical Papers, Volume II*. Oxford: Oxford University Press.
1986c. "Causal Explanation". See Lewis (1986b), 214–40. First published in this collection.
1986d. "Events". See Lewis (1986b), 241–69. First published in this collection.
1986e. "Probabilities of Conditionals and Conditional Probabilities II", *Philosophical Review* **95**, 581–89. Reprinted in Lewis (1998), 57–65.
1987. "The Punishment that Leaves Something to Chance". In *Proceedings of the Russellian Society (University of Sydney)* **12**, 81–97. Also in *Philosophy and Public Affairs* **18** (1989), 53–67. Reprinted in Lewis (2000a), 227–43.
1988a. "Desire as Belief", *Mind* **97**, 323–332. Reprinted in Lewis (2000a), 42–54.
1988b. "The Trap's Dilemma", *Australasian Journal of Philosophy* **66**, 220–23. Reprinted in Lewis (2000a), 95–100.
1988c. "What Experience Teaches". In *Proceedings of the Russellian Society (University of Sydney)* **13**, 29–57. Reprinted in Lewis (1999a), 262–90.
1989a. "Academic Appointments: Why Ignore the Advantage of Being Right?". In *Ormond Papers*, Ormond College, University of Melbourne. Reprinted in Lewis (2000a), 187–200.
1989b. "Dispositional Theories of Value", *Proceedings of the Aristotelian Society, Supplementary Volume* **63**, 113–37. Reprinted in Lewis (2000a), 68–94.
1989c. "Mill and Milquetoast", *Australasian Journal of Philosophy* **67**, 152–71. Reprinted in Lewis (2000a), 159–86.
1990. *Parts of Classes*. Oxford: Blackwell. Appendix co-authored with J. P. Burgess and A. P. Hazen.
1992. "Meaning Without Use: Reply to Hawthorne", *Australasian Journal of Philosophy* **70**, 106–10. Reprinted in Lewis (2000a), 145–51.
1993a. "Evil for Freedom's Sake?", *Philosophical Papers* **22**, 149–72. Reprinted in Lewis (2000a), 101–27.
1993b. "Many, But Almost One". In *Ontology, Causality and Mind: Essays on the Philosophy of D. M. Armstrong*, K. Campbell, J. Bacon & L. Reinhardt (eds), 23–37. Cambridge: Cambridge University Press. Reprinted in Lewis (1999a), 164–82.
1993c. "Mathematics is Megethology", *Philosophia Mathematica* **1**, 3–23. Reprinted in Lewis (1998), 203–29.
1994a. "Humean Supervenience Debugged", *Mind* **103**, 473–90. Reprinted in Lewis (1999a), 224–47.
1994b. "Reduction of Mind". In *A Companion to the Philosophy of Mind*, S. Guttenplan (ed.), 412–31. Oxford: Blackwell. Reprinted in Lewis (1999a), 291–324.
1995. "Should a Materialist Believe in Qualia?", *Australasian Journal of Philosophy* **73**, 140–44. Reprinted in Lewis (1999a), 325–31.
1996a. "Desire as Belief II", *Mind* **105**, 303–13. Reprinted in Lewis (2000a), 55–67.

David Lewis

1996b. "Elusive Knowledge", *Australasian Journal of Philosophy* **74**, 549–67. Reprinted in Lewis (1999a), 418–45.
1996c. "Illusory Innocence", *Eureka Street* **5**, 35–6. Reprinted in Lewis (2000a), 152–8.
1997a. "Do We Believe in Penal Substitution?", *Philosophical Papers* **26**, 203–9. Reprinted in Lewis (2000a), 128–35.
1997b. "Finkish Dispositions", *The Philosophical Quarterly* **47**, 143–58. Reprinted in Lewis (1999a), 133–51.
1997c. "Naming the Colours", *Australasian Journal of Philosophy* **75**, 325–42. Reprinted in Lewis (1999a), 332–58.
1998. *Papers in Philosophical Logic*. Cambridge: Cambridge University Press.
1999a. *Papers on Metaphysics and Epistemology*. Cambridge: Cambridge University Press.
1999b. "Why Conditionalise?". In Lewis (1999a), 403–7. Written in 1972, with an introduction dated 1997, and first published in this collection.
2000a. *Papers in Ethics and Social Philosophy*. Cambridge: Cambridge University Press.
2000b. "Causation as Influence", *Journal of Philosophy* **97**, 182–97. See Lewis (2004a).
2002. "Tensing the Copula", *Mind* **441**, 1–13.
2004a. "Causation as Influence" (extended version). In *Causation and Counterfactuals*, J. Collins, N. Hall & L. A. Paul (eds), 75–106. Cambridge, MA: MIT Press.
2004b. "How Many Lives Has Schrödinger's Cat?", *Australasian Journal of Philosophy* **82**(1), 3–22.
2004c. "Void and Object". In *Causation and Counterfactuals*, J. Collins, N. Hall & L. A. Paul (eds), 277–90. Cambridge, MA: MIT Press.

References

Adams, R. M. 1974. "Theories of Actuality", *Noûs* **8**, 211–31.
Adams, R. M. 1987. "Flavors, Colors, and God". In *The Virtue of Faith and Other Essays in Philosophical Theology*, 243–62. Oxford: Oxford University Press.
Armstrong, D. M. 1978a. *Universals and Scientific Realism: Nominalism and Realism, Vol. 1*. Cambridge: Cambridge University Press.
Armstrong, D. M. 1978b. *Universals and Scientific Realism: A Theory of Universals, Vol. 2*. Cambridge: Cambridge University Press.
Armstrong, D. M. 1980. "Against 'Ostrich' Nominalism: A Reply to Michael Devitt", *Pacific Philosophical Quarterly* **61**, 440–49.
Armstrong, D. M. 1983. *What is a Law of Nature?* Cambridge: Cambridge University Press.
Baxter, D. 1988. "Many-One Identity", *Philosophical Papers* **17**(3), 193–216.
Braddon-Mitchell, D. & F. Jackson 1996. *The Philosophy of Mind and Cognition*. Oxford: Blackwell.
Carnap, R. 1963. "Replies and Expositions". In *The Philosophy of Rudolf Carnap*, P. A. Schlipp (ed.), 958–66. La Salle, IL: Open Court.
Cartwright, N. 1983. *How the Laws of Physics Lie*. Oxford: Oxford University Press.
Chalmers, D. 1996. *The Conscious Mind*. Oxford: Oxford University Press.
Chandler, H. 1976. "Plantinga and the Contingently Possible", *Analysis* **36**, 106–9.
Chisholm, R. 1967. "Identity Through Possible Worlds: Some Questions", *Noûs* **1**, 1–8. Reprinted in *The Possible and the Actual: Readings in the Metaphysics of Modality*, M. J. Loux (ed.) (1979), 80–87. Ithaca, NY: Cornell University Press.
Cohen, S. 1998. "Contextualist Solutions to Epistemological Problems: Scepticism, Gettier, and the Lottery", *Australasian Journal of Philosophy* **76**, 289–306.
Collins, J., N. Hall & L. A. Paul 2004. *Causation and Counterfactuals*. Cambridge, MA: MIT Press.
Colyvan, M. 2001. *The Indispensability of Mathematics*. Oxford: Oxford University Press.
Davidson, D. 1984. *Inquiries into Truth and Interpretation*. Oxford: Oxford University Press.
DeRose, K. 1992. "Contextualism and Knowledge Attributions", *Philosophy and Phenomenological Research* **52**, 913–29.
Dretske, F. 1977. "Laws of Nature", *Philosophy of Science* **64**, 248–68.
Frankfurt, H. 1971. "Freedom of the Will and the Concept of a Person", *Journal of Philosophy* **68**, 5–20.
Graff, D. 2000. "Shifting Sands: An Interest-Relative Theory of Vagueness", *Philosophical Topics* **28**(1), 45–81.

Heller, M. 1998. "Property Counterparts in Ersatz Worlds", *Journal of Philosophy* **95**(6), 293–316.

Hitchcock, C. 2001. "The Intransitivity of Causation Revealed in Equations and Graphs", *Journal of Philosophy* **98**(6), 273–99.

Jackson, F. 1977. "Statements about Universals", *Mind* **86**, 427–29.

Jackson, F. 1982. "Epiphenomenal Qualia", *Philosophical Quarterly* **32**, 127–36.

Jackson, F. 1986. "What Mary Didn't Know", *Journal of Philosophy* **83**, 291–5.

Jackson F. 1998. *From Metaphysics to Ethics*. Oxford: Oxford University Press.

Jeffrey, R. 1983. *The Logic of Decision*. Chicago, IL: University of Chicago Press.

Johnston, M. 1987. "Is There A Problem About Persistence?", *Aristotelian Society supplementary volume* **61**, 107–35.

Johnston, M. 1992. "How to Speak of the Colors", *Philosophical Studies* **68**, 221–63.

Kanger, S. 1957. *Provability in Logic*. Stockholm: Almqvist and Wiksell.

Kaplan, D. 1989. *Demonstratives*. In *Themes from Kaplan*, J. Almog *et al*. (eds), 461–563. Oxford: Oxford University Press.

Kripke, S. 1959. "A Completeness Theorem in Modal Logic", *Journal of Symbolic Logic* **24**, 1–14.

Kripke, S. 1963. "Semantical Considerations on Modal Logic", *Acta Philosophica Fennica*, **16**, 83–94.

Kripke, S. 1980. *Naming and Necessity*. Oxford: Blackwell.

Kripke, S. 1982. *Wittgenstein on Rules and Private Language*. Oxford: Blackwell.

Lewis, C. I. & C. H. Langford 1932. *Symbolic Logic*. New York: Dover Publications.

Loux, M. J. (ed.). 1979. *The Possible and the Actual: Readings in the Metaphysics of Modality*. Ithaca, NY: Cornell University Press.

Markosian, N. 1992. "Brutal Composition", *Philosophical Studies* **92**, 211–49.

Martin, C. B. 1994. "Dispositions and Conditionals", *Philosophical Quarterly* **44**, 1–8.

McDermott, M. 1995. "Redundant Causation", *British Journal for the Philosophy of Science* **66**, 523–44.

Menzies, P. 1996. "Probabilistic Causation and the Pre-Emption Problem", *Mind* **105**, 85–117.

Mill, J. S. 1956. *On Liberty*, C. V. Shields (ed.) [originally published 1859]. Indianapolis, IN: Bobbs-Merrill.

Montague, R. 1974. *Formal Philosophy*, R. Thomason (ed). New Haven, CT: Yale University Press.

Moore, G. E. 1925. "A Defence of Common Sense". See Moore (1959), 32–59.

Moore, G. E. 1939. "Proof of an External World". See Moore (1959), 127–50.

Moore, G. E. 1959. *Philosophical Papers*. London: George Allen & Unwin.

Nemirow, L. 1979. "Functionalism and the Subjective Quality of Experience", PhD thesis, Stanford University.

Nemirow, L. 1980. "Review of *Mortal Questions*, by Thomas Nagel", *Philosophical Review* **89**, 473–77.

Nemirow, L. 1990. "Physicalism and the Cognitive Role of Acquaintance". In *Mind and Cognition: A Reader*, W. Lycan (ed.), 490–99. Oxford: Blackwell.

Nerlich, G. 1976. *The Shape of Space*. Cambridge: Cambridge University Press.

Nolan, D. 2002. *Topics in the Philosophy of Possible Worlds*. New York: Routledge.

Noonan, H. 2001. "The Case for Perdurance". In *Reality and Humean Supervenience: Essays on the Philosophy of David Lewis*, G. Preyer & F. Siebelt (eds), 123–29. Lanham, MD: Rowman and Littlefield.

Oppenheim, P. & H. Putnam 1958. "Unity of Science as a Working Hypothesis". In *Concepts, Theories and the Mind-Body Problem*, H. Feigl, M. Scriven & G. Maxwell (eds), 3–36. Minnesota Studies in the Philosophy of Science 2. Minneapolis, MI: Minnesota University Press.

Oppy, G. 2000. "Humean Supervenience?", *Philosophical Studies* **101**, 77–105.

Pap, A. 1959. "Nominalism, Empiricism, and Universals: I", *Philosophical Quarterly* **9**, 330–40.

Pargetter, R. 1984. "Laws and Modal Realism", *Philosophical Studies* **46**, 35–48.

Preyer G. & F. Siebelt (eds) 2001. *Reality and Humean Supervenience: Essays on the Philosophy of David Lewis*. Lanham, MD: Rowman and Littlefield.

Price, H. & J. O'Leary-Hawthorne 1996. "How To Stand Up For Non-Cognitivists", *Australasian Journal of Philosophy* **74**, 275–92.

Priest, G. 1987. *In Contradiction*. Dordrecht: Kluwer.

Putnam, H. 1967. "The Nature of Mental States". Reprinted in Putnam (1975b), 429–440.

David Lewis

Putnam, H. 1970. "On Properties". Reprinted in Putnam (1975a), 305–22.
Putnam, H. 1971. *Philosophy of Logic*. London: George Allen & Unwin.
Putnam, H. 1975a. *Mathematics, Matter and Method: Philosophical Papers Volume 1*. Cambridge: Cambridge University Press.
Putnam, H. 1975b. *Mind, Language and Reality: Philosophical Papers Volume 2*. Cambridge: Cambridge University Press.
Putnam, H. 1975c. "The Meaning of 'Meaning'". Reprinted in Putnam (1975b), 215–71.
Putnam, H. 1977. "Realism and Reason". Reprinted in Putnam (1978), 123–40.
Putnam, H. 1978. *Meaning and the Moral Sciences*. New York: Routledge & Kegan Paul.
Putnam, H. 1980. "Models and Reality", *Journal of Symbolic Logic* **45**, 464–82.
Putnam, H. 1981. *Reason, Truth and History*. Cambridge: Cambridge University Press.
Quine, W. V. 1951. "Two Dogmas of Empiricism". Reprinted in Quine (1953a), 20–46.
Quine, W. V. 1953a. *From a Logical Point of View*. Cambridge, MA: Harvard University Press.
Quine, W. V. 1953b. "Three Grades of Modal Involvement". Reprinted in Quine (1966), 156–73.
Quine, W. V. 1953c. "Reference and Modality". In *From a Logical Point of View*, 139–59. Cambridge, MA: Harvard University Press.
Quine, W. V. 1960a. "Posits and Reality". Reprinted in Quine (1966), 233–41.
Quine, W. V. 1960b. *Word and Object*. Cambridge, MA: MIT Press.
Quine, W. V. 1966. *The Ways of Paradox and Other Essays*. New York: Random House.
Quine, W. V. 1969. *Ontological Relativity and Other Essays*. New York: Columbia University Press.
Raffman, D. 1994. "Vagueness Without Paradox", *Philosophical Review* **103**, 41–74.
Ramsey, F. P. 1990. *Philosophical Papers*, D. H. Mellor (ed.). Cambridge: Cambridge University Press.
Rescher N. & R. Brandom 1980. *The Logic of Inconsistency*. Oxford: Blackwell.
Robinson, D. 1989. "Matter, Motion and Humean Supervenience", *Australasian Journal of Philosophy* **67**, 394–409.
Rosen, G. & C. Dorr 2002. "Composition as a Fiction". In *Blackwell Guide to Metaphysics*, R. M. Gale (ed.), 151–74. Oxford: Blackwell.
Ryle, G. 1949. *The Concept of Mind*. London: Hutchinson.
Salmon, N. 1981. *Reference and Essence*. Princeton, NJ: Princeton University Press.
Soames, S. 1999. *Understanding Truth*. Oxford: Oxford University Press.
Sider, T. 2001. *Four Dimensionalism*. Oxford: Oxford University Press.
Sider, T. 2002. "The Ersatz Pluriverse", *Journal of Philosophy* **99**, 279–315.
Smart, J. J. C. 1963. *Philosophy and Scientific Realism*. London: Routledge & Kegan Paul.
Stalnaker, R. 1984. *Inquiry*. Cambridge, MA: MIT Press.
Stalnaker, R. 1999. *Context and Content: Collected Papers on Intentionality in Speech and Thought*. Oxford: Clarendon Press.
Suppes, P. 1970. *A Probabilistic Theory of Causality*. Amsterdam: North-Holland.
Teller, P. 2001. "Against Against Overlap and Endurance". In *Reality and Humean Supervenience: Essays on the Philosophy of David Lewis*, G. Preyer & F. Siebelt (eds), 105–22. Lanham, MD: Rowman and Littlefield.
Tooley, M. 1977. "The Nature of Laws", *Canadian Journal of Philosophy* **7**, 667–98.
Tooley, M. 1987. *Causation: A Realist Approach*. Oxford: Oxford University Press.
Unger, P. 1975. *Ignorance*. Oxford: Oxford University Press.
Unger, P. 1985. *Living High and Letting Die: Our Illusion of Innocence*. Oxford: Oxford University Press.
van Fraassen, B. C. 1966. "Singular Terms, Truth-Value Gaps and Free Logic", *Journal of Philosophy* **63**, 481–95.
van Inwagen, P. 1986. "Two Concepts of Possible Worlds", *Studies in Essentialism, Midwest Studies in Philosophy* **XI**, 185–213.
van Inwagen, P. 1994. "Composition as Identity", *Philosophical Perspectives* **8**, 204–20.
Williams, D. C. 1951. "The Myth of Passage", *Journal of Philosophy* **48**, 457–72.
Williams, D. C. 1953. "On the Elements of Being", *Review of Metaphysics* **7**, 3–18, 171–92.
Williamson, T. 2000. *Knowledge and its Limits*. Oxford: Oxford University Press.

Index

abundant properties 19, 21–2, 23
accidental intrinsics 68–9
Adams, R. M. 189, 234
alien properties 29, 62–3, 230
analysis
  causation 90–101
  content of language 163–5
  convention 158–63
  counterfactuals 74–9, 96–101
  de re modality 67–72
  dispositions 101–6
  laws of nature 83–9, 112–14
  mental content 135–56
  necessity and possibility 53–67
  objective chance 112–14
  value 179–85
  Lewis's defence of philosophical analysis
    213–27
  see also deservers, methodology, Ramsey–
    Lewis–Carnap method
analytic functionalism *see* functionalism
analytic philosophy 3
analyticity 3, 126–9, 134, 234
  first step in analysis as analytic 223–4
  theory of value as analytic 183–5
  unsharp analyticity (semantic indecision
    and variation) 113–14, 223–7
  see also analysis
Aristotle 6, 39
Armstrong, D. M. 3, 25, 88, 208, 229, 232

Baxter, Donald 38
belief and desire, nature of the content of
  135–47
  as properties/set of doxastic
    counterparts 138–42
  as sets of possible worlds 136–8, 234, 235
  beliefs in impossibilities and inconsistent
    beliefs 143–7, 235
  fragmentation/compartmentalization
    144–7

implicit content 142–3
  representation as holistic 142–3, 152
  see also credence, value, utility
beliefs and desires, fixing the content of
  151–5
  constraints of rationality (theoretical,
    instrumental) 153–5
  eligibility (naturalness) constraint 154–
    5, 206, 226
  functionalism 151–2, 154
  justification for rationality constraints
    153–4
  principle of charity 153
  rationalization principle 106–7, 110, 147
big bad bug 112–13
Braddon-Mitchell, David 234
Brandom, Robert 235

Canberra plan 223, 237
  see methodology, Ramsey–Carnap–Lewis
    method
Carnap, Rudolf 214–18
Cartwright, Nancy 232
causal closure of the physical 13,16
causal decision theory *see* decision
  theory
causal dependence
  and chance 100–101
  causal dependence and influence 93–4
  causation without causal dependence
    91–3
  counterfactual characterization of 90–
    91, 100, 232
  see also causation, counterfactual analysis
    of causation
causal role 14–15, 116–18, 125, 152
causation 89–101
  causal closure of the physical 13,16
  causal verbs 89
  causing past events 40
  chancy causation 100–101

David Lewis

David Lewis

Philosophy

"David Lewis's *oeuvre* spans an astonishing range of philosophical topics: from epistemology to mereology, from metaethics to mathematics, from materialism to realism, from explanation to interpretation, from chance to perdurance, from propositions to dispositions, from convention to causation – and much more. He was also one of the most systematic philosophers. Daniel Nolan has the breadth of knowledge and technical facility to produce this first-rate, user-friendly study of the Lewisian system. In doing so, he has provided a great service to both specialists and non-specialists."   – Alan Hájek, *California Institute of Technology*

"... essential reading for specialists and non-specialists alike in metaphysics, mind, epistemology and language, since even those who know Lewis's work on, say, counterfactuals and possible worlds will benefit from knowledge of his views on related topics such as semantics and convention. Daniel Nolan has given us a pellucid, lively and accessible overview of the diverse strands of Lewis's work; I know of no other treatment of Lewis that is as useful, comprehensive and well written."   – L. A. Paul, *University of Arizona*

The work of David Lewis (1941–2001) has influenced most areas of Anglo-American philosophy and remains of fundamental importance in current philosophical inquiry. Lewis's work provides a comprehensive philosophical system that answers a broad range of questions in metaphysics, philosophy of mind, philosophy of language, philosophy of action and many other areas. The breadth and unity of his ideas, however, have meant that a casual reader may miss some of the illuminating connections between apparently quite disparate pieces of work. Daniel Nolan's book not only makes Lewis's work more accessible to a general philosophical readership but provides a unified overview of his many contributions to contemporary philosophy.

The first part of the book examines Lewis's metaphysics – the area where he has had the greatest impact and which serves as the framework for the rest of his theories. The second section discusses Lewis's important contributions in the philosophy of mind, language and meaning. The book then explores some of Lewis's work in decision theory, metaethics and applied ethics, areas in which his work is both accessible and important. The final chapter focuses on Lewis's distinctive philosophical method, perhaps one of his most significant legacies, which combines naturalism with "common-sense" theorizing.

Daniel Nolan is Lecturer in Philosophy at the University of St Andrews.

McGill-Queen's University Press
www.mqup.ca

Philosophy Now Series Editor: John Shand

ISBN 0-7735-2931-4   Cover photograph: © Steve Pyke

9 780773 529311